The Navy in the
English Civil War

by
J. R. POWELL

with an Introduction by
C. V. WEDGWOOD

AB

ARCHON BOOKS
Hamden • London
1962

In a shorter form this study received the Julian Corbett Prize for modern naval history in 1956, awarded by the University of London.

Map labels:

Berwick
Newcastle, Tynemouth, Tees, Scarborough
Carrickfergus
Gainsborough
York, Hull
Galway
Dublin, Holy Is., Beaumaris, Pool of Aire, Liverpool, Conway, Chester, Newark
Bunratty, Limerick
Yarmouth
Waterford, Wexford, Duncannon
Cork, Youghal, Kinsale
Pembroke, Swansea, Gloucester, Oxford, Harwich
Milford Haven, Cardiff, LONDON
Lundy Is., Holmes, Bristol, Deal, Dover, Dunkirk
Barnstaple, Bideford, Minehead, Calais
Exeter, Lyme, Portsmouth, Boulogne
Fowey, Plymouth, Weymouth, I. of Wight
Falmouth, Dartmouth, Dieppe
Scilly Is.
Cherbourg, Guernsey, Le Havre
Jersey
Ushant, Morlaix, St. Malo, Brest
Lorient

Fleet Stations during
the Civil Wars
Royalist and Privateer
Ports underlined

FLEET STATIONS DURING THE CIVIL WARS

The Navy in the English Civil War

Table of Contents

INTRODUCTION   ix

PREFACE   xii

CHAPTER I
The Winter of the Navy's Discontent   3

CHAPTER II
1642: Warwick Secures the Fleet for Parliament   14

CHAPTER III
1643: Warwick Challenges the King's Successes   33

CHAPTER IV
1644: Warwick Bends Back the Southern Prong of the
    King's Fork   56

CHAPTER V
1644: Warwick Helps to Break the King's Northern
    Prong   71

CHAPTER VI
1645: The Change in Naval Command   83

CHAPTER VII
1645: Batten and Penn at Work   97

CHAPTER VIII
1646: Batten Meets the Scots at Newcastle   111

CHAPTER IX
1647: Batten is Replaced by Rainsborough   131

CHAPTER X
1648: The Revolt of the Fleet   146

CHAPTER XI
1648: Warwick and the Revolted Fleet   161

CHAPTER XII
1648: Warwick Fails and Is Replaced   176

APPENDICES — SHIP LISTS   193

KEY TO REFERENCES   225

NOTES   229

INDEX   234

Maps and Illustrations

Fleet Stations During the Civil Wars   Frontispiece

Robert Rich, Earl of Warwick *(From an engraving by Wenceslaus Hollar)*   2

The Town of Hull *(From an engraving by Hollar. By kind permission of the Trustees of the British Museum)*   15

The Siege of Plymouth *(From an engraving by Hollar)*   34

Map of the District around Pembroke   57

Map of the Engagement at Pill   60

Map of the Siege of Lyme   64

Map of Pembrokeshire   79

The Siege of Duncannon *(By kind permission of Trinity College, Dublin)*   84

Sir William Penn *(From the portrait by Lely. By courtesy of the National Maritime Museum)*   98

Map of the Siege of Youghal   100

Map of the Siege of Bonratty   112

Colonel Thomas Rainsborough *(By kind permission of the Bodleian Library)*   132

Sir William Batten *(By courtesy of the National Maritime Museum)*   147

Chart of the Mouth of the Thames   162

The *Constant Reformation (From a drawing by W. Van de Velde. By courtesy of the National Maritime Museum)*   177

Introduction

Although three centuries have gone by since the English Civil War it plays almost as large a part in English historic memory as does the American Civil War in the memory and traditions of the United States. This armed conflict between King and Parliament, between the gallant Cavaliers of King Charles on the one side and the stubborn Puritan Roundheads on the other, is of central importance in the history of England, but it is also deeply relevant to ideas of liberty and government as we know them in the English-speaking world today. King Charles the doomed monarch, Oliver Cromwell with his Bible and his sword, Prince Rupert the daring young leader of the Cavaliers, and Thomas Fairfax, his blameless and chivalrous opponent — all these and many more have a place not only in the history books but in the traditions of the English countryside and the English people.

But the English are above all a sea-faring race. It is therefore almost inexplicable that the naval side of the Civil War has had to wait until the twentieth century for its historian. For the Navy played an important part in the defeat of the King.

At the opening of the English Civil War the Navy supported Parliament. This had two vitally important consequences. First, it induced foreign powers to give their support, officially or unofficially, to Parliament rather than to the King. The reason was simple. What mattered to France and Spain, to the Dutch, and to other European nations, was not so much who controlled the *land*, but who controlled the *seas* round England. A King of England with no naval power was, in diplomatic terms, a person of very little consequence. A second result followed from the first. Owing to Parliament's control of the sea, no foreign power seriously contemplated armed intervention in the English fighting.

During this same epoch, in Germany, the Thirty Years War was raging. The German conflict and the sufferings of Germany were confused and prolonged by the armed intervention of Sweden, Denmark, France and Spain. In France, during the religious civil wars of the sixteenth century, German and Spanish intervention had occurred. But, owing to the parliamentary watch on the seas, the conflict in England was kept within bounds — apart from a few mercenaries — foreign troops and generals, and the interests of foreign powers, were not involved. This is an inestimable blessing for which Englishmen have cause to thank the Navy.

Mr. Powell fully describes in these pages the character of the war at sea, of the men who fought it and of the ships in which they fought. He describes the numerous occasions on which the course of the land war was modified or altered — sometimes vitally —by intervention from the sea. It is an enthralling story full of interesting incidents and memorable men.

First and foremost there is Parliament's admiral, the Earl of Warwick. His picture, by Sir Anthony Van Dyck, can be seen today in the Metropolitan Museum, New York. It was painted several years before the outbreak of the war, and the famous Court painter of King Charles has, so to speak, disguised the tough Earl of War-wick in the gorgeous, elaborate and most unpractical attire of a courtier. But the face which surmounts all the finery is the hard-bitten, weathered face of an old sea-dog, a face that belongs more to the adventurous days of Queen Elizabeth I than to the silken time of Van Dyck. During the peaceful years of King Charles Warwick had been concerned with Lord Saye, Lord Brooke and others famous in American history, in various colonial and naval ventures. But it was in the Civil War that he came into his own as a naval commander of readiness and resource.

One of the greatest and most famous of English seamen, Robert Blake, the hero of the Cromwellian navy, also played a part in the Civil War. He appears in Mr. Powell's book in his other capacity as a land commander. He was the valiant defender of the sea port of Lyme against the besieging Cavaliers, an epic defense in which he was assisted at a critical moment by the intervention of the Navy.

Mr. Powell has done valuable research in exploring the sources and putting together the complete history of the Navy during the English Civil War. This is a chapter of history important and interesting in itself. But it is also important in the larger context of the history of liberty among the English-speaking peoples. Here is a story fascinating alike in its details and its general consequences for which readers and students of all kinds have reason to be grateful to Mr. Powell.

C. V. WEDGWOOD

Preface

Most modern historians realize that the adherence of the Navy to the Parliament in the English Civil War did much to decide the issue. Yet the average Englishman is hardly aware that there was a Navy, or that it did anything in the struggle. Perhaps this is not surprising. For to his mind there is a great gulf fixed between the defeat of the Armada and the magnificent victories of the Commonwealth fleets, led by the genius and inspiration of Robert Blake. Save for the disastrous voyages of the Duke of Buckingham to Cadiz and the Isle of Rhè, and for the cruises of the Ship-Money fleets in the Channel, the Navy seems to vanish into the mists of obscurity. Then, like a meteor, with the advent of the Commonwealth, it flashes across the pages of history. In seven short years it drove Rupert's fleet from the seas and snatched from the Royalists the Scilly and Channel Islands. From the indomitable Tromp it wrested the Dutch mastery of the Narrow Seas. It affronted the maritime might of Portugal, Spain, France, and the Moor, and made them acknowledge England as the mistress of the Ocean.

Straight from the Civil War came the seamen Blake led in 1650. Four of his vessels had been at sea in 1642, while three of them had been built by Parliament in the Civil War. In almost continuous service at sea from 1642, they had learned the naval art. Instead of a gap there is continuity. An analysis of the men-of-war and armed merchantmen of the Summer and Winter Guards set forth each year proves this. For it reveals the large number of ships that were employed during the struggle.

Year		Rate						Total	Total		Reserve
		1	2	3	4	5	6	Merchantmen			
1642	Summer		9	6	2		1	18	24	42	
	Winter		3	2	2		5	12	28	40	
1643	Summer	1	7	8	3	2	9	30	50	80	
	Winter	No Record						22	24	46	25 Merchantmen
1644	Summer		2	8	6	7	7	30	22	52	
	Winter		1	2	5	3	7	18	10	28	

Year		Rate						Total	Total	Reserve
		1	2	3	5	4	6		Merchantmen	
1645	Summer		2	7	6	5	9	29	26	55	
	Winter			4	5	5	7	21	17	38	
1646	Summer	6	8	6	9	15		42	21	63	32 Merchantmen
	Winter			4	9	8	12	33	10	43	
1647	Summer		2	8	9	9	17	45	13	58	6 Second rate &
	Winter			2	11	6	6	25		25	26 Merchantmen
1648	Summer	1	6	12	10	10		39		39	
	Winter	2	2	11	5	12		32		51	

The absence of merchantmen in the last three Guards is due to the fact they had either been bought or taken into the Navy, and so were reckoned as men-of-war. But the lists show there was a Navy at sea, and that obviously it must have been active.

Confronted by this list of ships the average Englishman may still wonder what the Navy did. Historians have strangely neglected the work of the fleet in the English Civil War. Save for a short chapter by Mr. C. D. Penn in his book, *The Navy under the Early Stuarts*, little or nothing has been written. The military and political sides of the struggle have received ample treatment. But to ignore the work of the Navy is to view the struggle in false proportion and perspective. The names of Pym, Essex, Fairfax, Cromwell, and Rupert spring to mind as the great leaders in the Civil War. That of Robert Rich, Earl of Warwick is practically unknown. He it was who commanded, led, and directed the Navy. Under him were a galaxy of able Admirals — Batten, Swanley, Moulton, and Penn, equally obscure. Their names deserve to be added to the history of the Civil War.

To understand the conflict it is necessary to realize the points of contrast between the military and naval forces. First, there was no regular standing army. It is true that there were the local train-bands and the militia, but they were only called out in the case of emergency. They still tended to be feudal in character, following the lead of the local magnate. Both sides supplemented this irregular force by raising troops of their own. These armies suffered from the unwillingness of the rank and file, who feared for the safety of their homes and families should the enemy make an appearance, to serve outside their own district. Defeat or reverse led them to disperse with the cry of "Home, Home!" How to arm them became an important question. The private armories of the train-bands, or of the local magnate, supplied a certain quota. From the outset the possession of the royal arsenals at the Tower and at Hull became the objective of both sides.

The Navy stood out in strong contrast, as a regular standing force, manned by trained officers and men. The ships were well supplied with guns, powder, and munitions, ready for war. The men had no feudal ties, for their allegiance was to King and Parliament. Above all they were accustomed to serve at long distances from their home ports, and to continuous engagement and discipline.

In the matter of the high command the contrast was even stronger. The command of the parliamentary armies was entrusted to the Earl of Essex. But, as the authors of *The Great Civil War* have acutely pointed out, he "exercised a nominal power and control over the subordinate army commanders in the North, East Anglia, and the West. But in practice they seldom sought or regarded his infrequent instructions."[1] Nor had he the strategic ability to see the war as a whole. Instead he allowed himself to become bogged down in the concerns of his own army. Thus he fixed his headquarters in the Thames valley, instead of the obvious place, which was London. So, without realizing it, he allowed his wider powers to pass to the Committee for the Safety of the Kingdom, composed of members from the Lords and Commons, led by John Pym with Harry Vane as his second. Neither of them had any military experience, nor could the generals advise them, for they were absent in the field.[2]

With no co-ordinated plan of campaign, and with little or no central direction, the parliamentary strategy became a confused fumbling. Each emergency was dealt with separately. The various army generals had to conduct operations as best they could, ignorant of what was happening elsewhere. They frequently became jealous of each other, and subordinates would act as if they were independent.[3]

They had to contend against a royalist high command, centered in military and political matters in the King and his Council. Upon this sat the generals to advise. They were to produce a definite plan of campaign: to take the offensive and capture London, the nerve center of the rebellion. The wealth of the City, upon which Parliament depended financially, would no longer be available.[4]

The naval high command was to be in very different hands. Robert Rich, Earl of Warwick, was to serve first as deputy Lord High Admiral, and then as the Lord High Admiral himself. He was to keep the reins of office firmly in his own hands. Since Parliament was abysmally ignorant of naval affairs he was in a strong position. It is true that a Committee for the Navy was set up, but it was not to count for much. Every detail of administration was at Warwick's finger tips. He kept in intimate personal touch with his officers and men, proving himself a sailors' Admiral.

He made London his headquarters, where he would frequently return from his station in the Downs, or from expeditions with his ships at sea. He was thus in touch with the progress of the war as a whole. With his strategic ability he at once picked the focal points upon which to station his ships. He sat like a spider at the center of the web which he spun round the coasts of England with his ships at the circumference. Though his commanders had to operate at long distances from him, they were never allowed to become independent. They were expected to exercise initiative and action, but always as a unified force acting under his direction and orders. His squadrons, separate though they were, conformed to a planned purpose, directed by a single head.

Thus Warwick was able to weave into the pattern of the war isolated ports and local forces. Desperately struggling against their enemies and cut off from military aid, they had a sense of neglected isolation. With each parliamentary army operating on its own, with little or no central direction, their situation must have seemed desperate. The appearance of Warwick's ships, always at the right moment, gave them naval support, supplies, and reinforcements of both troops and seamen. The fleet transformed them into bastions against the Royalist armies. They realized the importance of their resistance to the war as a whole.

By the control of the outer lines of communication the ships could bring swiftly these supplies and specially heavy guns to any threatened spot upon the sea coasts. Often the seamen were

to be used as an amphibious force to aid the troops upon land.
Moreover they were free from naval opposition, whereas the armies
had to struggle over rough roads, often impeded by mud, to say
nothing of the Royalist armies.

The problems of foreign intervention, of protecting the merchant
shipping, and of intercepting gun-runners and privateers, Warwick
saw as parts of his operations as a whole. He resolutely refused
to disperse his ships in order to deal with these problems separately,
although frequently urged to do so by popular clamor. From this
parochial outlook he rescued the Navy by preserving it as a unified force.

From the outset Warwick recognized that First and Second
Rate ships were not so useful to him as the Third, Fourth, Fifth
and Sixth Rates. The bigger ships required more men and money;
the smaller were cheaper in both respects. He required smaller,
swifter vessels that could operate in shallow waters, to pursue both
the gun-runners and the privateers. Constantly he urged the need
for such, if he was to deal with the Royalist vessels adequately.
Yet it was not until 1646 and 1647 that Parliament built seven new
Fourth-Rate ships. As the sphere of naval operations extended
widely he was to be hampered by the need for more vessels. Only
by his ability in placing his squadrons at the strategic positions was
he able to do so much with so few vessels.

It has often been said that the Navy was never so well supplied
and paid as it was by Parliament. Warwick's despatches tell a different story. Constantly he had to beg for supplies, victuals, money
and ships. For the Navy fell into the hands of Parliament as a
ready-made gift from the gods, whereas they had to raise aand equip
their armies. They became obsessed with the military needs, and
they tended to regard the Navy as a useful Cinderella. It was already
equipped and furnished, officered and manned, so that they did not
need to worry about it. Parliament began the war far better equipped
by sea than by land, and they expected the Navy to look after itself.
Like the workhouse board they expected the fleet to subsist on the
"supper allotted by the dietary." They were horrified when Warwick,
in the capacity of Oliver Twist, asked for more. But in Warwick
they met their match. He was not afraid to beard them with their

neglect of the fleet, and to make known its needs in and out of season. As a good Puritan he followed the example of the importunate widow.

With the two differences between the Navy and the Army in mind this book endeavors to show the part the fleet played in the Civil War, to reveal the influence it had on the struggle. It has for its purpose the answer to two questions: why the Navy joined the Parliament, and how Warwick achieved so much with so little. Out of the confusion of 1643 there begin to emerge significant facts. The contest for the possession of Hull, Plymouth, Milford Haven, and even North Wales, was in reality the attempt to secure or to deny the fleet important naval bases. The securing and support of these places by the Navy had a direct bearing on the course of the war. The fleet held the ring for the Parliament. Gradually it prevented any support from reaching the King from outside England. Time and again Warwick's mobile squadrons were to call check to the King's armies. They moved in perfect co-ordination to a master plan, directed by a master brain. Had the Navy failed, the outcome of the Civil War might have been far different. How it succeeded, in spite of great handicaps not of its own making, is related here, for this comparatively unknown story is worth the telling.

I must express my gratitude to Miss C. V. Wedgwood for so generously contributing an Introduction, and for reading the manuscript. Professor Lewis and Brigadier Peter Young have also done so. To all of them I am indebted for advice, suggestions and criticisms, both military and naval. Doctor R. C. Anderson and Commander J. H. Owen also have given me much valuable information and help. Messrs. Collins, Eyre and Spottiswoode, and the Clarendon Press have kindly allowed me to quote from *The King's Peace* and *The King's War*, by C. V. Wedgwood, *The Great Civil War*, by Brigadier Peter Young and the late Lt. Colonel Burne, and from *Cornwall in the Civil War*, by Mary Coate. The Editors of the *Mariner's Mirror* and the *Irish Sword* have kindly permitted me to make use of my articles, first on the "Siege of Lyme" and the "Siege of Bonratty", and secondly from the "Siege of Duncannon" and the "Siege of Youghal". Messrs. Allen and Unwin have kindly given permission to quote from Professor Lewis' *Navy of Britain*.

I am indebted to Mr. A. L. Leach and Messrs. H. F. Witherby for permission to reproduce the two maps of Pembrokeshire from *The Civil War in Pembrokeshire,* and also to Sir J. F. Rees and the University of Wales for the map of the engagement at Pill from *Studies in Welsh History.* I am most grateful to Jean Reeves for her drawings of the maps.

To my wife I owe much, for her help, criticism and encouragement.

The Navy in the English Civil War

Robert Rich, Earl of Warwick

CHAPTER I

The Winter of the Navy's Discontent

Through the windows of the Guildhall, in the City of London, closed against the frosty morning air of January 9th 1642, came the mingled sound of marching feet and cheering men. The Committee of the House of Commons raised their heads and listened expectantly. They had fled here dramatically for safety, after the King's failure to seize five of the members, for John Pym, the King's principal opponent, well understood the art of window-dressing and of publicity. The City should protect Parliament from the King. As the sounds drew nearer, the Committee could distinguish cheers for the Earl of Warwick, the Vice-Admiral of England, and in present command of the fleet. They moved to the windows and saw in the street below some two thousand mariners, who had come from Ratcliffe and the districts below the bridges. A deputation detached itself from the crowd and entered the Guildhall. In a moment they stood before the Committee. Their spokesman respectfully explained they had come to offer their services for the defense of Parliament and for the Protestant Religion, as it had been established in the days of Queen Elizabeth.

Then he presented a Protestation proclaiming 'the chief and main reason" of their coming. "We, who are used to tempests, never stood in fear of a greater than this on land. That great vessel, the Parliament-House, which is so richly fraught with no less value than the price of a Kingdom, is fearfully shaken, and in great danger. Rome has rocks, and Spain quicksands, to swallow her up." The document was obviously the work of a far abler hand than that of an ordinary seaman, as it cleverly put into words their old fear of Spain and Popery, and their present alarm at the trend of events.[1]

The Committee thanked the deputation and promised to present their Protestation to Parliament. Two days later that body received it, and returned their gracious thanks. To parliamentary sympathisers as well as to the seamen, the Protestation must have recalled the Spanish Treaty of 1630 — how the King, in order to balance the budget, had arranged that Spanish gold should be brought to England to be minted into coin and then transported in English ships to Antwerp to pay the Spanish troops, fighting against the Dutch. The King, of course, received a part of the gold for his own mint. And yet were not the Dutch Protestants the natural allies of the English in the fight against Spanish and Papal dominion? As the ships carrying the money belonged to England, the Dutch could neither attack nor capture them. No wonder they protested against such an interpretation of neutrality, while to the Englishmen it seemed, in Miss C. V. Wedgwood's apt phrase, that "the King had become the pensioner and helper of Spain."[2]

More humiliating events had followed. The loss of Breisach cut the Spanish communications with the Hapsburg dominions in lower Germany. Instead English ships had been chartered to carry troops from Spain to Dunkirk. Then came the failure of the Scots' war in 1639, in which the troops had been driven back to England. The splendid Ship-Money fleet, under the command of the incompetant Earl of Hamilton, had cruised aimlessly between the Forth and Holy Isle in inglorious inactivity, and thus the King was forced to sign the Pacification of Berwick on June 9th. Even while it was being signed, Tromp, the Dutch Admiral, in the absence of the English fleet, had swooped down on three English ships in the Channel, carrying fifteen hundred Spanish troops. The English seamen were treated with courtesy, but the soldiers were made prisoner and removed.[3] Only one vessel escaped to Portsmouth. From here the troops were marched by London to Dover, where they were shipped to the Netherlands. The Spanish officers taunted the English seamen with cowardice in submitting to the Dutch in English waters, which naturally aroused their anger. Their anger reached fever-pitch a little later when five shiploads of Spanish troops were landed at Plymouth.[4] The rough sea-dogs of Devon had to watch the Spanish officers ruffling it upon the Hoe, ground that was to them still hallowed to the memory of Drake and the Armada. They were filled with fury at such desecration. Nevertheless, despite the protests of the Dutch Ambassador, these troops were allowed to reach the Netherlands.

In September a Spanish fleet, with ten thousand soldiers aboard, came up the Channel. Tromp left the blockade of Dunkirk and attacked it. After a fierce battle in which the Spaniards consumed all their powder, their Admiral, Oquendo, ran into the Downs for shelter, where Tromp blockaded him. The English fleet, under Sir John Pennington, watched both parties. Both the Spanish and Dutch Ambassadors appealed to Charles, but the King had no intention of getting involved or of risking his ships. He tried to pacify the Spaniards by selling them gunpowder — at exorbitant prices — while he ordered Pennington to prevent hostilities. As this could only mean action against the Dutch, which Pennington knew would lead to mutiny among his crews, when Tromp attacked, Sir John took advantage of a slight fog and a contrary wind to remain neutral. The Spanish fleet, with the exception of a few vessels which escaped to Dunkirk, was destroyed. And all England rejoiced.[5]

The disaster led Spain to offer Charles four million ducats in May, 1640, if he would give them a permanent escort of thirty-six warships to convoy their transports through the Channel. The King, who had just dissolved the Short Parliament, saw in the offer a dazzling financial prospect: he could be free of Parliament for some time. He promptly threw his principal opponents into the Tower — among them Pym, Hampden, and the Earl of Warwick, the idol of the seamen and a violent opponent of Ship-Money. Riots at once broke out, in which the seamen and the eager apprentices joined. One enthusiastic mariner smashed in the gates of Lambeth Palace — for which he was duly hung. And the royalist Lord Mayor quelled the mob only by calling out the train-bands. But Pym, Hampden, Warwick, and the seamen were acclaimed as martyrs to the Anti-Papal and Anti-Spanish cause and their ultimate release only added to their popularity.[6]

The Dutch now took a firm line. If the King continued to escort the Spanish troops, his ships would be treated as enemies. Since Charles could not afford war with Holland, the Spanish finan-

cial agreement had to be abandoned. The anger of the seamen was
further enflamed by the failure of the fleet to protect the Channel.
It had been hampered by the preparations for operations against
Scotland — known as the Second Bishops' War. Thus Barbary
pirates had landed at Penzance and had carried off men, women
and children, while twenty-four Dunkirk privateers had ravaged the
Kent and Sussex coasts. The Navy had actually been forbidden to
interfere, lest the King's hopes of a Spanish alliance might be damaged: the Dunkirkers were in an unofficial alliance with Spain.
They even flew the Spanish colours at their mastheads, sailing, as
it were, under a flag of convenience. Their operations boldly extended
as far as Ireland.

In Ireland in the absence of the Earl of Strafford, the Lord
Lieutenant, bloody rebellion had broken out, and the English had
been massacred by fire and sword. The anger of England had
forced the King to hand over the charge of Irish affairs to Parliament. The small army that had been sent over saved Dublin, from
which place the Lords Justices administered such parts as remained.
It was not much — a stretch of country round Dublin, with the
ports of Carrickfergus, Cork, and Youghal. Off the latter two lay
the Irish Guard, of two Third-Rates and eight armed merchantmen, both to secure the ports and to check the Irish and Dunkirk
privateers.

The failure of the Second Bishops' War forced the King to
recall Parliament, as he was at his wits' end for money. Strafford
was promptly impeached, and sent to the block on May 12th 1642,
while Archbishop Laud lay in the Tower awaiting a similar fate.
It was clear that an armed struggle was not far off. The thoughts
of both sides must have turned to the Continent in speculation as
to the probable attitude of the foreign powers. With the failure of
the Spanish Alliance the King had transferred his hopes to Frederick
Henry, Prince of Orange, to whom he had married his daughter
Mary. Frederick Henry was one of the richest nobles in Europe,
one who might well be expected to devote much of his wealth to
the cause of the English King. His subjects, however, were mostly
in sympathy with the parliamentary party, and could exercise their
power through their States, or Parliament. The King of France,

Louis XIII, was brother-in-law to Henrietta Maria, Charles' Queen. But Charles could expect no help from him. France and Spain were at war, and neither Louis nor his minister, Cardinal Richelieu, were prepared to risk their young navy in carrying troops to Charles' aid. Nevertheless, it was clear that much would depend upon which side could secure the Navy — King or Parliament.

Here was a weapon ready-made. Its creation was due to the interest the first two Stuarts had taken in the Navy. They had built some splendid ships, some of which survived to fight as late as 1673. Charles too had improved the dockyards and repaired James' ships. Then he built the Ship-Money fleet, in hopes of clearing the Channel of the Moorish pirates and of the Dunkirk privateers, who had even blockaded the mouth of the Thames and blackmailed the London merchants into paying a duty to let their ships pass in. Here, as Professor Lewis has aptly pointed out, lay the crux of the matter: The nation objected to the formula that the King controls, but the people pay; thus the issue touched the heart of the constitutional quarrel. If the King could collect money by such means as levying of Ship-Money, he need never call a Parliament again.

The fleet stood ready. A report by William Batten, Surveyor of the Navy, made early in 1642, shows the estimated fitness, with ordinary repairs, of each ship. So thorough was the survey that the sails and ropes that were either rat- or moth-eaten were listed.[7]

Rate	Ship	Date	Tons	Men	Guns	Fit for years
1	Sovereign	1637	1522	600	90	15
	Prince	1641	1187	500	70	20
	Merhonour	1616	946	350	40	5
2	Defiance	1616	857	250	38	2 (Summers only)
	Rainbow	1617	731	240	40	10
	Constant Reformation	1619	742	250	40	7
	Victory	1620	721	260	40	7
	Swiftsure	1621	746	260	46	5
	St. Andrew	1622	783	260	42	10
	St. George	1622	792	260	44	10
	Triumph	1623	776	300	44	7
	Vanguard	1631	751	250	40	5
	Henrietta Maria	1633	793	250	42	9

Rate	Ship	Date	Tons	Men	Guns	Fit for years
	Charles	1633	810	250	44	9
	Unicorn	1634	767	250	46	9
	James	1634	875	250	48	10
3	Assurance	1601	600	200	34	Perhaps 2 summers
	Dreadnought	1613	552	140	30	3
	Convertine	1616	621	200	34	3
	Antelope	1619	512	160	38	7
	Happy Entrance	1619	539	160	30	7
	Garland	1620	567	170	34	8
	Bonaventure	1621	557	170	32	8
	Swallow	1634	478	150	34	10
	Leopard	1635	515	160	34	10
	Lion	1640	620	170	40	20
4	Mary Rose	1623	321	100	25	4
	Expedition	1637	301	110	14	5
	Providence	1637	304	110	14	5
5	Eighth Whelp	1628	162	60	14	⎧ Perhaps 2
	Tenth Whelp	1628	186	60	14	⎩ Summers
6	Henrietta Maria					
	Pinnace	1624	68	25	6	⎧ 4 Years Harbor
						⎩ Service
	Greyhound	1636	126	50	12	7
	Roebuck	1636	90	45	10	
	Nicodemus	1636	105	50	6	Perhaps 2 summers

Non-effective Ships:

Rate	Ship	Date	Tons			
5	First and Second					
	Whelps	1628	105	Fitted for the Baracado at Chatham		

Not fit for Sea Service:

Rate	Ship	Date	Tons
2	Nonsuch	1603	619
3	St. Denis (prize)	1635	619
4	Adventure	1594	287
5	Third Whelp	1628	196

The ships varied in length: the First-Rates 100 feet and upwards: the Second-Rates up to a hundred feet: the Third-Rates up to ninety-six feet: the Fourth-Rates up to ninety feet: the Fifth-Rates up to sixty feet, and the Sixth-Rates up to the same. They were roughly a third in breadth in proportion to their length. Under good conditions they could sail about ten knots, but with lighter winds they were much slower, so that the smaller ships could outsail them. Charles' chief mistake was in not building enough small vessels fast enough to be capable of catching the slender swift-sailing Dunkirkers.

The principal guns with which they were armed were:

The Demi-Cannon	32 pounder, with a range of 340 yards.
The Cannon-Perier	24 pounder, with a range of 320 yards.
The Culverin	18 pounder, with a range of 400 yards.
The Demi-Culverin	9 pounder, with a range of 400 yards.
The Saker	5 pounder, with a range of 340 yards.

These guns were mounted as broadsides on the upper and lower decks. The Second-Rates carried four demi-cannon, four cannon-perier, thirty-two culverins and demi-culverins, and sakers, while the Third and Fourth Rates carried culverins, demi-culverins and sakers. The rate of fire was slow — ten to twelve shots per hour for the heavy guns, and rather more for the light ones. In action the best results were obtained by getting as close to the foe as possible, and then giving her a broadside. Between each shot the gun had to be sponged to avoid the risk of premature explosion, which partly accounted for the slow rate of fire.

The fleet was supplemented by the hire of armed merchantmen at two shillings per ton per month, though after 1642 the rate was altered to £3.15.6 per month. The owner armed and provided the ship, while the State accepted responsibility in the event of loss. Two fleets went to sea each year, the Summer Guard from May to October and the Winter Guard from November to April. The chief dockyards were at Deptford, Chatham and Portsmouth.

Naval administration was in the hands of the Lord High Admiral, and the parliamentary Committee for the Navy, which had been revived on November 3rd, 1642. It consisted of eighteen persons from both Houses, and dealt chiefly with finance. There was also a Navy Board comprised of the four principal officers, the Treasurer, the Comptroller, the Surveyor, and the Clerk of the Ships.

These probably worked through deputy officers, who did the real work. Their duties consisted of the care of the dockyards and the equipment of the ships with stores and victuals so as to keep them in proper trim.

Administration had been brought into some sort of order by the Earl of Northumberland, the Lord High Admiral, when Parliament had been recalled. The King's personal rule had resulted only in chaos, owing to the cutting off of supplies and money. His reported remark, when he heard of the march of the seamen to the City to offer their services to Parliament, "How is it that I have lost the hearts of these water-rats?", can best be answered in Pepys' acute saying years later: "Englishmen, and more especially seamen, love their bellies above everything else — any abatement from them in the quantity or agreeableness of the victuals is to provoke and discourage them in the tenderest point, and will sooner render them disgusted with the King's service than any one other hardship." Neither Spain nor Popery was their chief grievance — that was aimed at a far wider audience — but the conditions under which they had suffered.

Owing to the lack of money, seamen, whose time had expired, were transferred from ship to ship to avoid payment of their wages, while worn-out mariners were given, in lieu of their pay, worthless tickets which no sensible person would cash. The dockyard workers and their families had been reduced to starvation, and the officials could only keep the wolf from the door by means of peculation. The Victuallers, whose provisions stank to High Heaven (and here was the chief grievance, as Pepys recognized), might well be excused on the ground that this was the only means of calling attention to their unpaid bills. Ship-money had provided the King with his fleet, but he had no money to pay the seamen.[8]

It is not surprising, therefore, that to man the fleet fishermen and merchant-seamen were torn from their employment to mingle with raw landsmen and watermen. Their only means of escape from their miseries was desertion. In April, 1636, out of two hundred and fifty men sent to the *St. Andrew,* two hundred and twenty vanished.[9] Typhus was rampant and Mervyn, one of the Admirals, reported that the men "In this weather fall sick for want of clothing, most of them barefoot and scarcely rags to hide their skins." Sick men had to be kept aboard "or turned ashore in danger of starving, not to be received into any house so as some have been seen to die upon the strand." Well might he conclude with the warning, "now with what confidence can punishment be inflicted upon men who mutiny in these wants? These neglects be the cause that mariners fly to the service of foreign nations to avoid His Majesty's: His Majesty will lose the honour of the seas, the love and loyalty of his sailors, and his Royal Navy will droop."[10] Similar complaints from the Earl of Northumberland, Sir John Pennington and others fell on deaf ears. Those from the seamen were either ignored or treated as frivolous. There was no money.

Even with the recall of Parliament Northumberland could only make slow progress. He did his best to right the wrongs of the seamen. Even so, many sailors, in 1642, had received no pay for seven years. The best of the Captains were selling the masts and yards out of the ships to feed and clothe the starving and naked crews. Such was the long winter of the Navy's discontent. As Professor Lewis has written: "Charles I forgot that with sailors as with camels, there is such a thing as the last straw". Not that the seamen were politically-minded — most were simple, blunt, childlike men, upon whose minds the hardships of poverty, hunger, and cold weighed heavily, to the exclusion of everything else. They were matter-of-fact individuals with the greater part of their attention fixed on pay and food. It is quite beyond doubt that what now passed through the minds of these Ship-Money sailormen was simply this: "We know now what the King is like as an employer and a paymaster, and are not impressed. Let us give the other side a chance, and see what Parliament (which promises so much better things), can do for us."[11]

Of the support of the seamen, therefore, Pym and the parliamentary party could be fairly certain. But what of the higher command? Without the officers, as the Spanish Civil War has demonstrated, the fleet would be useless. Northumberland, it was true, had deserted the King, but he was a cautious man, too much so to become involved if he could avoid it. The Vice-Admiral, Robert Rich, Earl of Warwick, was very different. He was a stout Parlia-

mentarian and Presbyterian who had fought in the Low Countries.
He had been associated with Pym in the Providence Company and
in the founding of the Saybrook Colony in Connecticut, although he
had soon deserted the New Jerusalem there for the more lucrative
business of piracy against the Spaniard from Santa Catalina in the
Caribbeans. This policy he carried out with a fleet he had inherited
from his father. In any hopes Pym had of gaining the fleet, Warwick
must have taken a prominent place. In addition many of the officers
were on the side of Parliament, partly because of their dislike of
the King's Spanish policy and partly out of their sympathy with
the sufferings of their crews.

Strangely enough, the King was equally confident of the support of the seamen. After his failure to seize the Five Members he
had gone to Hampton Court, where he began to plan for war. He
appointed the Earl of Newcastle to be Governor of Hull, and ordered
Captain Legge to go north to secure the submission of the citizens
to their new Governor. He would thus gain possession of the arsenal
with the munitions stored there for the Scottish war. And here he
hoped to land Danish troops when the port was his. But the plan
was betrayed to Pym, and the younger Hotham was sent with orders
to his father, Sir John Hotham, parliamentary Governor of Hull,
to use the Yorkshire train-bands to secure the city. He was not
to deliver it up except "by the King's authority, signified unto him
by the Lords and Commons now assembled in Parliament". Thus
before Legge had started Hotham was riding hell-for-leather down
the North Road. When Newcastle and Legge appeared before the
city the Mayor refused to admit any troops whatsoever into the
town.[12]

Charles now decided to send the Queen, with her daughter
and the crown jewels, to Holland, where she could buy arms to send
across to him. She sailed from Dover on February 23rd, in the *Lion*.
The King's depression at the recent action of the seamen vanished
with the reception he got from the Captain, John Mennes, a devoted
Royalist, and from his seamen. He was now confident of their de-
votion to him, and of his naval strength.[13] After waving a long
farewell to the Queen from the cliffs until she was out of sight, he
rode to Greenwich. From Greenwich, on March 3rd, he left for

York, where he believed the people would rise in his favour. After securing the arsenal at Hull, and with the arms the Queen would send him, he would move on the rebellious City of London, which, blockaded by his ships, would soon be forced to surrender. George Goring, who had gone over to Parliament and been made Governor of Portsmouth, was prepared to declare for him at a suitable moment. Charles could ride confidently northwards.

Pym too was equally confident. He knew the King's plans. The principal ports, London, Hull, Bristol, Portsmouth and Plymouth, however, were in the hands of parliamentary governors. The seamen and many of the officers were on the side of Parliament. But the possession of the fleet was vital. How was it to be wrested from the King's control?

CHAPTER II

1642

Warwick Secures the Fleet for Parliament

The answer came quickly. Early in March the Earl of Northumberland, anxious not to be involved personally in the coming struggle, pleaded a convenient illness to exercise his constitutional right to appoint a deputy to take charge of the fleet. Both sides instantly saw that the control of the Navy was at stake. The King nominated Sir John Pennington, a devoted Royalist and an experienced seaman, but Parliament boldly claimed their right to appoint to the command at sea. They persuaded Northumberland to appoint the Earl of Warwick, the Vice-Admiral. Then, surprisingly, they suggested that Captain Carteret should be made the Vice-Admiral, for he was a stout Royalist. In fury at the rejection of Pennington the King refused to allow Carteret to serve under Warwick. His decision was to have dire consequences for his cause in the near future. William Batten, the Surveyor, a zealous Parliamentarian and Puritan, was selected instead.[1]

In Warwick, Parliament made an excellent choice. He was to prove a first-rate administrator and organizer, with a keen eye for the strategical positions for his ships. Moreover, he had the ability to see that the work of the fleet must be co-ordinated with the military position on land. Men spoke of him as a man "foremost in fight, capable of climbing mast and yard", and as "one immune from seasickness." Such qualities endeared him to the rough mariners, who saw in him a leader of the old school, sharing with them the hatred of Spain, since they knew him for a keen Protestant and Parliamentarian. Above all he was a just man who, though he was a strict disciplinarian, could understand and right their grievances. He could, as well, credit and respect the motives of those who differed

THE TOWN OF HULL

from him politically. Thus he won the trust and confidence of the Navy.

Warwick got to work at once. With the King at York it was clear that he would endeavor to secure the arsenal at Hull to arm his troops. The possession of this port would be essential for the landing of the munitions the Queen was gathering in Holland. Two armed merchantmen, the *Bonaventure* (28) *, under Captain George Swanley, and the *Mayflower* (28), under Captain Joseph Piggott, were sent to the Humber to lie off Hull. Three other ships were to cruise in the North Sea to watch for the Queen's ships, since the possession of Hull was vital also to the Parliament. Rumor too spoke of Lord Digby's endeavors at Elsinore to raise thirty thousand Danish troops (probably grossly exaggerated), which were to be brought over to capture Hull.[2] Parliament thereupon ordered Hotham to reinforce the garrison, and to guard against any attack by sea. He was not to admit any foreign vessels without search, nor any armed forces without the express permission of Parliament.[3]

They had good reason, for already the Queen had been lent 800,000 guilders from the Prince of Orange to buy munitions. He had also arranged for the pawning of the crown jewels, despite the protests of Roger Strickland, the parliamentary agent in Holland, who claimed they were state property. By this means another 1,265,300 guilders were raised.[4] As the possession of a port was essential for the landing of her munitions, the Queen wrote the King urging him to secure Hull, Berwick, or Newcastle.[5]

Parliament now gave the King notice that they intended to remove the arsenal from Hull.[6] This news stung the King into action: the port was his and the arsenal also; he would go to claim both. On April 22nd he sent the young Duke of York to the city with a small party. Although they entered unobserved, they were soon recognized, and there was no choice but to receive them officially, since they said they would leave next day. To Hotham's dismay, Sir Lewis Dyve arrived early next morning to announce that the King was on his way to do him the honor of dining with him. An invitation from the Borgia could hardly have been more unwel-

*Numbers in brackets after ships denotes number of guns.

come. Sir John Hotham at once called a council, at which it was agreed that, as the King had troops with him, entrance must be refused to him. The drawbridge was drawn up, the troops stood to arms on the walls, and the townsfolk were confined to their houses.

Hull stood on a broad flat plain, a city walled on three sides and protected on the fourth by the waters of the deep broad Humber, which was joined on the east by the river Hull. At the east and west ends the walls met the estuary, and here the two armed merchantmen could lie at all states of the tide to protect the flanks. Troops, supplies, and munitions could be safely landed, so long as the Humber remained open. Hull's defence therefore depended upon the water.

At eleven o'clock the King arrived before the Beverley Gate, the only one in use, since the others had been blocked up at the time of the threatened Scot invasion. With him were a few hundred horse and foot, among them the Heralds in their gorgeous tabards. The King demanded entrance. Sir John, who was standing upon the wall, answered that Parliament had entrusted him with the city, and that trust he could not surrender. He irresolutely qualified his refusal by adding that if his presence gave offence to the King, he would get himself discharged, if the King would withdraw. The King thereupon appealed to the soldiers standing upon the wall. And his own troops, weary with their march, shouted to them to throw Hotham over to them. But the garrison stood steadfast by their Governor. Hotham saw a possible compromise: his orders forbade the entrance of troops, but said nothing about the King. He suggested Charles should enter with twelve attendants. Charles promptly declared that his dignity required thirty. Fearful of a possible rising of the citizens in the King's favor, Hotham refused to agree. The King then declared he would proclaim him a traitor. This outburst forced Hotham dutifully to his knees, answering once again that he could not betray his trust.

Meanwhile the royal party within were being banqueted by the Aldermen of Trinity House. When they learned of what was passing they demanded to leave, but Hotham refused to let them depart until one o'clock. When they joined the King, this insult added fuel to Charles' wrath at this affront to his royal dignity.

At four o'clock the King gave Hotham a last chance. He allowed him an hour in which to change his mind. Much of England's fate now depended upon Hotham's decision. Would the King secure the city with its port, and the weapons from the arsenal with which to arm his troops? Hotham steeled himself to a final refusal. At once the Heralds stood forth. They solemnly proclaimed him a traitor, and those serving him to be guilty of high treason. Then, as it was impossible, with his tiny force and without artillery, to force his way in, the King retired to York.[7]

Parliament at once approved Hotham's action, and indemnified all those who served him. Then in true Puritan spirit they decided to remove temptation out of the King's way. The *Prosperous* (28), under Captain Driver, and the *Hercules* (28), under Captain Moyer, were sent to Hull, where the magazine was loaded upon four merchantmen to carry to London. They were escorted by the *Bonaventure* and the *Prosperous*. Warwick himself with two men-of-war met them on the way, as there was a rumor they might be intercepted at sea. On April 30th the precious cargo was safely brought to London.[8]

About the start of June, the Queen sent off the *Providence* (20), an armed merchantman of the Royal Navy, under Captain Strahen. She carried two hundred barrels of powder, two thousand arms, and seven field pieces. Agents in Holland had warned Warwick of her sailing, and his three ships watching for her chased her into the Humber. Here the *Mayflower* met her, and ordered her to follow her to Hull, but the pilot gave her the slip, and took the *Providence* into a small creek near Paul, east of the city. Owing to her draught the *Mayflower* dared not follow. The royal train-bands, who were on the outlook for her, came up and stood by. Though Hotham sent troops and small boats to secure her cargo, they were beaten off. The munitions were unloaded and carried off to York, but the ship had to be abandoned, and a little later she was taken by Piggott.[9]

The King and the Earl of Newcastle, William Cavendish, were now able to arm their forces. On June 10th Cavendish captured the town of Newcastle and thus gave Charles a badly-needed northern port. The affair of the *Providence*, however, had revealed to the King the long-armed reach of the Navy. He was furious, not merely with his repulse before Hull, but more by the fact that his own ship, executing his commands, had been chased by vessels of his own fleet. He must secure the Navy. He determined to put into execution a long-contemplated plan, still believing the seamen were devoted to his person — even that they might seize the Earl of Warwick and throw him overboard. He would therefore revoke Northumberland's Commission as Lord High Admiral, under the Great Seal, and thereby render Warwick's appointment void. Sir John Pennington should be sent to take command of the fleet. But Sir John pointed out to Charles that Parliament had already objected to him, and that if he went to the fleet his purpose would instantly be guessed. He therefore dutifully asked to be allowed to decline. Then the King had a brilliant idea: the fleet should come to Sir John. Orders were drafted to Northumberland dismissing him. Others bade the Captains to bring their ships to Bridlington Bay, ignoring any orders Warwick might give them. Northumberland's letter was given to May, one of the King's pages. He was to ride slowly, so that Villiers, carrying the Captains' letters, should arrive at the Downs at the same time as May reached London. Should the hare beat the tortoise all would be undone.

Hardly was May out of sight when Pennington unexpectedly reappeared. On thinking things over he had conceived it to be his duty to accept command. Feverishly new letters were drafted to the Captains, ordering them to obey Sir John, while another dismissed Warwick and bade him not to meddle further in naval matters. Villiers was to go to Sir Henry Palmer, a retired naval officers, who lived near the Downes, and who was known to be *persona grata* with the fleet. Both were to go aboard, and then, when Sir Henry judged the moment to be ripe, to send back to Pennington, waiting nearby in secret, to come and take command. But second thoughts in secret operations are rarely best, for no one seems to have thought how an old man, ignorant of what was planned, would re-act to such a situation. But to horse, and ride like the Devil: May was well ahead, and his letter would stir up a hornet's nest.

Sir John, however, could not keep up with Villiers' frantic pace, so he ordered him to ride ahead to Sir Henry. With youthful enthusiasm Villiers clattered on, without pausing for sleep, until, on July 1st, he was hammering on Sir Henry's door. He could not make the sleepy, bewildered old man understand that he must come aboard immediately. Villiers had to leave him behind and go aboard himself. The Captains received the King's letters respectfully, but Warwick was ashore, and Batten was in command. And it was solely due to the King that he was there: had Carteret been in his place there was a faint chance that things might have gone differently. The weary hours dragged on, and neither Sir Henry nor Sir John came, nor had Villiers anyone to send back to them. Unadventurously Pennington waited, instead of putting all to the test. At long last Warwick stepped aboard and, as he did so, Villiers handed him the King's letter.[10] For the moment the Earl was taken aback. As he wrote to Pym, "I was in great straits between these two commands that had so much power over me." Then he pulled himself together and called his captains to a council. They all came, with the exception of Sir John Mennes, the Rear-Admiral, and Captains Fogge, Burley, Slingsby and Wake. The Council decided that their first duty was to Parliament, and they stood by Warwick. He could thus rely upon his flagship, the *James* (50), *St. George* (46), *Unicorn* (46), *Vanguard* (40), *Mary Rose* (26), *Martin* (36), *Sampson* (20), and the *Increase* (36). With Mennes in the *Victory* (40), were the *Reformation* (40), under Fogge, the *Antelope* (38), under Burley, *Garland* (34), under Slingsby, and *Expedition* (18), under Wake. The two parties of ships eyed each other anxiously. Then at the last moment Burley brought the *Antelope* over to Warwick, though the other four stood aloof.[11]

By good luck May had arrived in London about the same time as Villiers did in the Downs. He delivered his letter to Northumberland, who craftily allowed the news to leak out. He was pressed to remain in office, but was too cautious to do so. Call then an emergency meeting of Parliament: confirm Warwick in his authority; and send it off to him post-haste.[12] Established in power, Warwick surrounded the disobedient ships, and summoned them. This brought in Mennes and Fogge. Slingsby and Wake still stood out. After firing a gun over their vessels, Warwick sent his ships' boats to board them. Though they were unarmed, the crews eagerly clambered aboard, seized the shroud, seized the two captains, armed though

they were with sword and pistol, and struck the yards and top-
masts. Then with the aid of the two ships' crews they brought the
Captains and their ships to Warwick. The fleet was in the hands
of Parliament. As Miss Wedgwood has observed, "the King had
lost the fleet, and with it his remaining reputation in Europe: a
King of Great Britain without a Navy was, in all interchanges of
diplomacy, no King at all."[13]

The five Captains were sent up to London, where the first three
were released, while Slingsby and Wake were sent to the Gatehouse.
At Warwick's request they were set free a little later, after engaging
not to serve against Parliament. This action was typical of Warwick's
understanding generosity to those who had served him faithfully
in the past.[14] They were replaced by captains and owners from the
merchant ships. No captain now remained who had commanded a
man-of-war before 1637. All the Royalist Gentlemen-Captains had
gone. Now slowly a new type of captain, drawn from a lower social
class, was to emerge.

The King next made a desperate effort to hamstring Warwick.
He ordered the Principal Officers and their deputies not to issue
any stores or provisions to the fleet without his royal warrant. On
July 15th the Parliament sent out contrary instructions. The unfortunate officials hesitated as to which set of orders they should obey.
Parliament promptly dismissed them all, and replaced them with
Commissioners of the Navy. There were twelve members, headed by
Sir Henry Vane. Four were paid £100 a year — probably the permanent officials. Batten and Phineas Pett, his deputy, were paid by
virtue of their office as Surveyors. The Commissioners' duties were
to survey the ships for fitness, and to deal with their rigging, equipment, and allowance of stores. They had to examine all books,
vouchers, and payments, and generally to perform "all things whatsoever appertaining to the well-government of the Navy." All Clerks
of the Cheque, Principal Masters, Master Shipwrights, and inferior
officials were to attend and assist them, or any three of them. The
Commissioners had power to punish any neglect of duty or misbehavior by loss of wages, suspension, or removal from office. Thus
the whole administration of the Navy had passed from the King
to Parliament. Then, as if to celebrate this victory, the seamen's

wages were raised from fifteen to nineteen shillings a month. Frequent broad hints from Warwick, that the sailors' actions could best be rewarded by an issue of pay, show that Parliament found it easier to promise than to find the money.[15]

The arrival of the *Providence* had alarmed the authorities at Hull, who feared it pointed to a new attack, and they appealed for help. Sir John Meldrum with five hundred soldiers and supplies arrived on July 6th by ship — just in time, for the Earl of Lindsey with three thousand men arrived before the city. He built two forts, east and west of Hull, at Paul and Hessle, both to command the Humber and to prevent supplies from coming in. Another fort, on the Lincolnshire shore, opposite Paul, was to complete the plan. A pinnace, laden with guns and arms for this fort, set out from Paul, but she was set upon at once by the *Mayflower*. After a stout fight she was sunk with all hands.

In Hull Meldrum set about strengthening the defenses. The walls were repaired and culverins and demi-cannon mounted on them. A half-moon battery was built before each of the three main Gates — Beverley, North and Myton — linked up by trenches and breastworks. The Hessle and Myton Gates were also rammed up with earth. The banks of the river Hull and of the Humber were cut so as to flood the country round the city. It was still possible, however, for Lindsey's troops to approach the town along the raised banks of the Humber, the Hull, and Derringham Dyke.

Soon the *Sampson* (20) and the *Jocelyn* (12), with fifteen hundred troops aboard, were seen coming up the Humber, escorted by Rear-Admiral Trenchfield in the *Unicorn* (46) and by the *Rainbow* (40). The soldiers were rushed ashore. The thunder of the city's guns, as they checked the advance of the royal horse splashing through the floods, now mingled with the roar of the naval cannon. Across the broad Humber drifted the rolling clouds of smoke from the ships' guns as they overwhelmed the light pieces in the three royalist waterside forts. Swiftly they were battered into ruins. The attempt to deny the use of the Humber to the fleet had failed. Warwick's ships had saved Hull by keeping the water-way open. The reinforced garrison then clinched the naval victory by a final sortie which forced Lindsey to withdraw his army. Now Hull was to become a bastion against the royal army in the North.[16]

About the same time as the *Providence* had sailed, the *Lion* (38), had also left for Newcastle with the two Princes, Rupert and Maurice, aboard. She was driven back by a storm to Holland, where the two, suffering severely from sea-sickness, were landed. The *Lion* then sailed for the Downs, hoping probably to join Pennington and the fleet. Warwick suspected this and, when the *Lion* came in, he dismissed Fox, her Captain. Though he denied any knowledge of Pennington, his ship was seized. Another powerful vessel had been added to the fleet.[17]

The two Princes went to the Hague where the Prince of Orange gave them a forty-six gun ship, and a galliot laden with muskets, arms and powder, with a hundred officers aboard. They sailed for Newcastle or Scarborough, hoping to join the King. Off Flamborough Head they were hailed by the *London* (16). Her Captain asked what they were doing and what the galliot was. Captain Colster, with Rupert by his side wearing a mariner's cap, answered that they were cruising, and that the galliot, which was flying Dunkirk colors, was a prize. When the *London's* Captain demanded to search the galliot Colster refused, and emphasized this by running out his guns. The *London* then fired a gun to leeward to call for aid, since she was no match for the Dutch warship. Rupert now took the galliot in tow and made northwards. The sound of the firing had brought up two ships which had been lying off Tynemouth, and Rupert, seizing his opportunity, ran straight into the unguarded waters and anchored. As the parliamentary ships dared not attack, the Princes landed, while the galliot got away safely to Scarborough under cover of the dark night. The parliamentary ships had missed the rich prize of Rupert, soon to be the King's daring cavalry leader.[18]

More trouble now threatened Warwick from the Dutch. Twelve merchantmen, escorted by the *Mary Rose* (26), were seized in August by Tromp. He was a strong supporter of the House of Orange, at the moment blockading the Spaniards in Dunkirk. He declared that the vessels were carrying contraband to the Netherlands, and he sent them to Holland. Warwick retorted by arresting two Dutch warships and other vessels, bound for the Straits. But Parliament, anxious not to be further involved with the Prince of Orange at such a delicate and critical moment, ordered Warwick to release the ships. Eventually Tromp did the same, although he asserted his right of search, adding that he would defend it by force if necessary, and that it was well that Warwick should know it.[19]

An alarming piece of news now startled both sides. Colonel George Goring, parliamentary Governor of Portsmouth, suddenly declared for the King. This premature act came as a shock for Charles as he was not yet ready for war. To Parliament it came as a bombshell, for they thought the town was in safe hands. Portsmouth was essential to the fleet, both as a base, and for supply and repair. Warwick acted instantly. He sent off Richard Swanley in the *Charles* (44), with seven armed merchantmen, to cut the port off from the sea. They arrived on August 8th, at once landing seamen on Portsea Island to hold it until Sir William Waller could bring up troops.[20]

On the 15th Brown Bushell, of the *Martin* (36), was sent in to cut out the *Henrietta* pinnace (6), which defended the mouth of the harbor. Under cover of the darkness the longboats pulled silently for the pinnace. Before the half-wakened crew had realized what was happening they were boarded and driven below. As the *Henrietta* was taken past the sleeping batteries, two corn ships were sighted, hailed, and captured. This daring exploit was followed by a land operation on September 5th. In the half-light of the grey dawn the seamen marched to Southsea Castle. Brown Bushell and a trumpeter swam the moat and summoned the Castle. The Governor, who was sleeping off a drinking bout, was rudely aroused from his slumbers. He bade them return later on, when he would be able to attend to matters. Seeing him in no condition to conduct the defense, the seamen planted their ladders against the walls, scaled them, and took the Castle without the loss of a man. The Governor received them sitting, with very good reason, and asked them to fire a gun to let Goring know the Castle was lost! The sound of the firing promptly brought about a mutiny of the Portsmouth garrison. Goring was forced to surrender, and on September 7th the parliamentary forces entered the town. Goring was allowed to sail for Holland and, as he left, he threw the town keys into the harbor.[21] Portsmouth had fallen without the ships firing a shot, thanks to Warwick's prompt action. It was a blow, wrote Clarendon, "that struck the King to the very heart."

The possession of the Isle of Wight, however, was essential for the security of Portsmouth. Boldly acting on his own initiative, and without orders, Swanley decided to secure it. On the 18th he took the *Charles* into Cowes, and the town yielded without opposition. At Yarmouth the Governor refused to surrender to the *Greyhound* (12), and so Swanley sailed there in Elias Jordan's ship, the *Caesar* (20). He found the Governor, Barnabe Burley, standing on the ramparts with a lighted linstock in his hands, which he vowed he would plunge into a barrel of powder by his side, before he would betray his trust. Swanley wisely gave him time to think things over and eventually the intrepid man tamely surrendered. The sight of the ships' guns was too much for him. The contagion spread to Hurst Castle, on the opposite side of the water, where the garrison allowed a guard to enter. A gunner from Sandown Castle then arrived, asking for an order from Swanley to hold the place for the Parliament. Now only Carisbrooke Castle stood out. Swanley and Jordan lost no time. On the 23rd they marched inland with four hundred soldiers and seamen, and appeared before the Castle. This display of force so terrified the garrison that they threw down their arms and forced the Governor to surrender. The Island had been taken without the loss of a single man. Swanley's initiative had demonstrated the power of the Navy used as an amphibious force. Seamen, acting as soldiers, could be swiftly carried to the right spot, landed, and set to work. Warwick's long arm had again reached out from the Downs.[22]

Warwick at once officially approved Swanley's bold action. Such commanders, capable of acting on their own, were essential to him, for his own hands were full. He wisely remained in the Downs with the greater part of the fleet. He had to consider the military and naval threat from Denmark, as well as the uncertain attitude of Tromp. Though he was blockading Dunkirk he was near enough to be dangerous. The Downs served as a focal point from which ships could be sent to threatened spots, and from which it was possible to guard against foreign intervention.

But the north was still Warwick's chief concern. Here Trench-field's squadron, reinforced by four collier ships, the *Hector* (20), the *Edward and Elizabeth* (14), the *Recovery* (11), and the *Dragon* (6), were busy. By cruising between Hull and Holy Isle they had already taken several of the Queen's vessels. One had been forced into Yarmouth by a storm and captured. But another, a smaller and swifter ship, had been chased by his larger and slower vessels, and had eluded them and got into the Tyne. Two others had also got away and had landed munitions at Holy Isle itself. Trenchfield suggested that four small ketches, armed with four guns, could deal more effectively and more swiftly with these gun-runners rather than his larger slower ships. He had put his finger on the chief weakness of the fleet — the need for smaller swifter vessels, which also would be cheaper to maintain and would require fewer men for a crew.[23]

Complaints now came from the Lords Justices at Dublin. The two powerful Third-Rates, the *Swallow* (34), and the *Bonaventure* (32), had vanished from Kinsale. They had received secret orders from the King to go to Newcastle.[24] The coasts of Ireland had thus been left open to the attacks of the Irish and Dunkirk privateers, the latter of which had actually hoisted the Spanish colors over Wexford. They were infesting the harbor of Dublin itself and seizing ships.[25] To deal with these marauders there remained the *Confidence* (10), under Captain Thomas Bartlett, whose loyalty was suspect, and the *Swan* (20), under Captain John Bartlett, which was absent. The only other vessel, the *Phoenix*, had been wrecked off the Great Orme. Warwick could only reply that he had no ships to spare: he was barely able to protect the ships coming up the Channel; nor was there any port in Ireland upon which he could base his vessels.

To complicate matters still further the Marquis of Hertford, after abandoning Sherborne Castle in Dorset, had marched with Sir Ralph Hopton to Minehead. Here he had embarked his men upon colliers and crossed the Bristol Channel to Cardiff. Hopton with a hundred and sixty horsemen had ridden off to Cornwall.

But Warwick's chief anxiety was the whereabouts of the *Swallow* and the *Bonaventure*. It seemed probable they might go to Holland to escort the convoy the Queen was busily preparing. Here too they might form the nucleus of a royal fleet that could raid the merchant shipping. It was essential to find and deal with them before they could do further mischief. So important was this that Trenchfield was recalled in the *Rainbow*, and replaced by Batten, with "two or three ships of force". Guessing that Newcastle might be their destination, he made for the port. Kettleby and Stradling had arrived there on September 22 and began to victual at Tynemouth, preparatory to going to Holland to escort the Queen's convoy to England. Here Batten found them. Seizing his chance, while they were unprepared, he sent in his long boats to board them. He relied, from his previous experience in the Downs, upon the probable disaffection of their crews. His gamble came off, for, as his boats drew near, Stradling escaped in his longboat and Kettleby was overpowered by his own men. Soon both ships were handed over. The two last powerful vessels belonging to the King had been taken and the final obstacle to Warwick's control of the sea had gone.[26]

Hardly had this danger been removed than Plymouth was threatened. It was a fiercely Puritan town, whose corporation had already withstood the King. The deep waters of its estuary could provide secure riding for the fleet, so that its safety was another essential to Warwick. Hopton had arrived in Cornwall on September 25. At once the train-bands flocked to his standard. Driving Sir Richard Buller before him, Hopton occupied Launceston, so securing the line of the Tamar. In great alarm the Committee of Public Safety sent horse and foot into Devon. There was urgent need for them. Hopton, knowing how difficult it was to persuade the train-bands to leave their own county, had raised a volunteer army of five regiments of foot, with five hundred foot.

The control of Cornwall was vital to the King, for it gave him the command of the tin trade. The tin had been pre-empted to the Queen at twenty shillings the hundredweight, instead of the usual price of fifty-six shillings. Two able men, Sir Francis Bassett and Sir Nicholas Slanning, dealt with its collection from the Duchy, in the royal fortresses of St. Mawes and Pendennis, opposite Falmouth. Sir Nicholas too had organized a fleet, both to carry the tin overseas, and to harry the merchant shipping coming up the Channel.[27]

In France Lord Jermyn, Doctor Goffe, and William Godolphin arranged for its sale. The proceeds were used to buy munitions, and to pay the interest on the jewels, pawned by the Queen in Holland. French, Flemish, and English ships were hired to fetch the tin, and to carry back the munitions. Despite the capture of several ships by Warwick's vessels, this traffic was very successful. By November ten thousand foot arms, two thousand horse arms, and twenty cannon had been landed at Scarborough, Newcastle, Weymouth, Dartmouth, and Falmouth.[28] To intercept this traffic, and to check the raiding of the Cornish privateers, Warwick posted the *Happy Entrance* (30) and another vessel off Land's End, where they were able to warn merchantmen not to put into Falmouth. Then to secure the Bristol Channel and to support the parliamentary forces forming in Pembrokeshire, Robert Moulton, in the *Lion* (40), was sent to Tenby. Already fears had been expressed that the Irish troops might land in Milford Haven, and Warwick was asked to send troops there. The *Fellowship* (28) and the *Hart* (12) were sent to Bristol, from where they could reach the Haven.[29]

In the tin and munition traffic the Channel Islands were to play an important part. Though the islanders were mostly parliamentarian in sympathy, they were held in check by the impregnable fortresses of Elizabeth Castle and Mont Orgueil in Jersey, and by Castle Cornet in Guernsey. These were held for the King by Sir Phillip Carteret in Jersey and by Sir Peter Osborne in Guernsey, ironically enough as deputies to Warwick, who had been appointed titular Governor by Parliament. Though the garrisons did not venture out of the shelter of their strong walls, neither were the islanders strong enough to attack them. The tin and munition vessels, if they were chased by the parliamentary ships, could run for shelter under the powerful guns of the fortresses. Here the two small ships, the *George* (12), under Captain George Bowden, and the *Elizabeth* (12), under Captain William Coppin, who guarded the islands, dared not follow. Storms could also force them from the dangerous anchorages round the coasts, while their prey lay in security beneath the Castles.

The Committee for Public Safety however had been much more concerned with the King's movements than with affairs at sea. Charles had by now advanced to Nottingham, where he was joined by the two Princes. Here on August 22nd he hoisted his standard on a wet and windy day, and Civil War began in reality. The road to London was barred by the parliamentary army assembling at Northampton, which waited for the Earl of Essex to come and take command. The King moved instead to Chester to recruit men from Wales, his chief source of man-power. Here came riding in the well-mounted gentry, with their tenants, and the yeoman farmers. Rupert set to work at once to train them to charge at full gallop, and to make them a cavalry much to be feared by the foe. The leisurely Essex did not leave London until September 8th, to find that the King had gone westward. He moved to Worcester, where he loitered, uncertain whether Charles would advance on London or down the Severn Valley.

On October 12th the King, with a greatly increased army, boldly set out for London. He slipped past Essex, and the road to the capital was open to him. The Earl gave chase, aand at Edgehill the King turned to give him battle. On that autumn day at the foot of the pleasant Cotswold Hills he won the victory. Essex had to turn aside to Warwick. He had failed to bar the road to London, and he had to allow the King to enter Oxford.

The alarm in London was intense. In the absence of Essex a new army was to be formed to defend the capital. A resolute, determined and able commander was needed. Thus on October 12th Warwick was summoned to take command. Already he had displayed the necessary qualities. Yet before he left the fleet he sent a ship, laden with arms and money, to threatened Plymouth. As there was now no deputy Lord High Admiral, the post was put into Commission. Nine members were appointed, among them Northumberland and Warwick, the two Vanes, with Thomas Smith as their secretary. Any three of them formed a quorum and they exercised all the usual functions of the Admiralty. They arranged for the Summer and Winter Guards, issued instructions to the Navy Commissioners, and

recommended suitable persons for vacant posts.[30] Batten was summoned from the North to take charge of the fleet.[31]

At Oxford the King paused, possibly to rest his troops. He should
instead have strained every effort to gain the outskirts of London.
He thus gave Essex the opportunity, by moving round his north-
east flank in a series of desperate marches, to reach London before
him. Had Charles got there first, with the new army still in the
throes of birth, his cause might have triumphed. By the ninth of
November the King reached Colnbrook. Then, on the 12th, Rupert
attacked Brentford under the cover of a thick mist. Suddenly ap-
pearing out of the fog, his dashing horsemen drove back the parila-
mentary forces with heavy loss. Only the arrival of Essex and
Hampden rallied the survivors, though Brentford was lost and sacked.
In the fading light of the wintry sun Sir Phillip Skippon, that veteran
of the Dutch services, led out the city train-bands to Turnham Green.
Here next morning the King found himself confronted by twenty-
four thousand men. Outnumbered badly, he decided to withdraw.
Covered by Rupert's horse, he fell back to Houndslow, and from
there to Oxford.

It might be extravagant to say that the King was foiled not
merely by the train-bands, so much as by Warwick's possession of
the fleet. Yet it would be largely true. Had Charles controlled it he
could have blockaded London. The city merchants would have been
faced with bankruptcy, and the citizens with starvation. Ruin and
hunger are powerful challenges to civilian loyalty. Had he also been
able to secure Hull, the Earl of Newcastle could have struck at the
West Riding and its cloth towns, Puritan to the core and the back-
bone of the tiny forces of the Fairfaxes. Then with the North firmly
secured, and free from the threat of a hostile fortress in his rear,
Newcastle might have been strong enough to join the King in the
South. Together they might have been able to take London, and so
end the war at the start. But Warwick's ships decided otherwise.

On November 22nd Warwick resumed the command of the fleet.
An unusually strong Winter Guard of twelve warships and twenty-
eight merchantmen had been set out.* Warwick would have full

*See Appendix B.

need of them, for his eyes were turned again on Plymouth. In December Hopton had closed in on the town. He cut off the water supply at Plympton, seized Saltash, Mount Edgecombe House, and Millbrook, only to find that he was not strong enough to blockade the city. He instead advanced to Exeter. Here General Ruthin, commanding a parliamentary force, advancing swiftly, slipped through his lines and reinforced the garrison, obliging Hopton again to retire to Cornwall. Ruthin brought up three "great ships" to force the passage of the Tamar. For a week they bombarded Saltash with their guns without doing much damage — when the foot tried to land they were driven back. But reinforcements enabled Ruthin to force the river, and compelled Hopton to fall back to Bodmin. Ruthin, eager to destroy Hopton before the Earl of Stamford, advancing with another parliamentary force, should supersede him, moved on to Liskeard.

Warwick now got news from Rotterdam, dated December 16th, that Goring was waiting for the first fair wind to sail for England. He had two Dutch ships, and three great trows, with 4,000 horse arms, twenty guns, ammunition wagons, two hundred officers, and £20,000 in cash aboard. Already he seems to have been in fight with the *James* (50) the *George* (48) and the *Greyhound* (18), somewhere about the 8th. He had with him seven ships. The *Greyhound* opened fire first, and Goring replied with a broadside. Then the *George* came up, and a four hours' fight took place, before Goring retired. The parliamentary ships claimed to have sunk two or three of Goring's ships. But this claim may have been made to cover up an unsuccessful action. For Goring got away. His ships were probably smaller and swifter than those of his opponents, who ought to have been able to have destroyed his little fleet. Before Warwick could act, Goring had safely slipped into Newcastle with his ships.[32] The Earl of Newcastle was now well supplied for his contest with the Fairfaxes. He was able to cut the direct route between Hull and the West Riding by the capture of Pontefract Castle. He then sent Sir John Henderson to secure Newark and the passage over the Trent. This enabled him to keep watch over Nottinghamshire and Lincolnshire. Sir Hugh Cholmley, however, managed to throw himself into Scarborough and to hold it for the Parliament. Neither he nor Hotham was much help to the struggling Fairfaxes, for they regarded themselves as independent, "as allies rather than subordinates", to quote the authors of *The Great Civil War*.

By the end of the year the fog of war had cleared sufficiently to show how the two contestants stood. The King held the North: Yorkshire with the exception of the West Riding, Hull, and Scarborough; all Lancashire, Chester, and most of Wales, with the exception of Pembrokeshire — the "Englishry" as it was termed. Oxford, too, with some of the surrounding country, was his, while Hopton maintained a precarious hold on Cornwall.

Parliament held East Anglia, most of the Midlands, and the Home Counties, which were overawed by London. Devon, Dorset and Somerset were theirs. It had the support of most of the towns, save a few cathedral cities. The chief ports of Bristol, Hull, Portsmouth, and Plymouth were in its possession, while Gloucester gave it control of the lower Severn. Above all it had the wealth of the City of London, and the magazine at the Tower.

Their most vital possession, however, was the Navy. It had fallen into their hands like a gift from the gods, ready-made and fully equipped for war, manned and officered. This had given them the control of the outer lines of communication by sea, which had already enabled support and supplies to be sent to Hull, Portsmouth, Plymouth, and Pembrokeshire. This ability of the naval arm to reach far beyond the army's capacity was to become increasingly important and decisive in the future.

The credit for this successful naval activity belongs to Warwick and his Captains. His keen eye for the strategic points had secured Portsmouth and saved Hull, and had envisaged the importance of Plymouth and of Milford Haven. His ships had indirectly foiled the King's advance upon London, and had held the ring free from foreign intervention. Now it remained to be seen whether Parliament knew how to make the best use of Warwick and the fleet, both in matters of supply and money and ships.

Chapter III

1643

Warwick Challenges the King's Successes

Fortune now dramatically veered in Hopton's favor. A fleet of forty sail, bound for London, were driven by stormy weather under the batteries at Pendennis, near Falmouth. Slanning seized them, with their rich cargo of arms, ammunition, and "a liberal store of money" aboard. He was able to arm his troops, to pay them their arrears of wages, with a fortnight's pay in advance.[1] As Slanning's ships had also, on January 8th, captured the *Richmond*, the *Little Richmond*, and the *Tiger*, belonging to Mr. Trelawney of Plymouth, with about eight hundred ounces of Plate aboard, Hopton could well afford to be generous.[2] With an army "encouraged to stand steadfastly" by him, Hopton at once advanced against Ruthin's army at Bodmin, which he found drawn up on Braddock Down. So confident was Ruthin of victory that he had waited neither for his own artillery, nor for Stamford's troops. Instead he was completely routed and fled back to Saltash. On the 22nd Hopton came up. By nightfall his troops had stormed their way in, as Ruthin's powder ran out. In panic Ruthin's men fled to the boats, to cross over to Plymouth, which became so overloaded that more men were lost by drowning than in action. A Newcastle ship, the *Frederick and William* (16), lying in the estuary, was taken without her firing a shot. On board were arms and stores.[3]

In Plymouth the drums beat a frantic alarm through the town, while from the church towers the bells took up the tocsin and the townspeople rushed to arms, or to help strengthen the defenses and earthworks. Unlike Hull, the country round could not be flooded, so that the defense lacked this advantage. A glance at Hollar's contemporary map shows the defenses clearly — the walled city, with

THE SIEGE OF PLYMOUTH

the outworks on a high ridge running from Stonehouse on the west
to Lipson on the east. These outworks ensured that the town itself
was out of range of hostile artillery. Various works protected the
Leerie and Cattwater, the most important being Mount Stamford,
on the opposite side of Cattwater to the Hoe. The Sound itself was
defended by St. Nicholas Island. The map also shows how supplies,
munitions and troops could be landed in safety, so long as the
ships could keep the approaches open. As at Hull, this was possible
since there was deep broad water to ride in at all states of the tide.

Hopton now crossed the river to the north and invested the
town. But he had not the men to do so completely, nor were his
troops strong enough to attack. Ruthin for his part was not powerful enough to make a sortie. Deadlock ensued. "Plymouth", wrote
Sir Bevill Grenville on February 22nd, "is still well supplied with
men and all sorts of provisions by sea, which we cannot hinder,
and therefore for my part I see no hope of taking it."[4] Even as he
wrote the royalist troops were suddenly attacked by James Chudleigh — Stamford lying ill at Exeter — to be driven back to Plympton.
Hopton had to withdraw to Saltash, with the loss of five guns, and
then to Tavistock. Warwick's control of the sea had enabled him
to throw in supplies and men by water. Plymouth's defense was
based on the sea.

In the north the capture of Newcastle had placed the coal
trade in the King's hands. By selling it abroad he was able to buy
munitions. The price of coal had already risen so high in London
that it had to be controlled, with the result that it was almost unob-
tainable. To allay the grumbles of the shivering citizens wood was
issued instead. Apparently, too, ships were running the blockade
to bring back this profitable commodity. An embargo therefore
was placed on this traffic: ships were forbidden to go to Newcastle,
in case they were seized there and turned into warships for royal use.[5]

But the proceedings of the Queen in Holland concerned Warwick
more nearly than coal. He could blockade Newcastle but not Holland. Parliamentary agents warned him that her convoy might sail
at any moment. They were right. On January 19th she left Schevenin-
gen with seven large and five smaller vessels, escorted by Tromp.
Almost at once they ran into a violent storm, which tossed the ships

to and fro off the Dogger Bank for several days. The Queen, nevertheless, was in high spirits, saying no Queen of England had yet
been drowned. Even amidst the roar of the tempest she could find
comedy, for she listened to the shouting voices of her seasick ladies,
as they confessed their sins to equally seasick friars. On the 27th
she was forced to return with the loss of two ships. Nothing daunted
she began at once to replace her lost vessels. In the Mase lay her
ammunition ship, closely watched by the *Greyhound* (18) and the
Providence (16), sent by Warwick for the purpose. They announced
they would either take or sink the ship. The Prince of Orange therefore sent Tromp with two ships to fetch her, only to be told by the
State Provincial, which was parliamentarian in sympathy, that he
was to arrest her, search her, and store her munitions ashore. This
stung the Queen to fury. She wrote to the States General that she
considered the arrest of her ship, freighted with her own goods,
to be a direct affront to the King, and a violation of the friendship
between him and Holland. With a feline touch she observed that
she had not asked for a license, since the States' order forbidding
the transportation of arms to either side had not been carried out.
Indeed she knew of large quantities of arms that had been allowed
to go to the rebels. Thereupon the State Provincial, a little uneasily,
excused their action by saying that they had thought the ship to be
a private one, which did not belong to the King. The States General
thereupon ordered the ship to be released, and Tromp was empowered
to resist by force anyone who tried to hinder her. He promptly
ordered the parliamentary vessels to lie at anchor till the ship got
to sea. Nevertheless, the *Providence* fired three shots at her, which all
missed. Tromp returned her fire, and the two ships withdrew.

The situation was a curious one. For despite the King's former
abuse of Dutch neutrality, they now found themselves able to indulge
in the lucrative business of selling and transporting munitions to
England. Both sides, the supporters of the Prince of Orange and
of the Parliament, had the sense to see that such traffic, though
mutually opposed, was in reality beneficial to both. The Dutch were a
commercially minded people. With England engaged in Civil War,
the carrying trade of Europe was falling into their hands, while in
the Indies they would now possess a monopoly.

On February 17th the Queen sailed again for Newcastle. Batten was sent there to intercept her, as it was her most likely destination. Off Scarborough the wind changed and the Queen was forced into Bridlington Bay. Here she lay until, on the 21st, Newcastle's cavalry arrived. That night she landed, and lodged in a house on the snowy quay. In the morning Newcastle himself came in with the foot. At night Batten in the *Rainbow* (42), with Haddock in the *Antelope* (36), and the *Recovery* (11), the *Edward and Elizabeth* (14), the *Dragon* (6), and the *Hector* (20), came in. Under the cover of the darkness a small boat landed men ashore, who enquired where the Queen was lodging. Suddenly at five o'clock next morning Batten opened fire, not on the obvious target of the ships, but on the village. He had no wish to be involved with the Dutch, and so he selected what he considered was a legitimate objective. Fire seemed to be concentrated upon the Queen's house for, as she wrote to her husband, "I assure you it was well marked." She and her retinue had to be hurried out in the bitter cold to the shelter of a snowy ditch behind the village. Nor did the Queen hesitate to go back to fetch her pet spaniel, Mitte, who had been left behind. Shots passed through her bedroom, and mud from a shot, killing a sergeant, bespattered her with slush as she lay crouched in the ditch. For two hours the cannonade continued until dawn, when it suddenly stopped. Tromp, lying farther out in the Bay, had intimated to Batten that unless it ceased he too would open fire. Batten had to obey, as a falling tide was forcing him to sea. The Queen returned. From her window all through the grey winter day she watched her precious cargo being carried ashore. Then, gaily styling herself "Generalissima", she carried it to York.[6]

Her arrival had instant repercussions, since both Hotham and Cholmley were wavering. Both disapproved of the lengths to which Parliament had gone, and of the unreasonable demands they were making on the King. Both had been in secret correspondence with Newcastle. Cholmley indeed declared for the King, and went to York to get his commission from the Queen. In his absence his nephew, Brown Bushell, with his brother Henry, surprised the Castle and took it. When Cholmley returned with some of Newcastle's troops, Bushell was persuaded to surrender it back. He had

previously written to Hotham for aid to hold the Castle, and two
ketches were sent to him. The Royalists seized them, and fitted
them as privateers. Brown Bushell "had the impudence" to return
to Hull, where Hotham "clapt him up close prisoner." Shortly
after he was released. He promptly joined the Royalists, who gave him
a ship, the *Cavendish* (12).[7]

As rumor still spoke of pilots being sent from Newcastle to
"bring the Danes upon these coasts", Parliament ordered Warwick
to take personal command of the Summer Guard of thirty warships and fifty armed merchantmen. Of these eight warships and
thirteen merchantmen were to form the Irish Guard.* There was
good reason, for from Wexford the Irish-Spanish privateers, to
the number of ninety ships, were preying on the English and Dutch
shipping. By using Breton ports, despite protests from the French,
they infested the western approaches of the Channel. Though as
yet they were not in open alliance with the King, the royalist captains knew them for friends, as they left their ships unmolested.
The King, too, had offered to cede the Orkney Islands to Denmark
in return for the services of their fleet. But the Danes, mindful of
the exploits of the late Gustavus Adolphus, had their eyes fixed on
Sweden, and nothing came of the proposal.[8]

The fluctuation of events in the west again claimed Warwick's
attention. Hopton had obtained munitions from a Bordeaux merchantman, which had arrived opportunely at Falmouth. By a
strange coincidence Chudleigh had also been able to re-arm his
men with fifteen hundred muskets brought by a Dutch ship to
Plymouth.[9] Hopton advanced against him, only to be routed at
Sourton Down. Again he had to fall back to Launceston. His baggage was captured, and from letters in it Stamford learned that Hopton was to have advanced into Somerset. He therefore crossed the
Cornish border to administer the *coup de grâce* to Hopton. Instead
he was utterly routed at Stratton on May 16th, with the loss of
thirteen guns, all his baggage, and £5,000 in cash. The whole of
Cornwall was in the King's hands.

The victory set free the Cornish privateers. On June 4th

*See Appendix C.

Captain Polhill, Admiral of Falmouth, in the *Mayflower*, with another ship commanded by Captain Jones, and a Yarmouth prize of ten guns was lying off Morlaix. Unknown to them Captain Thomas of the *Eighth Whelp* (18), and the *Charity* (6) under Captain Ralph Dansk, had put into the Isle of Basse. Here he met three captains whose ships had been plundered. They told him of the presence of Polhill and his consorts outside Morlaix. Thomas at once disguised his ships as merchantmen, covered up his paint with canvas, took in his guns, and sent his crews below. Soon Polhill saw him, and sent his lieutenant to board him. Thomas told him he had been chased by Moorish pirates, and that he had put into Basse in the hope of joining a convoy bound for London. The Lieutenant swallowed this fairy-tale, and returned to report an easy prey.

Now is Thomas' chance. Cut the cables and get to windward. She's coming up to us. Up on deck, lads. Up with the colors. Throw off the canvas. Uncover the guns and run them out. Now open fire and let her have it. Polhill is caught in a trap, and his ship is forced aground. Thomas anchors within musket shot, and for the next hour pours one hundred and twenty shot into his victim, who "answers very hot." At last Polhill and his officers scramble ashore, and the crew hang out a white flag. Thomas scents treachery and orders Dansk to run the *Charity* alongside to burn the *Mayflower*. Dansk has other ideas — he boards the ship, and she surrenders. He stops the leaks with the willing aid of her crew, who also do the same to the wounded *Eighth Whelp*. Then the two battered warriors are brought into Stokes Bay. Thomas is awarded prize money of one third to the crew, and two thirds to the State. Dansk, as a merchantman, gets one third for the crew, one third for the owners, and one third for the State.[10]

At Portsmouth Thomas found Warwick in the *James* (50), for the situation in the west had become alarming. Hopton, after leaving troops to contain Plymouth and Exeter, had pushed on to join Prince Maurice, sent to reinforce him, at Chard. On June 4th Taunton, Bridgwater, and Dunster fell to them, and they were sweeping on towards Bristol.

Warwick had come to relieve Swanley and the Irish Guard. The squadron was badly needed, both to check the privateers, whose exploits had aroused loud outcries from the merchants in London and Plymouth at the loss of their vessels, and to secure Milford Haven. Here the parliamentary party in Pembrokeshire urgently required support. Moreover, the Haven was essential as a naval base since no Irish ports were now available. The hard-pressed garrison in Galway was crying out for relief as well. Swanley in the *Charles* (46), with the *Jocelyn* (12), the *Mary Rose* (28), the *Crescent* (14) and the *Lily* (8) were despatched, while Moulton in the *Swiftsure* (46) was ordered to Tor Bay.[11]

Elsewhere fortunes had fluctuated. In Cheshire Sir William Brereton had driven the Royalists out of Nantwich so that, with the exception of Chester, he now dominated the county. In Lancashire Ralph Assheton had routed Lord Derby. In Yorkshire the two Fairfaxes had taken Leeds and Bradford, burst their way into Wakefield, and forced Goring's troops to surrender with the loss of all their equipment. Now they hoped to clear the West Riding.

In the center Rupert and the Marquis of Hertford had taken Cirencester, but a plot to betray Bristol to them failed, and instead they stormed Lichfield. They then returned to Oxford, to find that Essex had captured Reading and barred the road to London. Rupert therefore occupied himself by making sweeping raids with his cavalry round the countryside.

In London the situation was gloomy, despite the minor successes of the Parliament. After spending a chilly winter, the citizens now suffered from scanty larders, owing to the ravages of Rupert's horse, and from the seizure of wagons and animals for military purposes. The merchants grumbled at the lack of trade, at the ravages of the privateers, at the high level of taxation, at the forced loans they were compelled to make upon the dubious security of the "Public Faith".

The advance of Newcastle's troops southwards, under Cavendish, alarmed the Eastern Association, formed in December, 1642. Already the first of the Queen's convoy, forty wagon-loads of arms and munitions, with three hundred barrels of powder, had reached Oxford on May 15th. The Queen herself followed in June with three thousand men, nine guns, and a hundred wagons of arms and munitions. She left Newark on June 21st, and Cavendish, by capturing Burton-on-Trent on July 2nd, had enabled her to join the King on July 13th. None of the parliamentary armies had attempted to stop her. Her departure left Newcastle free to deal with the Fairfaxes. On June 20th he defeated them at Adwalton Moor. At this very moment Sir John Hotham was plotting to deliver Hull to the Earl of Newcastle. He was jealous of the Fairfaxes and even more furious at Cromwell — Cromwell had imprisoned his son, John, for threatening to fire on his men when they had clashed on a foraging expedition. John, however, managed to escape from Nottingham and to join his father.

Both were suspect. Thus a relative of Sir John's, John Saltmarsh, a parliamentary chaplain, was sent to worm his way into the Governor's confidence. Sir John was rash enough to trust him, and told him of his intention to change sides.[12] His first step was to order Moyer to leave port with the *Hercules*. Saltmarsh thereupon told Moyer of the Hothams' plot. Acting on this slimy reptile's advice, Moyer landed a hundred men to occupy the blockhouses, while the Mayor with fifteen hundred more secured the magazines and arrested the younger Hotham. Sir John, however, contrived to leave his house by a back way, got through the gate before the guard had been warned — only to be taken at Beverley by the hue and cry.[13] Both the Hothams were sent to London aboard the *Hercules*, where, after trial, they were executed at the Tower in January, 1644.

The alarmed and leaderless citizens of Hull sent post-haste to the Fairfaxes to come and take over the city. Undeterred by their recent defeat they rode full speed and flung themselves into Hull on July 4.[14] By their swift action they completed Moyer's movement in saving the port. Once again Warwick's ships had preserved the northern bastion.

By this time Warwick was off Studland Bay, about to go to assist in the siege of Corfe Castle. Here orders came for him to go instantly to the relief of Exeter. On July 1st he arrived off the mouth of the Exe with the *James* (50), the *Eighth Whelp* (16), the *Martin* (36), the *Charity* (6), and the *Golden Lion* (14). Moulton, in the *Swiftsure* (48), with the *Tenth Whelp* (14) and the *Cat*, was there already, since on June 27th he had sent in the *Tenth Whelp*, the *Cat*, the *Abraham* and the *John*, two small merchantmen, over the Bar to relieve the city. They took two vessels. Then they met with fierce opposition from a battery on the Red Cliff to the east of Exmouth Church and from two guns on the opposite shore. This forced them to try to recross the Bar next morning, but the wind took them and only the *Tenth Whelp* and the *Cat* got over. The other two ships were either sunk or captured.[15]

Warwick therefore decided that the approaches must first be cleared by taking the forts on either sides of the river. He began by capturing some small works at the river mouth, next sending in his smaller ships with some eight hundred seamen to tackle the larger ones up the river. He then sat down to write to the Admiralty Commissioners. Batten had asked him for reinforcements to guard against a possible Danish attack, but he had no ships to spare him: he could not even find an escort for the convoy of ammunition to Bristol. He wrote emphatically that "they must send out more ships, if they would employ so much, for in my life I was never so much put to it for want of ships, and there is but three on the West side of the Channel, which is much too little."

He was aroused from this routine work by alarming news. After two or three posts had been taken, a fierce charge of horse had driven the landing parties back to their boats. Though the ships poured a heavy fire upon the Royalists in a desperate attempt to retrieve the situation, a falling tide forced them to recross the Bar. According to the Venetian Ambassador, the Royalists had sunk three ships and two lighters in the Channel during the night, so that two ships were stranded on the mud and captured. The *Cat* was burned and her Captain, Turpin, made a prisoner.[16]

The attack was doomed to failure from the start, because it was based on false tactics. It was assumed that, as ships had been able to defend Hull and Plymouth from their deep broad estuaries, they could do the same under very different conditions. Here the river was tidal, wide though it was, and a falling tide reduced it to a narrow channel running between wide mud banks. Shore batteries, whose guns were firmly planted, were far more effective, powerful, and accurate than ships' cannon on a shifting platform on a rolling deck. Under such conditions ships could not provide continuous covering fire to landed troops, nor could they prevent the flanks of a town from being invested, if the river narrowed. Relief in this case must come by land. The lesson had to be learned by experience, and it was not assimilated during the Civil War, nor even long afterwards.

Warwick had to return to Portsmouth to revictual. There was much to cause him deep concern. With the Queen's arrival at Oxford, the King now outnumbered Essex. On that same day Hopton and Maurice virtually destroyed Waller's army at Roundway Down. Rupert joined them from Oxford, and on July 26th they stormed and took Bristol, the second city of the Kingdom. Its wealth, its arms, and its trade fell into the King's hands. Above all, eight ships were captured, including the *Fellowship* (28) and the *Hart* (12). Sir John Pennington was given command of this little fleet. The Irish Guard, which had at last reached Milford Haven, thus lost a victualling base, and would have to go to Portsmouth, or even further, to refit and victual. More important too, was the threat to the safety of the Haven itself, as Irish troops might be landed there.

This loss, coming on top of the defeat of the Fairfaxes, almost stunned the parliamentary party. Essex and Waller were at logger-heads. Waller complained that his defeat was due to Essex's negligence in not preventing Rupert's horse from leaving Oxford. Waller, however, was actually given a new army, independent of the Lord General. Essex retorted angrily that he was blamed for other men's failures, who were rewarded for losing an army by being given a new one. The peace party now proposed, as the King was victorious, and as it was useless to struggle further, to give him back control of the armed forces, and so make the best of matters.

Only Pym kept his sanity. Disputes must cease, and confidence must be restored in Essex, who threatened to resign. Pym saw that an alliance with Scotland, which he had been pressing upon his colleagues, was now an urgent necessity. It was an opportune moment, for the Covenanters were alarmed. They had learned from captured letters that the King proposed to use the Macdonnel Clan from Ulster to invade Scotland. Now that his forces had triumphed in the North, Charles might turn upon them. Herein, Pym saw, lay the way of salvation. He sent a deputation to the Scots, headed by the younger Vane, which since it was impossible to travel by land, sailed in the

Antelope on July 29th.[17] As a result, on September 26th the Solemn League and Covenant was signed. Vane cleverly persuaded the Scots to agree to a religious settlement "according to the word of God and the example of the best reformed churches." The Scots undertook to raise an army, under Alexander Leslie, Earl of Leven, and to enter the war.

Meanwhile Pennington had got to work. On August 3rd he sent the *Fellowship* and the *Hart* to secure Milford Haven. By good luck they found it empty, for Swanley in the *Bonaventure* (36), with his Vice-Admiral, William Smith, in the *Swallow* (34), had sailed to relieve Galway. Here Captain Brook, of the *Providence* (16), had already attempted to land supplies, only to be beaten back by the Irish boats. Faced with starvation, Colonel Willoughby had to surrender. A day later on the surge of the long Atlantic rollers Swanley and Smith beat into the Bay. They were too late. All they could do was to embark Willoughby, who had been allowed to march out with his men, and to sail for Kinsale.[18] On August 3rd they set out for Milford. As they sailed, they captured the *Fortune* (12) which they renamed the *Robert,* and then they were separated. Smith now learned from a cargo ship that Rear-Admiral Joseph Jordan, in the *Expedition* (14), had driven a Hamburgh vessel ashore at St. David's Head. Hoping to find Jordan, Smith bore in for the Haven. At the entrance a fishing smack told him of the presence of the two royalist ships.

Smith cleverly suggested to his crew that these ships might be laden with goods placed aboard by the Bristol merchants at the time of the siege. Scenting prize money, the crew cried out that they would support him to a man. So, on the 7th, he bore in, and saw his foes at anchor, but Captain Burley, of the *Fellowship,* had seen his arrival and made ready. As Smith came within range, Burley sent a boat, under a white flag, to offer Smith's crew a free pardon if they would carry their ship to Bristol. At this piece of bravado Smith angrily cried out that Burley was a pirate and that he would take or sink both his ships. As he was penning this answer to Burley in his cabin, the master ran in with the news that the *Fellowship* had cut her cables and was making off. Smith rushed up on deck, calling to the gunner to open fire. After a couple of shots the *Fellowship* ran aground, and Burley called out to Smith to hold his fire. He then boarded the *Swallow* and offered to surrender if he and his crew were set free: otherwise he would burn the ship. Smith ignored him, and instead offered the crew their wages, if they would yield. This unexpected offer the crew thankfully accepted.

The *Hart* meanwhile had fled up the Haven, closely pursued by the *Robert,* under Captain Rew. Both ships fired hard at one another until the *Hart* ran herself ashore in a creek. Here her crew abandoned her, but Rew got her off and took her back to Smith. On the 28th Swanley entered the Haven, though the *Providence* went on to Plymouth on what was to be Brook's last voyage.[19]

The Admirals now learned that Colonel Roger Lort had taken Tenby for the King. The fall of Bristol had encouraged the Royalists to flock to the banner of the Earl of Carbery, who had formed a royalist association in Pembrokeshire. Colonel Rowland Laugharne came aboard offering to retake the place, if Swanley would aid him, since his own forces were too few. With memories of his successes in the Isle of Wight, Swanley, since most of the Irish Guard had now come in, took the *Bonaventure* (36), *Swallow* (34), *Leopard* (34), *Expedition* (16), *Fellowship* (28), *Hart* (12), *Prosperous* (28), *Crescent* (12), and the merchantman *Leopard* (22), to Tenby. He bombarded the town with a hundred shots and then, by the irony of fate, a gun, loaned by Moulton to the town out of the *Lion,* shot one of his vessels through and through. Swanley at once withdrew. With Pennington's little fleet still in being he dared not risk the loss of a single ship. Moreover, it was clear that his guns had little effect upon the town. The jubilant Royalists now threatened to take Pembroke and so deny Swanley the use of the Haven. But they were forestalled by Laugharne, who threw a garrison into the town. Instead they started to build a fort at Pill, opposite to Pembroke, with the same object, for they had now recognized the strategic importance of the Haven to the fleet.[20]

After much deliberation the King and Rupert had decided to march on Gloucester. They were too weak to advance on London, nor could Newcastle move south as he was still held up at Hull. The capture of Gloucester would secure the line of the Severn Valley; it would also open the nearest road from South Wales to Oxford by which the Welsh recruits could travel. On August 10th the Royalists arrived before the city. As the losses at the storm of Bristol had been severe, it was decided to siege it rather than attempt a sudden storm — which probably would have been the better policy.

Parliament ordered Essex to go to its relief, reinforcing him with six London train-band regiments. The army set out from Uxbridge on August 26th, arriving in the very nick of time, for General Massey had only three barrels of powder left. As it approached, the King burnt his huts and raised the siege, and while these embers still fitfully glowed, Essex entered Gloucester triumphantly on September 8th. Yet the King's siege of the city had lured Essex from his base, and left the road to London open. Charles might yet again defeat him in the field, as he had done at Edgehill.

The loss of Bristol had resulted in an avalanche of surrenders. The Earl of Carnarvon over-ran Dorset, taking Weymouth and Portland, so that only Lyme remained true to Parliament. Prince Maurice with a western army was sent to complete the conquest of Devon, where Bideford and Barnstaple were now in royalist hands. At Plymouth, on August 29th, Sir Alexander Carew, the commander of St. Nicholas Island, a key to Plymouth's defences, was detected in a plot to betray it to the Royalists. He was arrested and sent to London, where he was eventually executed with the two Hothams. Hardly had the alarm died down than morale was further shaken by the arrest of Captain Brook. He had caught the infection too, since he was about to carry the *Providence* to the King. The arrival of a new Governor, Colonel James Wardlaw, bringing by sea £4,000 in cash, six hundred men, and two hundred barrels of powder, restored the citizens' confidence. It was badly needed, for Prince Maurice, after taking Exeter on September 5th, was advancing on the city.[21]

Nor had matters fared much better in the north. On July 20th Lord Willoughby of Parham had surprised Gainsborough, and so cut Newcastle's communications with Newark. Since Cavendish was still in the field, Meldrum and Cromwell were ordered to his support. North of Gainsborough they met and defeated Cavendish, who was killed in the action. Cromwell now advanced, hearing that a small body of Royalists was approaching. Mounting the top of a hill, he was astounded to see approaching the whole of Newcastle's army in battle array — retreat was the only course open. Skilfully using his horse to cover the retreat Cromwell enabled the Parliamentarians to retire to Lincoln. But Willoughby had to surrender Gainsborough on the 30th. Then, as his army began to dissolve, he had to abandon Lincoln also.

A direct order from the King now urged Newcastle to advance south on London. Instead he decided to lay siege to Hull, probably influenced by the alarm of the Yorkshire Royalists at the increasing strength of Thomas Fairfax, who had now built up an army of seven hundred horse and two thousand foot. They feared that if Newcastle advanced, their homes and estates would be at the mercy of the two Fairfaxes. The capture of Hull would also deprive the northern squadron of its base, for Haddock had been annoyingly active. He had captured the impregnable fortress of Holy Isle by the simple expedient of offering to pay the arrears of wages due the garrison. Early in August he had taken a ship, bound to Newcastle from Holland with a cargo of arms and munitions, within a league of Tynemouth, and he had also intercepted another vessel, as she came out of the Tyne, with a cargo of coal for Holland. She was searched and, buried deep beneath the coal, £4,000 in cash was found, which was to have purchased munitions.[22] So tight was the blockade, that the coal trade, on which the King had placed such hopes, had practically ceased. Coal stood piled high and useless upon the quays.

To meet the threat of a possible advance south by Newcastle, the Earl of Manchester was appointed to the command of the army of the Eastern Association. Since Newcastle was besieging Hull, he decided to put down a rising of the Royalists at Lynn, which fell on September 16th. He then shipped Meldrum with five hundred foot to reinforce Sir Thomas Fairfax in Hull. On September 2nd Newcastle had appeared before the city, with fifteen thousand men. The Mayor instantly wrote to the Speaker, begging for "two or three ships to lie in the Humber to keep the enemy from planting by the waterside — and debarring us from the sea and so hindering us of all relief that could come to our aid."[23]

As Newcastle had erected various batteries, whose guns out-ranged those of the city, Fairfax was forced to build emplacements outside the walls. The besiegers also entrenched themselves, and built a Fort Royal some distance from the North Gate. Fairfax countered these by opening the sluices on the 14th, so driving the Royalists from their trenches. Newcastle, observing, "You often hear us called the Popish Army, but you see we trust not our good works", moved his men to the top of the dykes. He then transferred his attack to the west of the city, at the same time building a bridge of boats across the Hull, out of range, so as to keep open his com-munications with Holderness. Attacks were made on the Hessle Gate, with the object of capturing the West Jetty fort, but they were enfiladed by fire from a battery at Myton Gate. On the 27th Willoughby and Cromwell boldly brought muskets and powder across the Humber, taking back with them the horses of twenty cavalry troops, which were dying from lack of fodder, due to the flooding. Once again the ships had kept the Humber open.

The Fort Royal, from which heated cannon-balls had been fired into the city, was now destroyed by a new parliamentary battery, which could rake it with its fire. On October 5th two large ships were seen coming up the Humber — the *Lion* (40), com-manded by Colonel Thomas Rainsborough, and the merchantman *Employment* (30), with Meldrum's five hundred men aboard. They came at a critical moment, for the West Jetty fort was being fiercely attacked: "a place of great importance for the riding of our ships before the town." The soldiers were rushed ashore and, with their aid, the attack was repulsed. On the 11th a feint sortie was made from the North Gate, while the real attack of five hundred muske-teers, led by Rainsborough, dashed out from the west side. In a wild charge they drove all before them, taking one work after another, until they had secured the royalist guns. But Newcastle had ready a hundred pikemen. As they came into the attack, the sight of the deadly levelled spears, against which there was no defense, threw the musketeers into panic. They broke in terror-struck retreat pell-mell from the captured battery, leaving Rains-borough a prisoner. At this dangerous moment old Lord Fairfax, calm and collected, organized a counter-attack, and drove the charging Royalists back. Such was the impetus of his onslaught that once again the guns were taken, including the Queen's "pocket pistols", Gog and Magog.[24]

On the other side of the Humber, Sir William Widdrington, who had gone to the relief of Bolingbroke Castle, clashed on this same fateful October 11, with Manchester, Cromwell, and the younger Fairfax at Winceby. His forces were defeated and scattered by Fairfax, who heard, as he fought, the heavy gunfire which announced his father's decisive sortie from Hull. This forced Newcastle to abandon the siege and with it all thoughts of an advance on London. Lincoln and Gainsborough were lost, and Newark itself was invested. Once again Warwick's ships, reinforced at precisely the right moment, by keeping the Humber open, had saved Hull. Newcastle's possible advance south was frustrated and the other victories made possible.

Meanwhile the King, after retiring from Gloucester, had determined to cut off Essex's return to London. Charles reached Newbury on September 20th, barring the road to the capital. In the ensuing battle he ran short of powder, and had to retire back to Oxford. A few days later Essex victoriously entered London.

In this fateful month of September another agreement was signed. It was the Cessation of Hostilities between the Catholic Confederacy at Kilkenny and the Earl of Ormonde, who signed on behalf of the King. Now Charles could hope that the secret orders he had sent to his Lord Lieutenant, Ormonde, on April 13th, to bring the Irish Army to England, would be put into effect.[25]

Nor did the faithful Ormonde disappoint him. At Dublin lay the *Confidence* (10), the *Employment* (20), the *Swan* (20), and the *Swan* pinnace (6). Other ships however were hard to obtain and their rate of hire was expensive.[26] The Earl of Inchiquin was the first to get ships away. From Cork he sent off troops under Colonel Sir John Vasascour and Sir John Paulet, troops suffering from lack of pay and food and ready to serve the King. They landed at Minehead on October 23rd, and were marched to Bristol.[27] The more direct route to Holyhead or Chester Water was dangerous, as six small parliamentary vessels, among them the *Charity*, based on Liverpool, threatened the crossing. Milford Haven also was in parliamentary hands.

At Conway, John Williams, the Archbishop of York, prepared for the reception of the Irish troops. His surprising presence there, instead of in his diocese, was due to that *enfant terrible*, the younger Hotham. He had threatened to remove the Archbishop's head, when he heard the Primate's comments on his father's action at Hull. To preserve both head and mitre the Archbishop had fled to his native place of Conway. Here he transferred his administrative ability from the passage of souls to Heaven to the transport of troops to England.

On October 26th Ormonde sent the Archbishop four small guns and some powder, as the *Employment* was not strong enough to carry heavy artillery. The Earl of Castlehaven hired three vessels of five hundred tons, and sent them to Dublin on November 7th. News of this reached Sir William Brereton, the parliamentary commander in Cheshire, who on November 15th wrote in alarm to the Speaker that there were eleven Bristol ships and fifteen Wexford barks waiting at Dublin to carry over three or four thousand troops. Ormonde, on the contrary, stated that Baldwin Wake, commanding the Bristol ships, only had two vessels and five barks.[28] Brereton was afraid that the Liverpool squadron was not strong enough to deal with them. Even as he wrote, Baldwin Wake had sailed with two thousand five hundred men in two parties. Stormy weather forced them into the Dee, and it was not until the 22nd that he was able to land them at Mostyn. On the way he had taken William Lurting's ship, the *George* of Liverpool, as she was carrying ammunition for that port.[29] The same stormy weather had probably prevented the Liverpool squadron from coming out to escort her.

Ormonde turned down a proposal on the 29th by Orlando Bridgeman, who had been sent from Oxford to Chester, that Wake's ships, with the Irish vessels, should attack and destroy the Liverpool squadron.[30] Ormonde's orders were to get the Irish troops across with all speed. Wake's ships were powerful enough to deal with any attack, while time would be lost in seeking out the Liverpool squadron. Brereton, however, was still convinced this might happen, for on the 21st he had written to the Speaker begging for ships to master

Wake's squadron: "otherwise Liverpool, your only haven, hazarded, and all these parts here in England and Wales subdued." He was fearful, too, that his army might be caught between the Irish forces and those of Newcastle, and he urged that the Scots "might be hastened and speeded before the counties be wasted and destroyed.[31]

The Irish troops were in wretched condition, ragged and without ammunition. By strenuous efforts they were clothed and fitted out for service. Their arrival aroused great indignation, for the regiments were reported to be composed of Irish rebels who had massacred the English. Even when it was clear they were the English troops, who had been sent over to Ireland, it was said that they would be followed by Irish Papists. Nevertheless, their coming forced Brereton to abandon Flint and to retire to Wrexham. The Archbishop had great hopes of them: "they shall be waited on by two or three thousand foot and horse, to the outskirts of England,"[32] meaning that the Welsh suffered from the usual reluctance to serve outside their own territories, from which the new troops would be free. He had many other difficulties to contend with. Wake demanded that the local authorities should revictual his ships. Sir John Mennes, the newly appointed Governor of Chester, disagreed with him over military matters. Affairs in North Wales, however, looked rosy for the King, with the promise of better things to come.

In the west, Prince Maurice, after taking Exeter, had turned aside to capture Dartmouth on October 5th. Forty merchantmen were captured in the river and many guns in the town. Yet had he moved straight to Plymouth, with the city's morale still shaken with suspicions of treachery, it might well have fallen. A storm had driven Captain· George Bowden in the *George* (12) into Dartmouth. He had completed his service off Guernsey, and had drawn his pay. He decided he might do well to serve his captors, although not from reasons of loyalty to the King, but because privateering seemed to be more profitable. He obtained a royal commission, and set forth in his new role.[33]

Not until October 20th did Maurice arrive before Plymouth, with five regiments of horse and nine of foot. He deployed them in a half-moon from Plymstock to Cawsand on the Cornish side, with his headquarters in the center of the line, opposite Maudlyn

fort. First he attacked the fort at Mount Stamford, so as to be able
to command Cattwater and the ships lying there. After three weeks'
fighting, culminating in a desperate nine days battle, in which points
were taken and retaken, the fort finally fell. Lipson fort was the
next objective, since its capture would open the way for an attack
upon the city itself. An outpost at Laira was surprised, but before
being taken it was able to warn Lipson fort. The Royalists poured
down into the valley, and up the steep ascent. Here they were held
up and then unexpectedly attacked in the rear by sixty men — a
forlorn hope. At the same moment Wardlaw launched a frontal
attack. Caught between two fires, the Royalists broke and fled.[34]

Wardlaw's defenses, however, were strained to the utmost, and
more so because the Mayor and Corporation refused to allow him
the control of the magazine. The stupidity of these local bumble-bees
made him protest to Warwick. On November 11th he asked for
powder and small and great shot to be sent him at once: "otherwise
the town will be in great danger to be lost".[35] On December 20th,
a wet, cold and stormy night, with the sentries crouching under
cover instead of being on the watch, the Royalists seized the chance
to build a new work near Maudlyn fort. Only after a long struggle,
in which every man had to be thrown in, were they driven back to
the lines. On Christmas Day Maurice gave up the struggle, and
marched away, leaving Colonel Digby to continue the seige.

For Warwick there was no respite. The Cessation had set free
great numbers of Royalist and Spanish-Dunkirk privateers, which
operated from the south Ireland ports, and from Cornwall. They
also used the Breton and Norman harbors, such as Dieppe, Havre,
Ushant, Morlaix, L'Orient, Belle Isle, Croisie, and Nantes. Their
ships made merry in the Channel, carrying their victims into "their
den of thieves at Pendennis." Loud and bitter were the complaints
of the Plymouth and London merchants that their trade was being
ruined by these pirates.

Yet the failure to check their activities, or to prevent the transport of the Irish troops, could not be attributed to any neglect on
Warwick's part. Even with a Summer Guard of thirty warships and
forty-three merchantmen, he had not enough vessels to cover the
extensive waters. On November 27 he reminded Parliament that he

had continually asked for more ships ever since August. He could not do his work with a mere handful, nor should "they think they had a fleet on the Irish coast strong enough to hold the rebels in check, as I cannot even protect the convoys." If any enemy fleet got to sea the sailors were likely to join them, since the prospect of pillaging the merchantmen was inviting, "as it is easy to give content out of other men's goods." There was no port in Ireland suitable for his ships. Already sixteen sail of enemy vessels were fitting out at Bristol and Barnstaple, and more were preparing. Once again he warned them that troops and munitions must be sent to Plymouth if the city were to be saved and held.[36]

These forceful, plain and unpleasant words made Parliament set out a Winter Guard of twenty-two warships and twenty-four merchantmen.* Eleven ships were allotted to the Irish Guard and five to the Severn, eight to the West, eight to the Downs, eight to Scotland, and six to north-east Ireland. Private ships were to be set forth to capture any of the King's vessels they could find. This last move so angered the King that he appointed the Earl of Marlborough his Admiral, with orders to fit out as many ships as he could at Dartmouth, the cost of which he airily suggested could be met by loans from the merchants there.[37]

Besides ships, Warwick needed money. As this was raised by loans from the City merchants and by the sequestration of the royalist estates, wages could only be paid as money became available. So irregular were the payments that the Venetian Ambassador reported that Warwick had to warn the authorities that the seamen threatened to march up to London to demand their pay. In October Warwick went personally to the capital to protest that unless the seamen were promptly paid there would be a mutiny in the fleet.[38] From the same cause arose complaints about victuals. On September 27 Captain Stevens, of the *Charles*, declared he had never been so badly supplied: beer, pork, and beef were "stinking". He indicated the unpaid bills of Victuallers, and also complained that if his warning to post a ship off Weymouth had been observed, a French-

*See Appendix C and D.

man, Jerome, could not have landed a hundred barrels of powder, arms, and munitions there. But Warwick had no ships to spare.[39]

The end of the year saw the summit of the King's successes. He had taken Bristol, Exeter, and Dartmouth. Devon, Cornwall, Somerset and Dorset were in his hands. So too was South Wales, with the exception of parts of Pembrokeshire. In the north he held Yorkshire, Lancashire, and Durham, with the ports of Newcastle and Scarborough. Already troops were coming to him from Ireland without let or hindrance. Still might he hope to put into action his plan for a three-forked advance on London: Newcastle from the north, Maurice and Hopton from the south-west, and his own army from Oxford. His prospects looked bright.

Yet Warwick already had done much to frustrate this plan. By his control of the outer lines of communication he had saved Portsmouth, Hull and Plymouth, because troops, munitions, and supplies could always reach them by sea which could never have come by land. His warships had always been at the right spot at the right time, to support the besieged from the water. Their presence not only kept up morale in these distant, separated and hard-pressed ports, but gave to them a much-needed sense of a co-ordinated planned operation centrally directed, which wove them into the pattern of the struggle.

As long as Hull and Plymouth stood firm neither Newcastle's men nor the western troops would advance. Haddock's northern squadron, composed of the *Antelope* (36), *Sampson* (20), *Golden Lion* (30), *Dragon* (6), *Hector* (20), *Edward and Elizabeth* (14), *Covenant* (12), and the *Lucy* (12), gave evidence of Warwick's eye for the strategic places, as did Swanley's squadron at Milford Haven, for this partly neutralized the royalist possession of Bristol, besides giving a base for future operations against Ireland. Swanley, for the moment, dared not leave the Haven, while ships were fitting out at Bristol, Bideford and Barnstaple. Without a port in Ireland he could not deal with the troops crossing from Ireland. Ships, it is true, had been sent to north-east Ireland, but their duty was to keep open the communications with Scotland for Munro's troops, which had just landed at Carrickfergus.

Despite the minimum of ships with which Parliament, in its

ignorance of naval matters, had supplied him, Warwick had done his work well. He had concentrated them at the strategic points, and he had seen the struggle as a whole. Resolutely he had refused to yield to the clamor of the merchants to open a second front against the privateers, and so to disperse his ships. This policy in itself had prevented any foreign intervention. Experience had shown him that the Third, Fourth, Fifth and Sixth Rate ships were better adapted for his purpose than the larger, clumsier vessels, which were more expensive to maintain, and required more men to man them. If he was to deal with the more numerous faster vessels of the Royalists, he would require more smaller ships with smaller crews. The larger First and Second Rates he could hold in reserve. Indirectly from the sea Warwick had played a great part in influencing the course of the struggle. Now he had his reward. On December 7, both Houses, in view of his "great and faithful service by land sea", created him Lord High Admiral.[40]

CHAPTER IV

1644

Warwick Bends Back the Southern Prong of the King's Fork

The year 1644 seemed to dawn full of good hopes for the King, but a chilling wind from Scotland was soon to wither them, for in icy weather, on January 19th, twenty thousand Scots crossed the Tweed. This second front now opened in the north was to prove the turning point of the war. The Earl of Newcastle hurried into Northumberland to try and dam the flood of invasion, to no purpose, for the Scots reached Newcastle. The town was garrisoned by five hundred men, with another four hundred in Tynemouth Castle. Powder and guns had been brought from Amsterdam and muskets from Scarborough in ships that had eluded Haddock's cruising squadron.[1] The town was summoned on February 3rd, but the resistance was stronger that the Scots had expected. As their artillery had not come up, they contained the place by seizing both banks of the Tyne towards the sea. Seven parliamentary ships blockaded Tynemouth and also guarded the Scots' communications.[2] Pym, slain by cancer on December 8th, had trumped the King's Irish card with the Scotch ace.

With Newcastle occupied by the Scots, Sir Thomas Fairfax was free to join Brereton at Nantwich. Together they defeated the five Irish regiments under Lord Byron and at a stroke the situation in North Wales was reversed. Parliament was now in the ascendant. Realizing the imminent danger of being caught between the armies of the Scots, the Fairfaxes and the Eastern Association, Newcastle sent an urgent appeal for help to the King.

Lord Digby, too, reporting this disaster to Ormonde, begged him to send over all the forces he could spare. These he would order

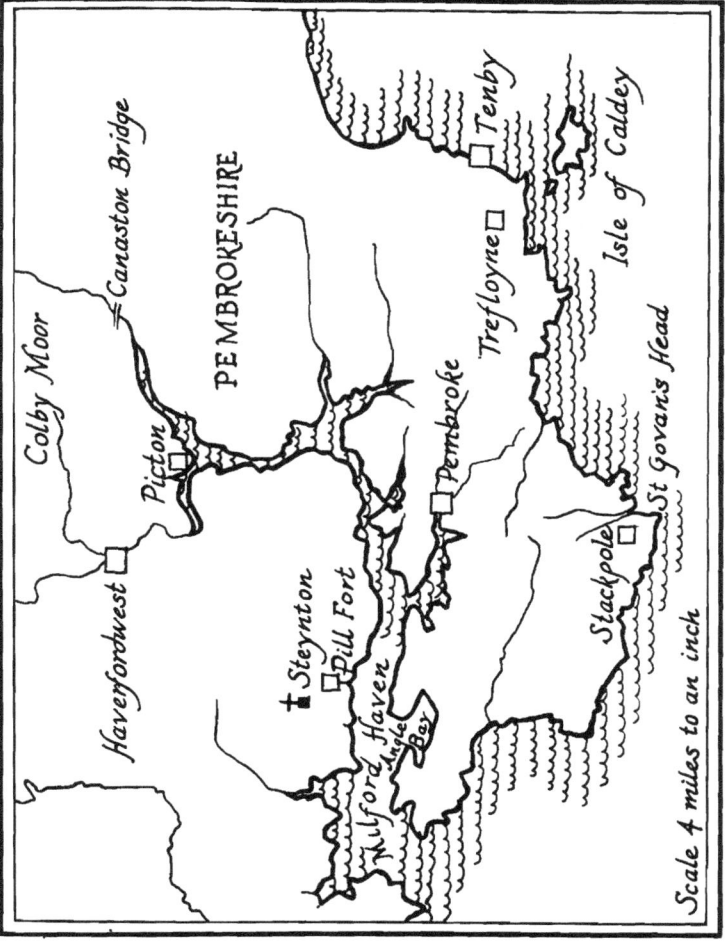

THE DISTRICT AROUND PEMBROKE

Wake, who was lying at Beaumorris with his ships, to transport
with all speed. On the way over to Dublin, however, Wake found
his ships "in so ill condition and his own men so disobedient" that
he had to tack about and return to Bristol.[3] Though two more Irish
regiments under Colonels Tillier and Broughton had been landed,
they had to be diverted to Shrewsbury. The squadron Warwick had
boldly sent to Carrickfergus, together with the Liverpool squadron,
were now blockading Dublin and making transport from there impossible. The naval arm had reached Ireland.

In South Wales it was very different. Swanley's squadron had
gone back to Plymouth, either to aid in its defense, or more probably
to revictual. Pembroke itself was hemmed in by Lord Carbery's
troops, and only the seaway remained open. In great alarm the
Mayor, John Poyer, sent off a small vessel to warn Warwick of the
town's danger. On the way she ran into the *Globe* (12) and the
Providence (10) and was captured.[4] Sir John Pennington had sent
them from Bristol with some barks, carrying guns and supplies, to
the fort the Royalists were building at Pill. Again the Royalists
were lucky, for when they arrived on January 15th the Haven was
empty. Swanley in the *Leopard* (44), with the *Swallow* (34), the
Crescent (14), the *Providence* (18), and the merchantman *Leopard*
(22), was battling his way through stormy seas round Land's End.
Not until the 23rd did he enter the Haven. The two royalist ships
at once retreated up the Pill River to shelter under a neck of land
behind the fort. After exchanging some ineffectual shots, Swanley
anchored in deep water off the fort, here to be joined by the
Prosperous (26) and two Liverpool vessels. Poyer, at the head of
a dejected Committee, came aboard to point out Pembroke's feeble
condition, and the strength of the Royalists. Swanley promised to
land guns, powder, and shot with two hundred seamen. Then, to
raise morale, he made them promise to join him in driving off the
enemy. Though Laugharne had only sixty foot and thirty horse, he
eagerly agreed to support Swanley. They decided to blood their
forces by attacking Sir Roger Lort's house at Stackpole near St.
Goven's Head. On the 30th, after a big gun had breached an outwork,
they stormed their way in. Striking while the iron was still hot,
they took Trefloyne House, near Tenby. Lord Carbery had committed

the usual fault of both sides, that of locking up troops in useless garrisons. Consequently he had no mass of manoeuvre to deal with a concentrated foe, a foe, moreover, who possessed an amphibious power of being able to land seamen and to use ships as a mobile artillery column to carry guns to any necessary spot.[5]

With Laugharne's men flushed with victory, Swanley felt able to tackle a much harder nut, the Pill fort. By night, on February 22nd, two hundred and fifty men were ferried in the ships' boats from Penmar across the Haven to Newton Noyes under the protection of the *Prosperous*. They landed safely, and at once manhandled a demi-cannon and a saker into position behind a small hedge on a hill overlooking the fort. Another demi-cannon on the Pembroke shore kept up a covering fire during this operation. Then the *Swallow* and the *Leopard* were posted off the west side of the Pill's mouth, while the *Prosperous* and the *Leopard* merchant lay off the east. The *Providence* was sent to Angle Bay to guard the ammunition ships there.

Laugharne, with five field pieces, now moved round the Pill river to Steyton, where he posted twenty musketeers on the Church tower to watch for a possible attack from Haverfordwest. At noon the hill battery and the ships opened fire on the fort. The noise of the cannonade brought out Sir Francis Lloyd from Haverfordwest, but the sight of the field pieces so alarmed him that he retreated without making contact. Laugharne's progress was hampered, however, by the difficulty of dragging the guns over the rough muddy roads. When night came on his men had to lie in the open fields, "being a bitter cold night."

Early next morning, as Laugharne again advanced, an ambush was discovered, and it was driven back into the fort. He at once pushed on into Pill village to attack it, but the fort had already surrendered before he could do so. Eighteen great guns, with the *Providence* and the *Globe*, were captured, together with the barks.[6]

The Royalists immediately abandoned Haverfordwest, and Swanley selected Tenby as the next objective. William Smith, the Vice-Admiral, with three ships, was sent to summon it. The garrison, however, remembered the previous naval failure and sat tight. Swanley and Laugharne, with five hundred horse and foot dragging

Thornton   Steynton

Priory

Liddeston

Castle Pill

Hubberston

site of
Milford
Haven

Pill

Hakin

Old
Chapel
St. Thomas

Demi-
culverin
and Sacre

The Fort

Newton
Noyes

MILFORD   HAVEN

N

0   1   2   3   4   5   6   7   8
                         furlongs

Royalist Ships
Parliamentary Ships

Angle
Bay

Demi-Cannon

THE ENGAGEMENT AT PILL

a heavy demi-culverin and a saker, were coming up by land, but again the roads were so narrow, rough, and muddy that it was night before they arrived. Once more the troops had to lie in the open.

Tenby was a walled town, defended by artillery, and impossible to attack from the sea, save for the few hours when the tide was favorable. On the morning of March 7th the ships opened fire, while Laugharne drove in some outposts. For three days smoke and fire poured from the ships on the town, but the garrison resolutely held the troops in check. As the seamen were now suffering from the bitter cold it was decided to attempt a storm the next day "lest they should lose heart." At dawn the great gate, "our only point of entrance", was smashed in by the cannon. Colonel Gwynne, the Governor, led out his men in a counter-attack against the stormers but they met so fierce a fire that the troops fled back, while Gwynne was hit and staggered back into the town to die. At once Captain Whitty, of the *Crescent,* led his seamen in a wild rush, followed by the *Swallow's* crew, with Laugharne and the horse close behind. The excited shouting mass burst through the gate and Tenby was theirs. All Pembrokeshire fell into Parliament's hands. Once again Milford Haven was safe for Swanley's ships, and Bristol could be held in check. Swanley had shown what could be done by a proper co-ordination of naval and military forces.[7]

About the same time, early in March, the Earl of Marlborough suddenly appeared before Jersey. His flagship (32) was accompanied by three other vessels of twenty-four, eighteen, and sixteen guns. He went on to St. Malo, where he chartered a ship (28) which he loaded with supplies and munition. He then sailed for England, but contrary winds drove his little fleet into Jersey. Meanwhile the Guernsey authorities had warned Warwick of his arrival, and Jordan in the *Expedition* (18), with five other vessels, was sent off to deal with him. They found him in St. Aubin's Bay. As Jordan had not expected to be confronted by such large and heavily-armed ships, he hove to. Marlborough shortened sail and trimmed a little, so that Jordan could come up to him, and Jordan did the same, keeping his distance. Then he opened fire, but the shots fell into the water, half way between the two squadrons. Marlborough replied

first with musket shot, and then with gun-fire, to try and lure
Jordan on. But for Jordan the odds were too great, and he held
off. As night came on, and the tide started to ebb, Marlborough
anchored under St. Elizabeth Castle. Here Jordan dared not approach, for fear of the fortress's heavy guns and instead he retired
to Guernsey. That night Marlborough sailed away, since he was
determined to keep his squadron in being. Rumor said he had gone
to the Barbadoes and Virginia to seize ships and fishermen to furnish
a royal fleet. The rumor was correct, for he vanished from the
naval scene. Jordan could not be blamed for not bringing him to
action. He dared not risk the loss of his squadron against such
heavy odds — every ship was precious to Warwick at this time.[8]

In reporting this action to the Houses, Warwick pointed out
that the Royalists now had two hundred and fifty sail of ships between fifty and six hundred tons (privateering and gun-running
must have been a profitable business). He needed fifty ships and five
thousand men, while he only had victuals for many less: small squadrons were essential to meet the threat of foreign intervention; money
and stores were exhausted, and the merchantmen had not been paid;
mayors had taken guns out of the ships for local defense, with the
result that the guns of the *Providence* had been lost at Mount Stamford; carrying troops by sea had consumed the crews' victuals and
had spread disease among them.[9]

The report stirred the Houses into action. Thirty warships
and twenty-two merchantmen were to form the Summer Guard,
while another twenty-five armed merchantmen were to be got ready
for reprisals, victualled by the state.* Only three Second-rate vessels were included, while about seven each of the Third, Fourth,
Fifth, and Sixth Rates were employed. In this way expense was
cut down, and sailors were set free for the smaller ships. With such
a fleet it was hoped to deal more efficiently with the privateers
which swarmed over the seas like mosquitoes.

In the north the royalist situation had become serious. After
Byron's defeat at Nantwich, most of Cheshire and Lancashire had
been lost, while Newcastle himself was hard pressed by the Scots.

*See Appendix E.

Newark, too, was invested by Sir John Meldrum. If it fell, the Eastern Association would be free to operate against the Earl of Newcastle. It was clear to the King and his Council that Byron was not the man to deal with any of these problems and Rupert was sent to take over the command. Gathering troops as he went, he reached Shrewsbury on February 19th, where he found the remnants of Byron's force and the two Irish regiments. At Chester Rupert received orders from the King to relieve Newark. On March 21st he routed Meldrum's army with the loss of all his artillery, muskets and arms. Then, as he was not strong enough to attack the army of the Eastern Association, Rupert withdrew again to Shrewsbury, only to be recalled to Oxford by the King.

Hopton had been sent to clear Dorset, Wiltshire and Hampshire, while the King detained Essex by operations north of the Thames. But on March 29th Hopton and the Earl of Forth, who had been sent to reinforce him, were defeated at Cheriton by Waller. All Hampshire was lost, and Forth fell back to Oxford.

At a conference here, on April 25th, a plan of campaign was decided. Rupert was to go north and relieve York, where Newcastle, after strenuously holding back the Scots by delaying retreat, had been besieged. Then jointly he and Rupert were to clear the north, preparatory to an advance on London. Maurice was to advance through the southern counties with the same objective. The King, with garrisons at Abingdon, Reading, and Banbury, was to manoeuvre round Oxford with a strong body of horse, always declining battle, but detaining Essex's army. On May 5th Rupert rode off for the north.

On April 20th Maurice, with some six thousand men, arrived before Lyme, on the Devon and Dorset border. He expected to take it at once. Though it had barely three hundred inhabitants, its importance was out of all proportion to its size, for it lay at the Channel end of a string of royalist fortresses that ran from Minehead through Dunster, Bridgewater, Taunton, and Langport. Its capture would therefore complete the royalist line barring the way to the west. The town lay in a "hole", commanded on on all sides by the surrounding hills. Blockhouses of turf, some twelve feet thick, were joined together by a rough improvised line, strengthened by

THE SIEGE OF LYME

four forts. Another three forts protected the Cobb, or ancient harbor, from attack from the sea.[10]

The Governor was the Mayor, Thomas Ceeley, but the real commanders were Colonel John Were, who wrote an account of the siege in a "Diurnal", and Colonel Robert Blake, the great Admiral-to-be. Many of the garrison had been besieged with Blake in Bristol, where the line had been far too extended for the available number of troops to defend. So Blake, who never forgot a lesson, contracted the front at Lyme. He saw too that the steep decline of the ground to the shore would largely neutralize the fire of the royalist artillery.

Maurice was suffering from influenza, so much so that the Parliamentarians referred facetiously to him as Maurice's ghost. Nevertheless he got to work, posting his four Cornish regiments on the north, the Devon men on the west, and the Irish regiments on the east. Batteries were erected at commanding points, particularly at Colway Meadow, roughly in the center, with another opposite the west gate. Fighting began almost at once, attacks and sorties meeting various results. The royalist batteries did a good deal of damage, both to west gate fort, and to Gaiche's fort, dismounting some of their guns. Soon the garrison learned caution, as a few men were killed "indiscreetly looking over the line." Maurice now realized that the east side of the town was the most vulnerable, and he built a "Fort Royal" as a threat to Davey's fort, "the stay of all", and new battery near it. It was feared this might make Davey's fort untenable and so it was strengthened with eight feet of earth.

Meanwhile the Committee of Both Kingdoms had written Warwick telling him of the town's distress and insisting upon its importance for the shipping in the west. They urged him to keep it supplied by sea, since nothing could reach it by land.

On the 28th Maurice launched a big attack. Stormers rushed forward, with trumpets sounding and drums beating, only to be met with volleys of caseshot. This so effectually checked them, that their horse could be seen slashing the unfortunate foot with their swords to force them back to the attack. But all to no avail. Off Portland the roar of the cannonade was heard by Captains Somaster and Jones, of the *Mary Rose* (26) and the *Anne and Joyce* (22), as they brought supplies from Portsmouth. Anxiously they crowded on full sail to come to the relief. They arrived only just in time, for their opportune coming "begat new life in the almost tired soldiers." Ammunition, match, bullet, the stores of which were almost run out, were landed, together with supplies of food, as well as a hundred seamen to aid in the defense.[11]

Heavy fighting continued almost daily. On May 8th the *Mayflower* (28) arrived with more supplies; followed on the 11th by four ships with three hundred men aboard, sent by Waller. They were escorted by Jordan in the *Expedition* (18) and by Mann in the *Cygnet* (18).[12] Under heavy royalist fire the men were landed, with a demi-culverin from the *Mayflower*. This was mounted on a new platform at Gaiche's fort, which enabled it to reply on equal terms to the battery at Colway.[13] Warwick was alive to the town's peril and was straining every nerve to keep it supplied.

Maurice now realized that unless he could prevent supplies from being landed — and more so artillery — he had little chance of taking Lyme. Under the cover of darkness he began to move his guns from Colway to a point on the west from which the Cobb could be commanded, for the Cobb was the key to Lyme. The uncanny silence of the royalist artillery led the town to think that they were drawing off their guns for a new attack on the east. Another demi-culverin was landed from the *Mary Rose* and placed in position near Davey's fort to meet this supposed new onslaught.

On the 16th the town had a rough awakening. "The ordnance we thought drawn off began to speak, which had not spoken in three days" — but from the west, not from the east. Sixteen guns opened a heavy continuous fire upon the Cobb, which damaged the shipping lying there. Sorties were made, one even managing to enter the Fort Royal, destroying guns, and bringing away prisoners, arms, and ammunition before it retired. Another attack hit the far more dangerous western quarter, before which the enemy withdrew. At night the Royalists were observed to be building another battery on the west, and a party sallied out, killed twenty of the workmen, and brought back their picks and shovels as prized souvenirs. All next day a continual fire was kept up on the new battery to prevent its repair, but the Royalists continued making breastworks against the Cobb. Early next morning an adventurous boy nipped down upon the Cobb, stole a ship's colors, while the crew slept, and returned triumphantly. His exploit was soon followed, for at seven o'clock sixty Royalists dashed down from the new battery on to the Cobb, where they hurled wild fire among the barges. Instantly fire, flame and smoke roared up from twenty ships ablaze. Desperate fighting, which reeled to and fro, took place upon the west, with Blake and Were in personal command. Now both sides had realized that the key to Lyme was the Cobb. Blake was wounded in the foot, and Were in the stomach, so intense was the battle. The town stood in a desperate position and, unless help came almost at once, it was lost.[14]

Next day, the 23rd, a fleet was sighted to the east. The anxious townsfolk crowded on to the cliff, straining their eyes in wild anticipation. Then they burst into a mighty cheer: streaming from the masthead of the leading vessel flew the flag of the Lord High Admiral. Warwick had come in person to their rescue and they were delivered. With him came the *James* (50), *Bonaventure* (36), *Dreadnought* (34), *Warwick* (22), *Greyhound* (12), *Hind* (12), and *Seaflower* (8). The fleet anchored off the town to the east[15] where it was out of range.

Blake went aboard at once to confer with Warwick. Thirty-eight barrels of powder, match and bullet, were sent ashore to replace the almost exhausted supplies in the town. Yet again that same night the Royalists repeated their exploit of the previous evening and burnt the remaining two or three barges in the Cobb. So touched were the seamen at the town's extremity that they generously gave one-fourth of their next month's allowance of bread together with boots, shoes, and stockings.

Maurice now strove vigorously to prevent the prize from slipping out of his grasp. His pressure upon the west was so intense that Warwick decided to make a feint of landing upon the east. He landed three hundred seamen to help hold the line, while he led seven ships, escorting boats filled with troops, in the direction of Charmouth. This forced the Royalists to move five troops of horse, and some hundreds of foot, parallel with the ships to prevent a landing. As soon as it became clear that Warwick's movement was only a feint, Maurice launched another heavy attack. The line near the west fort was breached, and the enemy came on six abreast with ladders to carry it. The line was held by the sailors, under fire for the first time, who began to waver and show signs of breaking, but their color bearer, Edward Moizer, "being a stout man both of person and courage", threw himself into the breach. He was bravely supported by a few soldiers and, by waving the colors, he rallied the seamen to their duty. He continued in the thick of the fight until the staff of the colors, with three of his fingers, were shot off. His courageous action probably saved Lyme. Three times the Royalists returned to the attack stoutly, only "to be repulsed by equal bravery and resolution". At sunset they returned to their works. Even the women had taken their places in the line to fill the bandoliers of the men.

Next afternoon fire arrows were shot into the thatch, which set alight twenty houses. Had not the wind changed, as by miracle, the whole town must have been burnt to the ground. Here again the women showed their courage: for one had her hands shot off and another her arms, as they brought up pails of water to quench the flames. [16]

Warwick by now had recognized that while he could support and supply the town, he could not raise the siege. Owing to the steep rise of the ground, his guns were useless against the foe. On June 1st he wrote to suggest that five hundred horse and five hundred dragoons could raise the siege from the land. A message accordingly was sent to Essex desiring him either to send a party to relieve Lyme or to dispatch Waller. At the time the King had slipped out of Oxford and was at Worcester, where he was more or less surrounded by the forces of Essex, Waller, and Massey. Fortunately for him, on June 6th Essex and Waller met at Stow-on-the-Wold. They agreed that Essex should relieve Lyme, while Waller watched the King. Essex was jealous of Waller. He thought of the west as his own sphere, and he was determined that, after relieving Lyme, he would march into Cornwall and cut off the King's supplies.

This division of forces alarmed the Committee, who had never dreamed of this interpretation of their orders. They hastily sent off another order, bidding Essex, after sending a force to relieve Lyme, to return himself to watch Oxford. It reached Essex at Blandford and his reply was petulant: he was carrying out his orders in the only way possible; after relieving Lyme, he would devote himself to the reconquest of the west. Waller he considered unfit for this task, although he was in a good position, after disposing of the King, to undertake the siege of Oxford. As for the proposal to send horse to Lyme, they could do no good service in those narrow passages: even if they broke through Maurice's army, how could they get out again? He wound up: "Consider what I have said, and if by following your advice the West be not reduced, Hopton's army recruited, and Lyme lost, let not the blame be laid upon your Lordships' innocent though suspected servant, Essex." Surprisingly he was allowed to proceed, even though he had abandoned his proper objective, the King.

On June 12th Warwick had again written to call attention to the alarming situation at Lyme. There was a shortage of powder, ammunition, and bullet. There were many sick and wounded, so that seamen had to be kept ashore to hold the line, and many of the crews were undermanned. Daily the enemy were drawing their lines nearer, and were being reinforced. He had no ammunition to spare the town. The only ships he had with him were the *James* and the *Reformation,* as the rest were elsewhere, either in the Irish Seas, or before Weymouth, Dartmouth, Exmouth, and Guernsey. Some were detained in the Thames for want of supplies, while others were kept in the Downs for convoy duty. [17]

Meanwhile Essex's lumbering approach alarmed Maurice for the safety of his rear. A deserter brought the news that Maurice was about to retire. So Blake went aboard Warwick to propose a renewal of the previous manoeuvre of sending ships eastward to draw off the Royalists, while a sortie was made to probe their lines. Next day, the 14th, this was carried out. Once again the Royalists came down to prevent a landing, but the seamen, who had been landed, drove off their horse and foot. Already the foe could be seen taking down their tents, and drawing off their artillery. To hasten them a continual fire was kept up from the town and by five o'clock in the afternoon Maurice had gone. After forty-six days the siege ended. Maurice had lost too many men to be able to continue his advance and he retired to Exeter. The prong of his fork had not merely been blunted—it had been bent right back.

Warwick's supplies to the town had enabled it to hold out, while the landing of heavy artillery had put the town on equal terms in this respect with the Royalists. With the dramatic instinct that is characteristic of the great leader, he had appeared in person at the moment of greatest stress. To Lyme, almost despairing of any military relief by land, Warwick brought a sense of leadership and planned direction which strengthened their morale. They felt they were part of a larger campaign, into which they were integrated by Warwick's naval strategy. No longer were they an isolated garrison, but an important part of the struggle as a whole. By his swift grasp of the fact that relief must come from the military forces on land, Warwick showed he knew the key to the situation, and he won the town's confidence. Nor did he leave Lyme until the solution he had propounded became a reality. Its relief was due to a commander who knew what ought to be done and who had the ability and strength of mind to see it achieved.

Yet strangely enough the siege had dislocated the plans of both sides. Maurice's advance had been foiled, but despite his failure Essex had been drawn away from dealing with the King, at the moment when it seemed that he had him trapped and at his mercy. The infatuated Essex moved on to Dorchester, while his horse took Weymouth. Here they secured sixty ships, and a hundred guns.[18] Now the Lord General was about to move on to complete disaster. And so, too, was Rupert.

CHAPTER V

1644

Warwick Helps to Break the King's Northern Prong

Swanley now left South Wales to go to the Downs to refit. Moulton remained behind in the *Lion* (42), with three warships and the merchantmen, to guard the Haven. Before Swanley left he had stained his name by an act of savage brutality. He had taken one hundred and fifty soldiers, under Colonel Willoughby, on board. He bound the Irish, seventy in number, back to back, and threw them into the sea, "to wash them", as he said, "from the blood of the Protestants that was upon them." Not a voice was raised in Parliament against this barbarous act, for the Irish were regarded as little better than savages.[1] On the contrary, Swanley and Smith stood at the Bar of the Commons, on June 4th, to receive gold medals and chains as a reward for their services.

On that same day Moulton wrote to Warwick. Hardly had Swanley gone, confident that South Wales was secure, than a brilliant new royalist commander appeared. He was Sir Charles Gerard, who had landed at Black Rock in Monmouthshire, with troops from Ireland. He swept through South Wales like a prairie fire. Soon all Swanley's gains were lost and the way to Pembroke itself lay open. Moulton appealed for help: if the Haven were lost, the Royalists would have access to South Wales, Bristol, and the neighboring ports; most of his ships were unserviceable from long duty at sea; he needed money to pay and revictual the merchantmen.[2] Laugharne seemed powerless to check Gerard's advance. Nearly all the gentry hundred seamen left and spoke of "our sad condition." Warwick and the train-bands were deserting to the foe. Moulton only had two could reply only that as soon as the *Swallow*, *Leopard*, and the *Provi-*

dence were refitted they should be sent. His own hands were tied, for at a Council of War with Essex, Warwick had urged him to march west. Warwick considered many would flock to the standard, and that, while he attacked Plymouth, the garrison would take the enemy in the rear.[3]

Warwick moreover had promised Essex to keep him company by sea with the fleet, probably hoping that these amphibious operations would lead to the reduction of Cornwall and the capture of the Cornish ports. The privateers would either be driven out or taken and a heavy burden lifted from the shoulders of the Navy. It was a bold and attractive plan, but it did not take into consideration that Essex would be advancing into an almost hostile country, and would therefore depend almost entirely upon the fleet for supplies. Nor was Essex the general to execute such a plan, with his notorious lack of the first principles of tactics and strategy.

Meanwhile, in view of Rupert's advance northwards, Ormonde was asked to send over three hundred men to secure Beaumorris, "so necessary to our communications with Ireland." He answered that while he hoped to send over Colonel Trafford's men for this purpose he had to consider the activities of the parliamentary ships, "which block up these coasts, some riding upon the point of Aire, near Mostyn." They had even taken seven barks "with much scandal and insolency out of the very port of Holyhead", laden with supplies for Chester. Trafford's men, with twenty barrels of powder and six guns, were already embarked upon the *Swan* (18). But they were unable to sail because two warships and a frigate blockaded Dublin. "The too good intelligence these ships have got from their friends ashore of all our actions, makes me unwilling to hazard so many good men and provisions." Swanley's brutal act was still fresh in his mind. "I would expose them", he wrote, "desperately to their mercies, who showed little Christianity of late to many of those who went with Colonel Willoughby, whose soldiers they cast overboard."[4]

Ormonde felt also that he must retain the *Swan* for the defense of Dublin harbor. The naval hold of the Parliament upon St. George's Channel was too strong for him to challenge. Rupert, however, moved on and captured Liverpool, though the ships, "richly laden and well furnished with ammunition", had got away to sea, since there were no royalist vessels to prevent them.

Rupert now skillfully outmanoeuvred the armies of the Scots, the Fairfaxes, and the Eastern Association, under Leven, Manchester, and Cromwell, and slipped by them to relieve York. Then in obedience to the King's order he moved out with Newcastle to meet the allied armies at Marston Moor. Here, on the fateful day of July 2nd, they suffered complete disaster. The northern prong of the King's fork had not been merely blunted again — it had been broken off. Newcastle fled overseas, but Rupert, valiantly gathering together six thousand horse, regained Chester and moved back to Oxford. The whole of the north, with few exceptions, such as Newcastle, Scarborough, and Carlisle, fell into the hands of the Parliament.

The Navy had indirectly played an important part in the victory. By supplying and defending Hull it had helped to prevent Newcastle's army from advancing. By keeping the Humber open it had enabled the army of the Eastern Association to advance into Yorkshire, with Hull protecting its right flank. The city had not only been a bastion against the Royalists; it was also the gate of the north; and Warwick's ships held the key of that gate, the Humber.

The northern squadron had done its work well and now could be entrusted with the blockade of Newcastle and Scarborough. Warwick could instead concentrate his attention on naval affairs in the south and west. On July 8th he sailed from Portland in the *James* (40) with the *Expedition* (18), and some smaller vessels; Batten, in the *Reformation* (46), with the *Paragon* (22), the *Warwick* (22), was off Falmouth, watching the Queen. She had left Oxford to give birth to a daughter and had asked for a safe-conduct to Bath to take the waters, but this was refused. The approach of Essex forced her to move from Exeter to Falmouth, where on July 14th, she embarked upon the *George*, escorted by some smaller vessels.[5]

As the *George* came out, Batten fired ten shots at her. Her captain, by superb seamanship, got to windward and crowded on all sail. Since the *George* had been newly tallowed, she began to leave the foe behind, until the *Warwick* came up and fire was exchanged. The Queen displayed her unfailing spirit, declaring that rather than surrender she would order the captain to sink the ship. Off Jersey the *George* was hit in the rigging and had to slacken sail. At this critical moment some Dieppe ships hove in sight. Batten, taking them to be Royalists, abandoned the chase. The Queen had not finished with her trials. A sudden storm scattered her escort before the *George* could make harbor. After some anxious hours she landed on the wild Breton coast, only to find her party was mistaken by the natives for pirates. They abandoned their opposition only when the Queen revealed her identity. Then the kindly fisherfolk gave her simple shelter in a rough hut. Batten excused his failure on the ground that his ships were foul, but he had now gained the distinction of having fired twice upon his Queen.[6]

Essex was still plodding on, unconscious of a danger that now threatened him from the rear. The King, in his absence, had escaped from the trap at Worcester, and regained Oxford. On June 20th he attacked and defeated Waller at Copredy Bridge. The beaten army fell back to Buckingham, where it was joined by Major General Browne, with four thousand five hundred men. But Waller's troops, shaken by defeat, raised the old cry of "Home, Home". The Essex train-bands even attacked Browne and wounded him in the face. Small wonder was it that the joint armies began to break up. Waller commented: "My Lords, till you have an army merely your own that you may command, it is in a manner impossible to do anything of importance." In this remark lay the germ of the New Model Army.

On July 7th a council of war advised the King to march after Essex. Anxious for the safety of his Queen, Charles agreed. By the time he reached Somerset, Essex had passed by Exeter and was moving on Plymouth. Here Grenville wisely withdrew before his superior forces to Horsebridge, to guard the passage of the Tamar. Encouraged by Lord Robartes, who pointed out to him the importance of the tin trade, Essex was more than ever determined to advance into Cornwall. He denuded the Plymouth garrison of one thousand two hundred men and in superb self-confidence began to enter a hostile territory. He brushed Grenville aside with ease, and reached Bodmin on July 28th, where he learned with a shock that the King was only twenty miles away at Launceston. It was his first news that the King was in pursuit. In alarm Essex made for Lostwithiel to keep his communications with the sea open, for now he depended entirely upon Warwick's ships for provisions.

Warwick had reached Plymouth on the 20th. On the way he had been dealing ceaselessly with the matters of powder, match, and shot for the defenses of Weymouth and Portland, with gun carriages for Essex, and with discipline. Captain Wheeler, of the *Greyhound,* had to be dismissed for disobedience to the Vice-Admiral. Thomas Cook, boatswain of the *Garland,* "did not use fitting authority over the crew, since he loves his bed too well." On the other hand Warwick saw to it that Wilkinson, gunner of the *Greyhound,* had the cost of his journey to London to collect stores refunded to him.[7]

At Plymouth he was horrified to find that Essex had left only eight hundred men to hold a front of four miles. The people would not supply victuals to the troops, who, in their turn, were clamoring for pay, having had no money from Parliament. The Mayor and the Governor were, as usual, at logger-heads and Warwick had to map out their various jurisdictions. He had only two ships with him, though five royalist ships had been captured in a sudden raid on Fowey. On August 18th he wrote to say that would be forced to leave unless victuals were sent to him before the end of the month. "If Essex", he wrote, "were defeated Plymouth would be in great danger." He closed on an ominous note, that was almost prophetic: the wind was blowing hard at west, so that he had been unable to send Essex any supplies.[8]

What he feared happened, for Essex, now desperately short of provisions, made for the sea at Fowey. Here he hoped to find Warwick, but the Lord High Admiral was tightly gripped by the wind in the Sound. Essex had pinned himself in a narrow valley, surrounded on all sides. Only his cavalry managed to break out. He was caught in the trap he had baited himself. With an amazing belief in his own value, Essex escaped by boat to Plymouth, leaving Skippon in command. On September 2nd that luckless general had no choice but to surrender.

All eyes were fixed upon the King. Would he attack Plymouth? Already £20,000 for the pay of Essex's army had been sent there. Warwick had been forced back to revictual at Portsmouth, but not before he had recalled Batten, with eight ships. Lord Robartes was now Governor, as Wardlaw had died. The town was in deep depression and alarm at Essex's defeat, "the soldiers low in their courage, loud in their complaints, the townspeople cold and indifferent, weary of a two years' siege, and over all a deadness of spirit." But Batten's arrival, together with many of Essex's foot, who had been allowed to march away to avoid the need to feed them, wrought a wonderful change. Batten could write of "the happy encouragement of the Lord Robartes that hath roused the spirits of the inhabitants, so that they resolve to stand it out to the last man."[9]

When the King arrived before the town on September 9th, the sense of common danger, together with resolute leadership, bound the city in a united resistance. After an attack on the western end of the line, Charles was repulsed with heavy loss and marched away. Had he been able to attack immediately after his victory, it might have gone hard with Plymouth. Once again, Warwick, by calling up Batten's ships, had preserved this essential bastion in the west.

Back at Holborn House Warwick dealt with routine naval matters. A Winter Guard of eighteen warships and ten armed merchantmen was set out.* Nor did he forget individuals: a poor woman of Deal had nursed and fed James Bushell, gunner of the *Spy*, when he was sick; James quietly went off without paying her; Warwick at once ordered that the amount due to her was to be stopped out of James' pay.[10]

On October 29th he penned a strong letter to both Houses, pointing out that though he had continually put forward the needs of the Navy they had as continually ignored them. Without supplies it would be impossible to set out the Guards. Ships were lying idle in the Thames, at the cost of £100 daily, because there was no money to equip them. The long delays between the going out and the coming in of the Guards resulted in ports being unwatched, enabling privateers to harass trade. Dutch ships had actually to be hired for convoy duty. The efficiency of the fleet was being impaired by the poor quality of the victuals. At Chatham and Portsmouth the Victuallers had refused to deliver supplies because of the debts owing to them. To such a state was the Navy reduced. Only the trust and confidence

*Appendix F.

of the sailors in Warwick's leadership, in the face of all these handicaps, had allowed him to hold the control of the seas.[11]

He was still ably supported by his Captains. In the north the only royalist activity had been a sudden raid from Scarborough by Cholmley, in which some London coal ships were captured.[12] This was balanced by the recapture of Liverpool. Moulton still held stubbornly on to Milford Haven. But the defeat at Marston Moor had led to the recall of Gerard, relieving the pressure upon Moulton and Laugharne. In July Moulton had captured nine East Indiamen, laden with wine and tobacco for Bristol. It was a well-earned reward for his tenacity, and it is to be hoped he enjoyed a drink and a smoke.[13] In August Abraham Percy, who had been abandoned off Land's End by Plunkett in the *Crescent*, brought in the *Amy*, laden with ammunition for Liverpool. Luckily for him, Moulton still held the Haven, for he was in great fear that he might be captured by the Bristol ships.[14] Now at last Moulton's real chance came.

The Earl of Inchiquin, who alone supported the Protestants and Settlers in Munster, had expected to be made President of the Province by the King.[15] When this post was denied him, he realised that Charles had neither the desire nor the power to put down the Irish revolt. The defeat at Marston Moor convinced him that only from Parliament could the Protestants look for support. He therefore transferred his allegiance from the King to Parliament. Straightway he seized the ports of Cork, Youghal, and Kinsale, and ejected the Irish. He sent the news to Moulton. Grasping at this unexpected opportunity for the Irish Guard to obtain bases, Moulton collected merchant ships to send across. On August 24th eleven vessels landed horses, arms, and ammunition at Cork; another eleven arrived at Youghal, and six at Kinsale.[16]

Inchiquin got to work at once. On September 11th he sent Captain Bright in the *Jeremy* (22) to Duncannon, a fort guarding the approach to Wexford, that stronghold of the Dunkirk and Irish privateers. It was held by Lord Esmond, a fervent Royalist and Protestant. The majority of his soldiers, however, were Parliamentarians. Under him were Major Capron, another Royalist, and Lieutenant Larcan, a Parliamentarian. Larcan was now practically in command, though Esmond still remained so nominally. After being promised food and pay, all the soldiers took the Covenant, although Esmond, Capron, and a few others declined to do so. The troops thereupon refused to obey Capron, who was therefore conveniently sent away with despatches to Dublin. Duncannon was now virtually in Parliament hands. Since it lay almost opposite Milford Haven, it would be useful as a naval base and its possession would prevent the sailing of the privateers from Wexford. Larcan soon extended his operations to the country round, becoming so dangerous that the Catholic Confederacy at Kilkenny decided that Duncannon must be wrested from him. General Preston, an able soldier who had fought in the Spanish Netherlands, was sent off for this purpose.[17]

Meanwhile Swanley and Smith, in the *Leopard* (38) and the *Swallow* (36), beat into the Haven from Plymouth, bringing £1,000 in cash and munitions. Laugharne was able to refit his troops: then, with the aid of the seamen and a demi-cannon from the *Leopard*, the town of Laugharne was taken. Cardigan was selected for the next attack, but heavy rains prevented any attempt until late in the year. The town soon fell, although the stout walls of the Castle defied all attempts to breach them. Another demi-cannon from the *Leopard* was sent for, but owing to the appalling state of the roads it took a fortnight to bring up. The trouble was justified when the gun smashed in the half-moon before the main gate. In a fierce attack the soldiers and the seamen stormed their way through the opening and the Castle was theirs. The remnants of Gerard's troops were now either mopped up or driven off. Once more the long arm of the Navy had reached inland into South Wales.[18]

Off Dublin the fleet was still active. Ormonde had embarked commissioners on a ship to go to England, who were to consult the King about some points connected with the Cessation. But a parliamentary frigate, lying off Dublin harbor, prevented their sailing. A friend of the captain's was persuaded to lure him ashore, for the captain, though a Puritan, believed strongly in the Biblical adage that wine rejoiceth the heart of man. His friend kindly induced him to drown his cares in strong drink until he was past worrying. By this trick the commissioners were able to slip out.[19] On their return they were not so lucky. After sailing from Carnarvon, they fell in with Captain Coachman, of the *Truelove* (18) on December 1st.

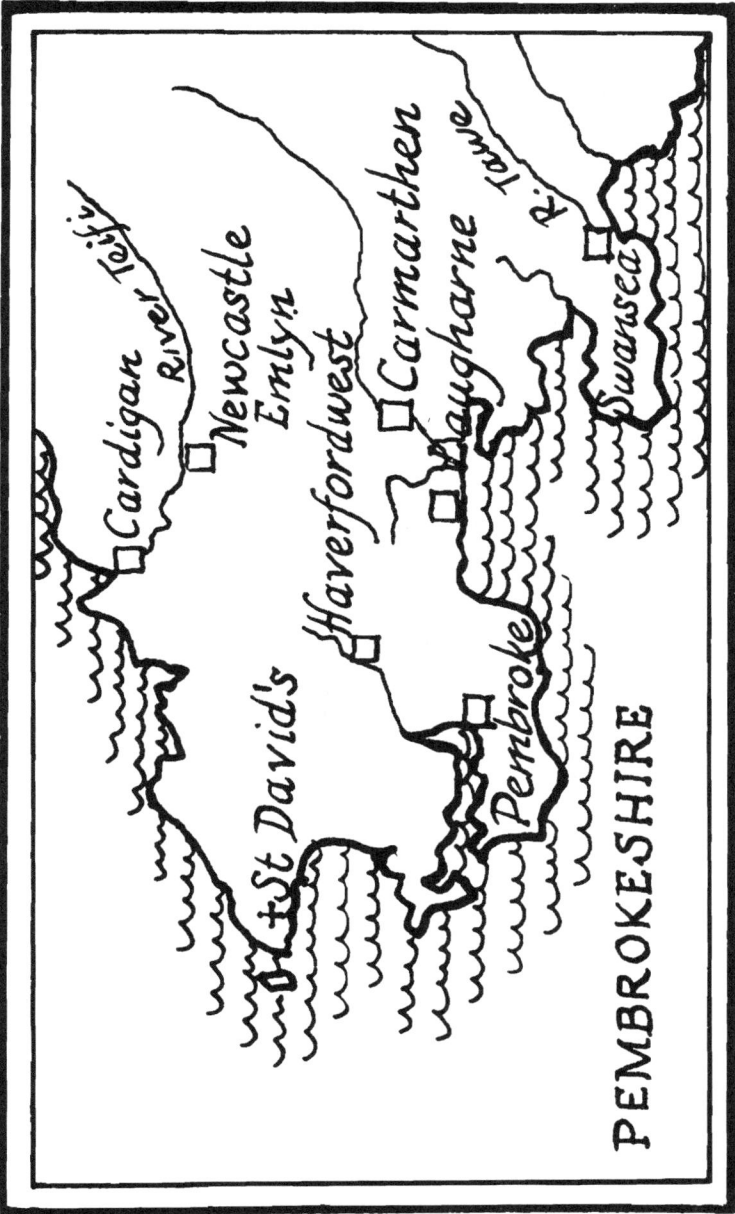

PEMBROKESHIRE

Before he boarded them, they managed to throw overboard a packet containing the King's reply. In disgust Coachman sent them to Swanley at Milford.[20]

In the north the Scots, at long last, took Newcastle on October 22nd, but only after mine and storm. Haddock, with ten ships, had blockaded the Tyne, so that neither supplies nor arms could reach the Royalists.[21] Newcastle proved a rich prize, since the Scots now had the control of the collieries. By taxing the sale of coal, much to the annoyance of the owners, they could pay their troops. Great indignation arose at this action among the poor of London, where the wood-sellers continued to reap a rich harvest. The effect upon shipping and trade had been disastrous. In 1641, 3043 vessels had entered the port, of which 2836 were English. In 1643 only twenty-eight English and nine foreign vessels cleared the river from January to June, while from June not a single ship sailed. Yet after the surrender, one hundred and forty six English and five foreign vessels cleared the river. The mountains of unsold coal upon the quays testified to the tightness of the blockade.[22] Scarborough was now the only northern port left to the King.

While these events had been taking place upon the circumference, the King, after leaving Plymouth, had marched to the relief of Donnington and Basing Houses. Then, on October 27th, he was confronted by the united armies of Essex, Manchester, and Waller. Essex lay sick at Reading, so that the command devolved upon Manchester. There appears to have been little co-ordination among his forces — it has even been suggested that Cromwell, in command of Manchester's cavalry, was sulking. Otherwise the King, outnumbered by two to one, ought to have been captured with his whole army. As it was, the intervention of night saved him and under the cover of darkness he was allowed to slip away to Oxford. His army was still intact, as were his besieged garrisons.

Though the Parliamentarians had won the victory, they had missed a much bigger one. As a result bitter quarrelling broke out among the generals. Cromwell made Manchester his target by accusing him of inefficiency. Manchester retorted by reminding Cromwell of his remark that he would fight the Scots as willingly as the Royalists, should they attempt to enforce Presbyterianism. He further alleged that Cromwell had deliberately filled the army with sectaries, who would agree to no peace unless it suited their own ideas.

Besides the quarrelling generals, the Eastern Association complained that the army they had equipped and paid was constantly being used in other parts of England. This burden they could not continue to bear: the army ought to be organized and paid for on a national basis. Waller had already suggested this and his idea was beginning to bear fruit.

To solve the problem of the quarrelling generals, Zachary Tate proposed that no member of either House should hold any naval or military command. The Self-Denying Ordinance was about to come to birth.

But this threatened Warwick's position as Lord Admiral. His loss would be a blow to the Navy. In the critical year of 1644 his squadrons had helped to preserve Hull, Plymouth, Lyme, and Milford Haven. They had put an end to the transport of the Irish troops to England, and now they were about to try to deal with the privateers from Ireland. They had indirectly, but decisively, contributed to the blunting, the bending back, and the breaking off, of the prongs of the King's fork. Above all they had brought to remote forces, isolated and cut off from military support, the sense that they were nevertheless part and parcel of the struggle as a whole. This was due to Warwick's conception of command: he alone must direct and control the fleet. By his strategic ability he had co-ordinated the work of his squadrons with the military situation. By assuming command at sea at a critical moment he had contributed a sense of personal leadership and direction to the officers and seamen. By this common touch he had held their confidence, trust, and affection. His constant attention to detail, as the few instances quoted reveal, shows the care he bestowed not merely on material, but also on individuals.

This sense of a planned leadership had communicated itself to the hardly pressed and isolated ports and forces. They now saw themselves as focal points of resistance. The presence of Warwick's ships had inspired them to renewed efforts. They were essential units in the struggle as a whole, and they derived this new knowledge from the consciousness that Warwick acted upon a pre-determined plan.

To appreciate the greatness of Warwick's achievements it is

necessary to remember his difficulties in the matter of keeping his
ships at sea. Warwick's continuous requests for supplies, victuals,
money, and ships, emphasized how hard was his task. Only a great
leader and organizer could have done what Warwick did, in the face
of such neglect and handicaps. Had Parliament been alive to his
abilities, instead of being lulled to sleep by his successes, they would
have applied the lesson to their military campaign. The Navy had
acted as a unified force under a single command. Only now were
they beginning to awaken to the need for a regular Army, under a
single commander.

Warwick had preserved them from dangers by sea. But already
there were whispers of a coming storm by land, not indeed so much
from the Royalists, as from the growing divisions among themselves.

CHAPTER VI

1645

The Change in Naval Command

Aloof from the struggles which now convulsed the parliamentary parties the Navy continued its work. A new young naval commander now made his appearance. William Penn, who had served with his father in the merchant service, had become a lieutenant and now at the age of twenty-three had been given command of the *Fellowship* (28), a Fourth-Rate. On his way from the Downs to Carrickfergus, he had to put into Portsmouth, where, on January 9th, he went into action. Colonel Goring's troops had swooped down on Gosport and plundered it. At night, about one o'clock they set fire to twenty-four houses. As the flames and smoke lit up the night sky, the *Fellowship*, with the *Swiftsure* (48) and the *Mary Rose* (28), opened fire upon the raiders and drove them off.[1]

About the same time Grenville made a determined attack upon Plymouth, beginning his operations with an attack upon the Maudlyn fort, into which his troops forced their way. Since this was a key point, holding together the outer defenses, a fierce counter-attack wrestled its possession from the Royalists, and drove them back to their lines. After re-organizing his troops, Grenville made a night attack, on February 17th, on Mount Stamford. It had been badly battered in previous attacks and was partly in ruins, but it was still held by the garrison. As the fort gave little shelter, the garrison was soon driven out, and the Royalists built up a protecting wall of fascines around it. Its capture threatened not only Plymouth, but the safety of the ships lying in Cattwater and the Sound itself — it must be recaptured. A cannonade was therefore opened upon it from the ships that lay in Cattwater and the Sound, thus taking it in the flanks. Next day a party of seamen was ferried from Plymouth across

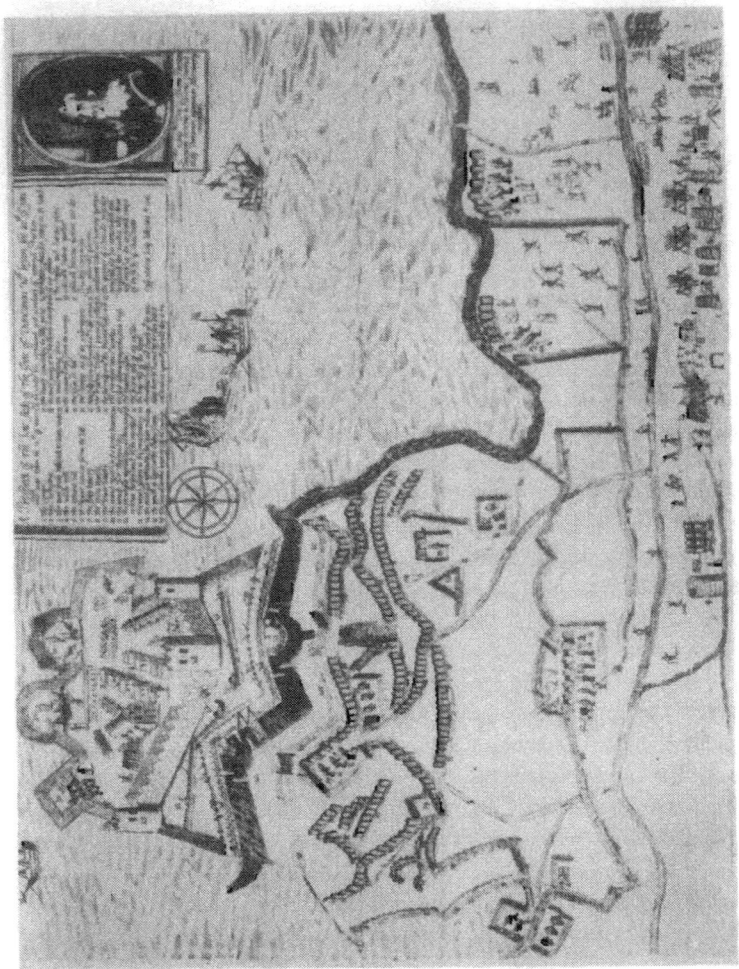

THE SIEGE OF DUNCANNON

Cattwater, under the covering fire of the ships' guns. As they emerged from the smoke, the Royalists poured a heavy fusilade upon them, but the seamen forced a landing, throwing themselves upon the fort. At the same time, in order to prevent the Royalists moving their main forces from the north to the support of their newly-won position, a feint attack was made from Penny-come-Quick. The seamen pressed on with their assaults, tore away the fascines, and burst their way into the ruined fort. Soon the defenders began to break, and the jubilant stormers drove them headlong to their lines.

Lord Robertes reported: "all the sea Captains behaved them-selves very stoutly, and Captain Thomas of the *Warwick* frigate was eminent. The seamen did very considerable service, whose ships of war I have for the present stayed here." Every preparation was made against a renewed attack. Mount Batten's defenses were improved. Food, pay, and equipment for the garrison was provided, together with medicine for the sick and wounded. Even shrouds for the dead were got ready — surely a strange way of improving morale! But Grenville, much against his will, had been ordered to join Goring for his spring campaign in Somerset. Once again the Navy had come to the rescue of Plymouth.[2]

January indeed was a busy month for the Navy. In South Wales Gerard had made a dramatic re-appearance. Learning that Cardigan was short of provisions, on January 4th he swooped down upon it with twelve hundred horse and a thousand foot. Rice Powell, the Governor, refused to surrender. Gerard at once broke down the bridge across the Teifi, to prevent any relief from reaching it and opened fire with his artillery upon the castle. He followed this up with several attempts to carry the Castle by storm, only to be repulsed with some loss. Laugharne came speeding up with six hundred horse and three hundred foot, of which a hundred were Swanley's seamen, to be brought up short by the broken bridge. As he stood fuming on the wrong side of the river, a dripping messenger, who had swum across, brought the alarming news that the Castle had only eight days' food left. Laugharne immediately filled a boat with supplies, guarding it on either side with two boats of musketeers to check the fire of the Royalists, who lined the river banks. Then, with the bullets whistling across the water, the seamen bent lustily to their oars, and brought in their precious cargo, with the loss of two men.[3]

By cleverly spreading a false rumor that fresh troops were coming to his support, Laugharne induced Gerard to draw off, though he left behind a small body to continue the siege. Seizing his opportunity, Laugharne shot an arrow, with a message bound round it, into the Castle, telling Powell that he intended to attempt to cross the river and asking him to make a sortie at the same moment. Rough repairs had been made to the bridge with wood and faggots, across which the troops scrambled. Powell's nicely timed sortie prevented the Royalists from opposing them. Then the joint forces combined to drive the Royalists in some confusion to Newcastle Emlyn.[4]

On January 17th an urgent appeal for help reached Swanley from Duncannon. But Gerard's re-appearance had tied Swanley's hands, so that he could spare neither seamen nor troops. He undertook, however, to send ships to Cork for Inchiquin to transport troops to Duncannon. Here a squadron of four small ships, commanded by Captain Beale, in the *Great Lewis,* lay off the fort. They had landed thirty-eight seamen with supplies to aid in the defense. Though his ships made abortive attempts to drive off the Royalists by gun-fire, the inexperienced gunners could not place their shots anywhere near the foe.

The garrison were in wretched state. They had only a hundred and fifty men, no proper water supply, and neither doctor nor surgeon. Preston, commanding the Royalists, had one thousand five hundred foot, with cannon and mortars. Under the direction of Lalue, a French engineer, batteries of cannon and mortars were erected, commanding both the land side of the fort, and the approach by water. As the contemporary map shows, two approach trenches, protected by baskets, were joined by a communication line and then divided again to run on to both ends of the curtain. This work was carried out under the protection of a heavy battery in the rear. But the work was difficult, owing to the rocky nature of the ground, coupled with violent storms and continuous rain. Preston fixed his headquarters near the chapel and burying ground, while Lalue stationed himself near the ship battery. Miners were set to work against the walls. Frequent sorties from Duncannon, with heavy loss on both sides, failed to prevent Preston from cutting the fort off from the land.

At sunrise on the 24th, the seaward batteries opened fire on Beale's ships. Their plunging shots were so effective that the vessels were heavily damaged, and Beale was forced to cut his cables and sail out of range. He was followed by the other three ships, which had to abandon their anchors. The exultant foe recorded this as "a most enjoyable sight." But worse was to come, for, as Beale withdrew, an adverse wind and tide held up his retreat and he came under heavy fire from the confederate mortars. All his guns were silenced; his masthead and sails shot down; two young men who were unfurling the Parliament flag had the rigging shot from under them. They came down on deck, as the jubilant foe noted, "almost in a single stride." At last a light breeze sprang up to relieve Beale from his predicament and he drifted slowly out of range. But so damaged was his ship that it sank with the loss of most of the crew. On the 28th Beale sailed in another ship for Milford.

In answer to Beale's tale of woe Swanley told him that he had sent the *Elizabeth* and the *Magdalen* (20) with a pink to take Inchiquin's troops to Duncannon. The *Mayflower* (28) was already at Cork for the same purpose. To Swanley's dismay Beale told him none of these ships had arrived when he left. Swanley at once ordered William Smith, his Vice-Admiral, to sail in the *Swallow* (36), with the *Duncannon*, a ship that Esmond had handed over, and Beale's ship. They arrived at Duncannon on February 19, having apparently picked up the *Magdalen, Mayflower,* and *Elizabeth* on the way. They had no soldiers on board, as Inchiquin said he had none he could trust. Smith now anchored under Creedan Head, in full view of the fort, but, by Beale's advice, out of range of the enemy's plunging fire.

After a heavy bombardment on the 11th, Preston sent in a drummer with letters to Esmond. Contrary to the customs of war, Esmond fired on him, so Preston instead bound a letter round an arrowhead and shot it into the fort. He bade the garrison desert to him, with the threat that the conditions he had offered Esmond would never be renewed. The letter apparently created a fifth column within: as the royalist trenches drew nearer, messages bound to lead bullets, giving information about the state of affairs in Duncannon, were thrown into the trenches.

When Smith arrived, he took advantage of thick darkness to throw much-needed supplies into Duncannon. Preston then launched an attack, but the musketeers of the storming party had the priming of their pieces suddenly blown away by a whirlwind and their pans filled with gravel. Though the attack was driven off with great loss, a chance shot decided Duncannon's fate. Larcan, the mainspring of the defense, was hit by a bullet which rebounded from a wall. As there was no surgeon to attend his wound, he died, and without his inspiration the morale of the defense gradually went to pieces.

The fort was now continually bombarded, despite stones and pieces of iron hurled upon the besiegers. On March 4 a tempestuous south wind sprang up, forcing the ships to weigh anchor and put to sea. Several roofs were blown off in the fort by the storm's fury and the two boats attending the seamen ashore were smashed to pieces on the beach. On the 8th Smith sent a letter of congratulation for their service to the seamen ashore. The next day James Frankyn and Abraham Mootham replied. They reminded Smith of his promise not to leave a man ashore and to send boats to fetch them off; they lacked water to drink or to cook with; their trenches were so commanded by the enemy that they dared not go out to fetch it; many were sick and there was no surgeon to attend them; it was impossible to hold the fort much longer since it was undermined in three places and the Irish were almost under the ramparts; they had unanimously resolved to stay no longer.

Smith replied in a letter to Esmond. He opened in pessimistic vein: "if the rebels take the fort by storming it, they will put you all to the sword, which would be much lamented." He could send no more supplies — he had only twenty days' victuals aboard, which would oblige him to sail at the first opportunity. "Your Lordship hath but two things to consider of: first the potency of your enemy; next, your abilities to subsist. For, before any relief can overtake you, it will be 10 or 8 days at soonest." Smith continued in high-minded fashion: "Our Saviour Jesus Christ gives you the best counsel, who sayeth, agree with thine adversary while thou art in the way. And so life and liberty may be maintained." He concluded by saying that even if the guns were of beaten gold he had no means of bringing them off. Then he piously expressed the hope that the Almighty would direct Esmond's decision "to His glory and your safeties", adding casually that "if I stay in the road tomorrow I shall take it for a great honour to receive your Lordship's resolution."

In reply the luckless Esmond could only say that he had been encouraged to hope for help that never eventuated. He begged Smith to leave his seamen ashore, as he was about to employ a stratagem by asking for a Protestant garrison, to be named by Ormonde. But Smith seems to have sailed almost at once.

His departure naturally led to an uproar among both the soldiers and seamen. Esmond pacified them by reading them the correspondence with Inchiquin, Swanley, and Smith. He told them he was writing to Preston to ask for a parley, to which they all agreed. Preston answered that though there was a Cessation, it was not between the Irish Confederacy and the Parliament. If Esmond surrendered he would clear his loyalty to the King; if not, Preston would take Duncannon by force.

Three days later, on St. Patrick's Day, Preston opened a heavy cannonade against the Castle, and soon the walls were breached. A forlorn hope of a hundred and fifty men leaped into the ditch to storm. Bullets, stones, pieces of iron were rained down upon them from the walls, but at last they broke into the Castle. After a truce to bury the dead, it was agreed to surrender Duncannon with all its contents, while the garrison was to march out with full honors of war, with bag and baggage, to Youghal or Dublin. The gallant old Esmond died a few days later, on his way to his manor house at Limerick. Once again it had been shown that naval force alone could not relieve a port. There must be military force to co-operate from the land.

Matters ended on a note of comedy. Not knowing that Duncannon had fallen, Captain Plunkett, "the scourge of the Irish Sea", came into the harbor with supplies from the Parliament. He actually sent his purser and six seamen ashore, who were taken prisoner. After paying a ransom, they were sent to Limerick. Cash was more useful to their captors than their persons. One wonders if Plunkett had to find it — if so it must have been gall to his grasping soul.[5]

The numerous Wexford privateers were free again to come and go. The nervous John Poyer, at Pembroke, foresaw a worse danger: Irish troops might be landed there. Then, "should the enemy gain the towns of Pembroke and Tenby, they will soon beat forth the ships of the Haven, and then from Waterford and other places of Ireland land their forces, which may prove dangerous to this Kingdom."[6]

Swanley was capable, however, of dealing with this unlikely threat. Elsewhere the Navy had its hands full. At Weymouth, on February 9, Sir Lewis Dyve, supported by the garrison of Portland, suddenly attacked the forts, before they had realized his troops were in action against them. The Chapel and North forts were rushed, and the town was taken, but help was speedily at hand. On the 14th Batten, in the *James*, (50) anchored in the Bay, at once landing three hundred seamen. Together with Colonel Sydenham, the Governor, he led the united forces and drove the Royalists out of Melcombe and Weymouth with heavy loss. Many were drowned in the river and Dyve was forced to retire to Dorchester.[7]

About the same time, Sir John Meldrum took Scarborough. Sir Hugh Cholmley tried to escape in his pinnace, but the boats of the blockading squadron drove him back into the Castle. Five Dunkirk ships sought to defend the town, but after two had been sunk by gunfire, the rest fled out to sea. Many ships were captured in the harbor, though Sir Hugh managed to hold out in the Castle until July 11th, when the last port the King held in the north was lost.[8]

With his ships engaged in these far-flung operations, Warwick was again calling attention to the wretched condition of the fleet. As the victuals of the Irish Guard were almost consumed, it would have to be withdrawn. The *Providence*, the *Expedition*, and the *Warwick*, off the west of England, were in the same condition. The *Swallow* and the *Leopard* would soon have to be relieved at Milford. Merchantmen would have to be taken up, victualled, supplied, and sent to the Irish Guard. This alarming situation was probably once again due to the unpaid bills of the Victuallers.[9]

A yet more serious danger threatened the Navy. The Self-Denying Ordinance had been passed, and the New Model Army was to be raised, to be formed largely from troops from Essex, Waller, and

Manchester. It was to be paid by taxes levied on the counties least affected by the war — shades of Ship-Money! And Sir Thomas Fairfax was to be in command. The Navy was to be paid in the same way but, as Professor Lewis has pointed out, it was no longer the King's Navy, controlled by him; it was now the State Navy, paid for and controlled by the people.[10]

Though by this move the incompetent Essex and Manchester had been eliminated, Warwick was *ipso facto* involved. On April 28th he accepted the situation, resigning his commission as Lord High Admiral. The office was put into commission, made up of six members from the Lords, and twelve from the Commons. But who was to command the fleet? The Commons, obsessed with the committee complex, wanted a body of three. But the Lords wisely replied that it would be better to have one person, who should be one of themselves. Clearly they saw the dangers of a divided command, from which the army had just been freed, and of changing not indeed horses, but riders. They obviously wished to retain Warwick. In single command he had done his work well and faithfully, and he was *persona grata* with the fleet. Plainly they considered him the only possible person for the post. The Commons, without consulting the Lords, directed the Admiralty Commissioners to appoint Batten for six months. The blow was softened by making Warwick head of the Commission, which was given power to select and nominate all officers of the Navy, and which was to continue in office until October 1st.[11]

It says much for the greatness of Warwick's character that he served as a Commissioner without rancor or anger. Indeed, he dominated the Commission by the strength of his personality, by the wisdom of his strategy, and by his wide knowledge and experience. But the arrangement had the serious drawback that Warwick was no longer in intimate touch with the seamen.

He got to work at once. On May 14th he proposed that twenty-nine warships and twenty-six merchantmen should be set forth as a Summer Guard*, nine for Ireland, seven for Scotland, seven to blockade Bristol, three to watch the Channel Islands, five for convoy

*Appendix G

duty in the Downs, five to refit or victual, and thirteen to lie before enemy ports in the west or before Ostend, St. Malo, and Dunkirk, to intercept the privateers and gun-runners. He pointed out that ships with the King's Commission were daily taking merchantmen and so menacing trade. The report shows the increasing distances the Navy now had to cover.[12]

How active the privateers were is shown by the arrival on May 3rd, of John Haesdonck, who had been granted letters of marque by the King on October 26th, 1643. He brought to Dartmouth four frigates with six Scotch prizes valued at £3,500, with cargoes valued at £1,800. His frigates had brought muskets, carbines, swords, match and brimstone.

Sir Nicholas Crisp, responsible for the royalist naval organization in Cornwall after Sir Nicholas Slanning's death, had twenty-nine ships, Jermyn five, and Ormonde eleven. Sir John Pennington and Baldwin Wake also had vessels operating from Bristol, besides those set out from Bideford and Barnstaple.* There were also some ninety Dunkirk and Irish ships raiding from Irish and Breton ports, while there were at least twenty Captains working from the Channel Islands. Warwick's estimate of two hundred and fifty royalist ships appears to have been a fairly accurate one.[13]

Crisp's task was no easy one. Slanning had controlled the entire organization, such as the seizure of ships, the valuation of prizes, and the customs on wool and other exports. After his death the work was divided among various officials, resulting in continual friction between Crisp, Pennington and his captains on the one hand, and the Vice-Admirals of Cornwall, Francis Bassett in the north, and Sir Charles Trevanion in the south, on the other. They now made the valuations. They also fought with the collectors of the customs for the Duchy, who were responsible for the duties on imports and exports. The Vice-Admirals claimed a tenth of all prizes brought into the ports under their jurisdiction, and so did the Judge of the Vice-Admiralty Court of Cornwall. He objected that Crisp's commission, entitling him to a tenth of the prizes his ships took, encroached upon his jurisdiction. To this Crisp retorted that the matter really rested

*Appendix P

with the High Court of Admiralty, represented by the surrogate in the west, Sir George Parry. How the matter ended is unknown.[14]

Difficulties arose over the tin traffic, upon which the King depended. It had increased from two hundred and twenty-seven thousand weight in 1644, to five hundred and ninety thousand weight in 1645 — the Stannary thousand weight being one thousand two hundred pounds. To carry this traffic English and Flemish ships had to be procured, the French and Dutch Governments had to be persuaded to allow these ships to unload in their ports, and steps had to be taken to see these captains did not play false, and sell their cargoes in parliamentary ports instead. Above all the gauntlet of the three frigates posted by Warwick off Cornwall had to be run.

Paradoxically the strength of the royalist ships lay in the fact that most of them operated under no central command, nor upon agreed plan. The attraction of securing prizes made each captain play for his own hand. Even if they could have been formed into a fleet, they would have been no match for the more powerful ships of the Parliament. As it was, Warwick had far too few ships to deal with them individually. Instead he wisely blockaded their ports, especially those in France, since the royalist defeat in the north had set free some of his ships.

In South Wales, on April 12th, Laugharne laid siege to Newcastle Emlyn. Out of the blue, on the 27th, at six a.m., Gerard, who had been sent back again, fell upon him, driving him headlong to Haverfordwest, to Pembroke, and Tenby. The garrison of Cardigan did not wait for him, but set the buildings ablaze, and fled by boat to Pembroke. By the first week in May Gerard had shut up Laugharne's troops in Pembroke and Tenby, and once more had made himself master of the Shire. He asked Pennington for ships to block up the Haven, where he was about to build another fort to prevent Swanley from moving up to the support of Pembroke. His rapid advance had forced Swanley to retire for safety to Angle Bay. In great alarm the Committee of Both Kingdoms asked the Navy Committee to send three hundred men to Pembroke. For ten weeks the blockade of Pembroke continued. In vain Gerard offered Poyer preferment and £5,000 if he would surrender, but the Governor stood firmly by his principles.[15] Relief, when it did come, was to

come from an unexpected quarter — for Swanley was pinned to
Angle Bay, which he dared not leave. So it was that some ships,
laden with Spanish bullion, had recently to surrender at Bristol,
whither they had gone for refuge from storm and piracy. Their
cargoes, worth £200,000 came as a godsend to the King, which
enabled him to pay and fit out his army.[16] Had Swanley been free,
this might not have happened.

Meanwhile Rupert was watching Massey in Gloucestershire. He
wanted the King to bring his artillery from Oxford to Worcester,
preparatory to a move to relieve Chester, and then to recruit in
Lancashire and Yorkshire, with the hope of helping Montrose,
recently victorious at Inverlochy.

The New Model at Windsor was ready to take the field at the
end of April. With incredible stupidity the Committee of Both Kingdoms repeated their old error of dispersing their forces. Cromwell,
who was about to resign his commission, was sent with a brigade
to prevent the Royalists from transferring their artillery to the
Severn valley. This he did by sweeping up all the horses around
Oxford. Fairfax was sent off to relieve Taunton. He reached Blandford on May 7th. On that same day the King left Oxford, and joined
Rupert at Stow-on-the-Wold, despite the efforts of Cromwell to stop
him. Here a council of war debated whether to march north or to
deal with Fairfax. Rupert, anxious to avenge Marston Moor, was
for the northern move; Goring and Digby, Rupert's bitter enemy,
wanted to give battle to the New Model. Disagreements were so
fierce that the King compromised. He gave Goring the command in
the west, sending the Prince of Wales, with Hopton, Digby, and
Culpepper to form a Council of the West at Bristol. The rest of his
forces were to go north. He too had dispersed his army.

Fairfax relieved Taunton on May 11th and the Committee
recalled him to siege Oxford. Unconsciously it made a wise move,
for Fairfax was now within easy reach of any new orders. But
Montrose had defeated Sir John Urry at Auldearn on May 9th with
the result that Leven and the Scots decided not to march southwards.
Instead Leven moved into Westmorland to prevent the King from
joining Montrose.

Appeals for supplies now reached Charles from Oxford, where

Fairfax had begun the siege on May 21st. The royalist army therefore marched on Leicester to relieve the pressure on Oxford. The city
was taken and sacked, a proceeding which horrified and alarmed the
Committee. They acted with prompt decision and messages were sent
out to collect their scattered forces.

Still the Royalists were bedevilled by divisions. Rupert was
firmly for going north, Digby for attacking the New Model and then
to move against the Eastern Association. Charles could make no
decision, but remained at Daventry, collecting supplies for the relief
of Oxford.

On June 8th Fairfax held a council of war, at which it was
decided that the objective must be the King's army. On the 9th the
Committee did what they ought to have done from the first and gave
Fairfax a free hand to do what he thought fit. He appointed Cromwell
his second-in-command, in charge of his cavalry. On the fateful day
of June 14th the two armies met at Naseby. Under the inspiring lead
of its two generals the New Model proved its worth and discipline.
The King found disastrous defeat: nearly all his infantry were slain
or captured; his artillery and eight thousand arms were lost; his
correspondence, which revealed his intrigues and double-dealing,
became the prize of the victors. Charles escaped with four thousand
horse, and retreated to Hereford, where he scrapped together some
three thousand foot. Gerard, with another three thousand infantry
was recalled from South Wales, never again to return. The only army
left to the King was in the west, for Byron was shut up in Chester
by Sir Thomas Middleton and Sir William Brereton. Charles' only
hope was to try to join him.

The Navy had done much to contribute to the King's ultimate
defeat. Yet defeat came only when Parliament realized that the sole
hope of victory lay in a regular army, under a single commander.
Fairfax demonstrated this fact at Naseby. The successes of the Navy,
could Parliament have recognized it, had been due to this very
fact. Here was a regular force, under a single command, led and
directed by a man of great ability. But Parliament had removed
Warwick from actual command although he was still head of the
Admiralty Commissioners. At the very same moment they had
promoted Fairfax to supreme command in the Army. What was

worse, Parliament had limited Batten's command to six months. Uncertainty as to the length of tenure of office does not make for
strong control, but Batten carried on Warwick's work with efficiency.
Nevertheless, doubts must have risen in his mind as to his future,
doubts which were to play a great part in the future events.

CHAPTER VII

1645
Batten and Penn at Work

With the victory at Naseby Swanley's difficulties had vanished. He was now free to send help to Youghal, besieged by the Earl of Castlehaven. His Vice-Admiral, William Smith, had died: when Penn came in from Carrickfergus in the *Fellowship,* Swanley promoted him to be Vice-Admiral, and gave him the *Entrance* (40). On June 15th the *Duncannon* came in from Tenby with Mr. Powell on board, who protested against the ships lying before the town being called away. It was agreed that the *Globe* (24), the *Anne and Joyce* (20), with the *Magdalen,* should ride before Tenby until the enemy retired. Three days later Captain Howett told Swanley that the crew of his ship, the *Duncannon,* had refused to go to sea. Swanley at once paraded the officers and men, rebuking them severely before he allowed them to sail to Youghal. On the 30th Penn sailed for Cork with the *Mayflower* (28), where she was to embark such men as Inchiquin could spare. Penn then moved on to Kinsale to embark soldiers for the defence of Youghal. With the *Duncannon* in company, he reached Youghal on July 8th, and at once went ashore to consult with the Governor, Sir Percy Smith, about the town's defense.[1]

Youghal stood on the west side of the harbor. It consisted of one long street running north and south along the water's edge. Behind the houses was a hillside with gardens sloping up to a ridge. On the landside the town was protected by a high wall, running along this ridge, with flanking towers at intervals. At the south end of the wall there stood a small fort for cannon, protecting the town from attack by sea. Near it was a mole for shipping. At the north end was a gate with a tower above it. Near this gate, and within the wall, there was a church or abbey with a square tower some fifty feet

SIR WILLIAM PENN

high at its north end. The entrance to the harbor was dangerous, as there was a bar which could not be passed until half flood. There was no high ground from which the enemy could command the town. The danger spots were therefore the flanks at the north and south ends of the town, and the land on the east side of the river.

In planning his attack Castlehaven had evidently realized that his problem was how to prevent the enemy's naval forces from reaching and supplying the town. To this end he erected a small battery of six guns on the east side of the harbor, opposite the fort. He also proposed to blockade the town on the west side, but at some distance from the wall. To meet these threats the Governor asked Penn to post the *Nicholas* off the south end of the town, while the *Duncannon* rode off the north end. He hoped that their guns would thus prevent the enemy from attacking at these points. Penn rather unwillingly agreed. Realizing the danger to the ships from the enemy's battery, he ordered the captains to take special care of their vessels. As he was returning from this visit an unfortunate accident occurred. In answering the Governor's salute of five guns with three from his barge, the last gun exploded, while the gunner was ramming home the cartridge. The gun had not been properly sponged and the luckless man had his hand blown off.

On July 12th Castlehaven began to move his troops away, an operation which could not be seen from the town. Penn, however, observed it from his ships, and sent a letter to inform the Governor. Penn decided in consequence to keep aboard the ammunition he had promised the town, in case it might be more urgently needed elsewhere. Next day the Governor replied that the enemy were still within two miles of the town with their whole army, and he asked Penn to remain in the harbor until further orders from Inchiquin. To this Penn agreed. That day some royalist cavalry appeared on the east shore of the harbor, and both the *Nicholas* and the *Duncannon* opened fire on them, but without effect.

On the morning of the 16th, while a barge was landing ammunition, the *Nicholas* suddenly opened fire. Penn hastened aboard to find out the reason. The captain pointed out some men busily digging near the top of a hill, with the apparent object of placing guns there

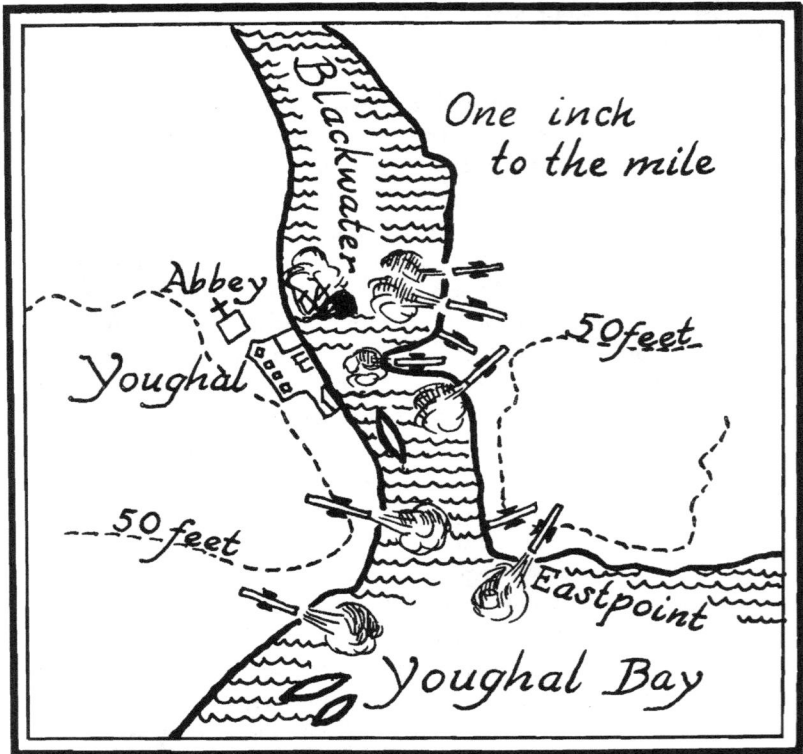

THE SIEGE OF YOUGHAL

"to beat the shipping out of the harbor." Fire was opened on this new target, only to discover it was out of range.

That night, Castlehaven, under the cover of darkness, got three guns, protected by cannon baskets, into position on the east side of the harbor, opposite the fort. At dawn they suddenly opened fire on the *Duncannon,* to which she replied. Then, to Penn's horror, she blew up with a tremendous explosion, and sank in shallow water with her stern still above the surface. A woman in the powder magazine, carrying a lighted candle, literally lost her head when it was blown off by a shot that entered. She dropped the candle into the powder. Two men were killed, with fifteen men who were on deck before the mast, and seven others were severely injured. It must have been one of the luckiest shots in the Civil War.

That afternoon, while Penn was dining with the Governor, two Irish boats were seen coming down the river laden, it was supposed, with ammunition for the new battery. Penn sent his barge in pursuit, but the boats landed before it could come up with them. Penn and the Governor, who were watching the chase from the wall of the fort, unexpectedly found themselves under fire from the battery. Stones flew thick about their ears and, though they both escaped harm, Colonels Badnedge and Loftus, with two soldiers, were killed at their sides. Later on the injured men from the *Duncannon* were brought aboard the *Entrance.* Penn then ordered her captain to salvage the sails and rigging, while her gunner was to get out the starboard guns. The ship had heeled over to port and all the guns on that side were under water. The carpenters of the *Nicholas* were sent to cut away the *Duncannon's* ports, so as to get the guns out more easily. The *Duncannon's* crew protested that they had lost all they had and that they did not wish to hazard their lives as well, "the enemy's work being so near, and they having no shelter for themselves, if the enemy should ply them with case-shot, as might be in all probability."

Penn wisely did not press the nerve-shaken men. Next morning he sent his barge to assist the *Duncannon's* crew "to save what might be, without any eminent or apparent danger, procured out of her." The crew still refused to co-operate. Therefore six of Penn's gunners, under his personal direction, got out the two best guns, and one hundred and forty-two shot, which were sent to aid in the town's defense. In writing his report to Swanley, Penn commented: "to the shame of the *Duncannon's* men be it spoken." He added, however, that the captain and master had been active and were deserving of commendation.

Before daybreak, on the 19th, a gun, planted at the mouth of the harbor, opened fire on the *Nicholas*. Her captain returned it and, mindful of the *Duncannon's* fate, weighed anchor. Before he could get the anchors aboard, two of his men were hit, two were wounded, and the ship hit several times. Only with great difficulty did he get under sail and anchor alongside Penn. Penn sent twenty barrels of powder ashore by his barge, which returned with a message from the Governor to say that a fire would be lighted on the church tower whenever he wished to communicate with Penn. Matters remained quiet until the 28th, when three enemy formations appeared on hills near the town, which prevented Penn sending ashore shot and royal paper, used for making cartridges. That evening, as Penn returned from supping with the *Mayflower's* captain, two lights were seen on the church tower. He at once sent his yawl ashore with the shot and the paper.

On the next night the signal was made again, but Penn, whose yawl was still ashore, did not venture to send another boat. It was a bright night and, in addition to their great guns, it could be seen that the enemy had lined both shores with musketeers. They also had posted an eighteen-oared boat at the mouth of the harbor. Next day Penn tried to send in his barge, only to find that the enemy had advanced to the west point of the harbor mouth, so that she had had to retire. At ten o'clock the yawl came out, forced to run through a fierce fire of great and small shot. But she came through unharmed. In the afternoon, escorted by the barge, she tried to get in again with medicine oil, shot, and letters from Inchiquin for the Governor. So heavy was the fire that she had to return. All that afternoon and night the enemy plied the town with very heavy shot. Penn sent his barge and pinnace to guard the west side of the harbor, while the *Mayflower's* longboat and pinnace did the same on the east. They had arranged a signal whereby to recognize each other at a distance.

Early in the morning the weary crews returned, but, as a

number of enemy boats had appeared, the barge and the longboat were furnished with fresh crews and sent out again. Five boats chased the longboat. As the barge was far away to the west, Penn sent out pinnaces to her relief and the enemy retired. That night heavy fire was again exchanged between the town and the attacking forces. On the water, Penn's vigorous measures took immediate effect and the enemy did not venture out to challenge his little flotilla. The continual patrolling, however, began to tell on the wearied men and on August 2nd Penn kept them on board for a well-deserved rest.

Two days later the *Charles* (6) came in with supplies for Youghal, but Penn could not deliver them since the Irish had cut off his communications with the town. His journal records quaintly: "not long after, the soldier, being closely besieged within the town, and we being able to do them no good, nor at present to gain intelligence of their condition, it was unanimously agreed upon for the soldier's encouragement, as if some extraordinary news were now arrived to us, to fire some guns on board each ship. Whereupon we shot seven, the *Mayflower* and *Nicholas* five apiece."

Penn sent back the *Charles* with a report to Swanley. "The enemy", he wrote, "hath quite blocked up the harbour: having planted great guns, whereof they have store (from whom God knows), so that we cannot pass in or out to relieve the distressed place, nor gain any intelligence from it: but if God give a blessing to it, we are now upon a design to effect and make no question of compassing it. I confess it is somewhat desperate, yet I know desperate disease requires desperate cure." He begged for ammunition and victuals to be sent him with all speed, "or else a speedy order to quit this place, which yet cannot without great hazard be done. One of the two must with all celerity be performed, for I have not a fortnight's provision on board."

On August 5th a bark from Cork arrived with provisions for the town. Though the master had a wife and family in Youghal he flatly refused to risk taking his ship into the harbor. Penn fiercely upbraided him with cowardice and neglect of his family, telling him he would have him tied to the mast and carried in. At this threat the master gave way. Fourteen barrels of powder and oil for the sick were put on board and four men from each ship were sent as a crew, each man being given half a crown as an encouragement. When all was ready the wind dropped completely! At nine o'clock a south-south-east breeze sprang up and the bark set sail. Although greeted with a heavy fire, to everyone's astonishment she got through without even being hit. "The soldier", commented Penn, "was much encouraged thereby." Penn also learned that the firing of the guns aboard the ships had so filled the garrison with hopes of good news that they had sallied out, spiked a gun, and killed three hundred of the enemy. They took another gun, but had been forced to throw it over a cliff as it was too heavy to bring back.

Penn then sailed for Cork, where he was greeted with the cheering news that the Irish had withdrawn some distance from Youghal. On the 13th the *Charles* and the *Trial* came in with ex-Royalists from Naseby, who had taken the Covenant to serve in Ireland. But also on board the *Trial* was John Crowther, who had been appointed Vice-Admiral by the Admiralty Commissioners. This caused some murmuring in the ship's company. Though his super-session must have been a blow to Penn, he dealt with the matter at once, "fearing it should beget or break forth into some mutinous distemper." After some argument he pacified the crew, so that he was able to hand over the *Entrance* to Crowther.[2]

At Youghal affairs dragged on. Preston, who had been sent to assist in the siege, withdrew in pique when he found he was merely to be second-in-command to Castlehaven. At long last Lord Broghill relieved the town with troops he had brought from England. As his troops began to desert for want of pay, Castlehaven went into winter quarters. Command of the sea had enabled Penn to support Youghal, and Crowther too, by resolute efforts to supply it, until relief came by land.[3]

To his surprise Penn found Moulton in command at Milford instead of Swanley. Swanley had been recalled to London to answer charges against him, although what they were is impossible to discover. Probably they were concerned with a quarrel between Poyer and the Pembroke local committee, which had complained of "his insatiable and insolent oppression." As Poyer was the blue-eyed boy of the Committee of Both Houses, he had been retained on the local committee. Batten himself had been sent to order Swanley back, and he had arrived on July 26th in the *Andrew* (45). "Swanley", he wrote, "was very obedient to the order, standing much on his justification, which being clear, and the information false, I am confident the House will vindicate him for the good service he has done." In this Batten was right, for Swanley was acquitted.[4]

Hardly had Swanley left than an appeal came to Batten from Laugharne. He had moved out with six hundred men to prevent the Haverfordwest garrison from burning the cornfields, only to find himself unexpectedly outnumbered by two to one. Batten sent off the *Warwick* (22), with two hundred seamen aboard, who were landed two miles below Canaston Bridge, far up the Haven. The royalist commanders, Major Generals Randolph Egerton and Sir Edward Stradling, were blissfully unaware of this landing, for their scouts had been captured by Laugharne. Next day, August 1st, as the Royalists marched to Colby Moor, they were attacked by two troops of horse and a hundred foot, though Laugharne's main body had not yet come up. A fight "very fierce and doubtful near the hour" pinned the Royalists down until Laugharne arrived. Then a fierce charge broke the royalist cavalry, some four hundred and fifty strong, and Laugharne's men chased them in headlong flight to Haverfordwest. The remainder of his horse fell upon the royalist foot and cut them to pieces. A hundred and fifty were killed and three hundred made prisoner. Without pausing, Laugharne marched straight on to Haverfordwest. For three days the stout walls of the Castle were bombarded — even a demi-cannon, sent from the *Lion*, could make no impression. Then Captain Thomas of the *Warwick* offered to storm the place, if his seamen were allowed plunder. "Which was promised", noted Batten, "but not observed." The seamen scaled the walls and so got possession of the Castle, and the Major Generals had to surrender.[5]

Batten was now requested by Fairfax to transport six hundred prisoners, taken at the fall of Bridgwater, across to Pembrokeshire. Ships were sent to him for this purpose. After Naseby, Fairfax had marched into Somerset to deal with Goring's army. Fairfax turned his flank by defeating him at Langport and relieved the gallant Blake at Taunton, after enduring a prolonged siege. Bridgwater, thought to be impregnable, fell next, and Fairfax advanced on Bristol.

The King, meanwhile, had decided to try to join Goring, and had come to Cardiff to cross the Bristol Channel. Moulton, however, forestalled him by swooping down and capturing sixteen ships, lying about the Holms Islands in the Channel, which were to have carried Charles' troops across.[6] This fresh disaster, coupled with the loss of Bridgwater, ruined the King's plan, and he retired to Raglan.

Batten had now returned to Plymouth, to learn of two naval engagements. John Mucknell, master of the East India Company's ship, the *John*, of 600 tons and 26 guns, had seized her for the King's service as he returned from the Cape of Good Hope, although not without some difficulty, for he is said to have nailed to the mast the ears of such of the crew as opposed him (a task of some skill surely). He then released them by cutting them free with his sword. He was also alleged to have put twenty-three other seamen on a desert island, leaving them to the mercy of the savages. The tale may only reflect the anger of the Company with their master. Mucknell took the ship into Bristol and seems to have been knighted for his exploit.

Sir John now set out on a privateering expedition. On July 19th he sighted three ships off Land's End, the *Constant Warwick* (26) under John Gilson, the *Expedition* (18) under Joseph Jordan, and the *Cygnet* (18) under John Mann. Between them they mounted sixty-two guns. Apparently they were at some distance from each other, for the *Cygnet* came up singly and alone. She offered Mucknell quarter, if he would surrender, whereupon Sir John stuck his sword into his quarter-deck and exclaimed "that is my quarter." Broadsides were exchanged, in which the *Cygnet* got the worst of it and sheered off. When the smoke had cleared away, the *Expedition* was seen coming up. She was received with another broadside in which Jordan was wounded in the leg. In the confusion that followed the loss of the captain, the *Expedition* drifted off. Up came the *Constant Warwick*, which managed to lay the *John* aboard. Gilson shouted that he would give ten pounds to the first man who should bring him the *John's* flag. Two seamen tried to clamber aboard, but one fell into the sea and was drowned, while the other ran up the rigging and hid himself in the main top. Then the grapnels broke, and the *John's* main-top-sail-yard carried away the *Constant Warwick's* main-top mast. At the same moment she sprang a leak and so had to break off the action. The man hiding in the main-top was ordered to come down. He did so and, seizing his only chance, he jumped into the ship's boat towed astern, cut her free, and escaped. Later on Batten himself rewarded the sailor with a gratuity. After a final broadside from the *Constant Warwick,* as night came on, the *John* got clean away. Sir John made for the Scillies, only to be wrecked at the entrance to the Islands by the carelessness of his pilot. He had out-manoeuvred and out-fought his opponents, though his gun-power was greatly inferior. Why the three captains did not combine is a mystery: did they hope to secure prize-money for each captain alone? The action was not one upon which the Navy could congratulate itself.[7]

Against this discreditable affair could be offset the victory of that respectable and valiant old lady, the *Eighth Whelp* (16) under John Kearse, and the *Robert* (8) under William Rew. Off Portland, about the same time, they met and took the *Cavendish* (12), Brown Bushell's ship, though he managed to get ashore in the ship's boat. The *Cavendish* was taken into Weymouth, renamed after the town, and added to the fleet.[8]

Fairfax had now arrived before Bristol and Moulton was ordered to sail there. He took the *Lion* (40), the *Mayflower* (28), the *Anne and Joyce* (22), the *Nicholas* (12), the *Defiance*, the *Spy* (6), and two shallops, capable of carrying 300 men apiece.[9] Much to his disgust, Penn was left to guard Milford Haven.[10] Moulton had instructions to take or burn all ships which should oppose him, or which were bound for Bristol. He began by securing the fort at Portishead and so cut the city off from the sea. At a conference with Fairfax, on August 21st, it was decided that he should send his seamen to join Colonel Thomas Rainsborough's brigade in storming the Watergate fort on the Avon. But a failure of the tide prevented the seamen from coming up by water and instead they were used to assist in storming the line and defenses.[11] As the Parliamentarians had previously learned, there were too few troops available for Rupert to hold the extensive line of earthworks. Though his guns took a heavy toll, the attack broke through and he had to withdraw into the Castle. Recognizing that resistance was hopeless, Rupert wisely surrendered, and was allowed to march away to Oxford with his men on the 10th. He had, however, to leave behind his supplies and fire-arms, his artillery and magazines. Bristol was lost to the King, and with it the last base against the Irish Guard, which now had no menace to fear. For Rupert the consequences were disastrous. He was dismissed by the King and went overseas. He would serve the royal cause again, but this time at sea.

Free from opposition, Laugharne made himself master of Pembrokeshire. He soon took Carmarthen, then advanced into Glamorgan. The King was not far off at Raglan, where he had decided to go north to try and join Montrose. When an urgent appeal for help came from beleaguered Chester, he moved eagerly to its relief, for it was the only port left to him where it was possible to land Irish troops. Charles still hoped, as a result of the Earl of Glamorgan's secret intrigues with the Confederates, that some troops might be sent across to him. On September 27th he entered Chester, only to watch from its walls the utter defeat of his troops at Rowton Heath. Then, after wandering aimlessly about the Midlands, he entered Oxford for the last time on November 5th. His hopes had perished on September 15th, when Montrose was routed at Phillip-haugh.

Fairfax now marched back into the west to complete its conquest, sending Cromwell to mop up the royalist strongholds in Hampshire. After taking Tiverton, Fairfax was about to move on Plymouth, when sickness among his troops forced him into winter quarters near Exeter. Hopton, who had taken over command from Goring, had retired before Fairfax into North Devon, while the Prince of Wales had wisely withdrawn to Falmouth, off which Batten had posted ships to prevent his escape.

On September 23rd the list of the Winter Guard was approved: twenty-one warships and seventeen merchantmen.* On the same day information was brought by Peter Cary from Russell, parliamentary Governor of Guernsey, that Haesdonck was gathering a fleet of thirty ships at Falmouth with which to secure the island as a naval base. He begged for ships to be sent to the Islands and Batten gave

*Appendix F

him seven vessels, which sailed from Portsmouth and arrived on October 7th. They lay idle for the greater part of the winter, on the Great Bank, waiting for an attack which was never likely to come.[12]

Now there sailed, on October 18th, from La Rochelle, in the *San Pietro*, a small frigate, a most important personage. He was Rinuccini, the Papal Nuncio appointed to Ireland. He took with him arms, ammunition, and, most valuable of all, twenty-eight thousand crowns, supplied by Cardinal Mazarin. On the 20th the ship neared Ireland, and there was every prospect of reaching Waterford the next day. Suddenly seven ships were sighted — probably Crowther's squadron — two of which took up the chase of the *San Pietro* for four hours. However the ship outsailed them and they had to abandon the pursuit. As the next day brought fog and rough weather with it, it was decided to keep out to sea to avoid possible wreck. At dawn, on the 22nd, a ship under full sail accompanied by a frigate was sighted some two leagues distant. The sailors with dismay recognized the ship as the *Discovery*, commanded by Plunkett, "that scourge of the Irish Seas." Instantly all superfluous articles were thrown overboard, the guns run out, and the passengers ordered below. Rinuccini, who had a vivid imagination, placed his confidence in the protection of St. Peter, though adding that "this confidence only increased with the horror of seeing the passengers and the sailors slaughtered, and my friends committed to my care lying dead before my eyes, and the ship stained with blood. Rather than this, I should have been inclined to yield maganimously where I could not resist." Amid stormy seas and roaring winds the chase continued all day. Then suddenly, just before daylight failed, the *Discovery* changed her course, and broke off pursuit. All aboard attributed their delivery to St. Peter, and sang a hymn of thanksgiving. But history compels a descent from the sublime to the ridiculous. Plunkett's cookhouse had caught fire! Had Rinuccini known this he might have reflected that if a saint had once met martyrdom by being fried on a gridiron, it must have been the first time that a Papal Nuncio found salvation by means of a flaming frying-pan. And it could have been small consolation to the Protestant cook to know that he had been the unconscious author of the miracle. Who shall assess the credit due to him or to St. Peter? Anyhow, the hunted Nuncio eventually landed at Kenmare, on the Kerry coast.[13]

Plunkett's failure was slightly compensated for by the capture of the *Swan* (18). She was lying at anchor in Dublin Bay, with a Flemish vessel, on December 8th. Most of her crew were ashore with her Captain, Bartlett, since he had no money to pay their wages. Captain Robert Clarke, of the *Jocelyn*, (12), came into the Bay, having been told of the *Swan's* whereabouts by some fishermen. He determined to take her. On the night of the 5th he sent in his long-boat with twenty men to seize her. The surprise was complete and no resistance was offered. The Flemish vessel too became a victim. Skeleton crews were put aboard and the two ships were sent into the Dee. This loss was a severe blow to the morale of the Royalists still holding out in North Wales. Chester, desperately in need of supplies, now knew that the only vessel strong enough to reach them was gone.[14]

The first Civil War was practically over. The increasing number of parliamentary victories had built up Roundhead morale, while defeat had lowered that of the Royalists. The Parliament's resources were greater, while those of the Royalists tended to diminish. In this the Navy had played a great part, preventing troops, arms, and supplies from reaching the King from overseas — lack of munitions cost the King at least one battle. Yet it was precisely because the Navy had been able to maintain supplies of all kinds that Hull, Lyme, Plymouth, and South Wales had been able to hold out.

Batten and his captains had faithfully carried on Warwick's works. They had prevented the King from joining Goring in Somerset and then they helped to recapture Bristol. Batten himself had contributed to this by his support of Laugharne in South Wales. Now his ships were active in Ireland, already making the operations of the privateers difficult. Batten must have hoped that the command of the Navy would be given to him as Lord High Admiral, but his uncertainty still clung to him.

Chapter VIII

1646

Batten Meets the Scots at Newcastle

The collapse of the royalist cause in England, and particularly in South Wales, left the Irish Guard free to devote itself to Irish waters. The immediate problem was the privateers. Lord Thomond, an Irish Protestant, in December 1645, after discussions with Moulton at Bristol, had decided to hand over his Castle at Bonratty to Parliament, since the Catholic Confederacy had sequestrated his estates. Its possession, it was hoped, would serve as a naval base from which to check the privateers at Limerick.

The Castle lay upon the west bank of the Orgarney river, which joined the Shannon at right angles, about a mile south. To the east the ground was mostly marsh, called locally a "corcasse". To the north, about three hundred yards from the Castle, was an earth ridge, with a deep broad ditch without. Beyond this an open space, some hundred yards wide, terminated at a rocky limestone hill, a hundred feet high. The ridge and ditch ran on to the west where they turned south until they reached another corcasse, adjoining the Shannon and the Orgarney. Thus to the north, west, and south there was a spacious plain upon which the garrison could graze their horse and cattle.

Within this ring stood Bonratty Castle, with an earthen platform, the remains of the ancient bailey. To the west was a small castle or fort and beyond was a church and a pigeon house, built upon a corner of the churchyard. All these stood on slightly rising ground. At the mouth of the Orgarney, where it joined the Shannon, stood Quay Island, which could be approached from the southern corcasse at low tide across sands and rocks.

The Siege of Bonratty

Moulton and Penn sailed from Milford Haven on January 24th, leaving Crowther in the *Expedition* (18) to watch South Wales. At Cork, on February 21st, Moulton ordered Penn to take command of the squadron going to Bonratty. Penn hoisted his flag in the *Peter* (10), as his ship, the *Fellowship* (28), was set to act as guard ship at Cork. With him went the *Trial, Increase* (14), *Roebuck* (10), *Green* frigate (6), *Antelope* (36), and the *Anne Percy* (32). Penn had obviously chosen the *Peter* so that he could direct operations in shallow waters. He arrived on March 11th and lay in the Shannon, sending the *Antelope* a mile up river toward Limerick to watch for vessels and fireships reported to be coming out. He then landed to consult with Colonel McAdam, in command at Bonratty, about the defenses. They decided to pull down walls so as to get a field of fire, to mount a big gun near the pigeon house, and to build defenses on Quay Island. The garrison numbered eight hundred foot and sixty horse, which Penn reinforced with some Welsh troops who had taken the Covenant after surrendering at Naseby. Raiding parties were sent out to secure cattle and supplies and to drive off any Irish .troops which might be near.

These operations alarmed the Catholic Confederacy, who feared not only that the place might become impregnable, but that the safety of the privateers in Limerick might be endangered. The Confederacy gathered some three thousand foot and horse and placed them under the command of Lord Muskerry. The Papal Nuncio, Rinuccini, supplied the necessary money for the troops. Muskerry began his operations on May 11th with the capture of the two outposts, manned by Welsh troops, who proved so unreliable that they surrendered at once. Penn summed up his disgust briefly: "we believe the soldiers were hanged, as justly they deserve." Muskerry made his camp behind the hill to the north and proceeded to entrench himself. As the hill was too steep and rocky to dig, fascines had to be used instead. Wood was secured from the ground between the hill and the ridge. To prevent these works being constructed McAdam determined to attack. He asked for the assistance of some of Penn's seamen to deal with the enemy's guns, "as being more skillful in drawing them away, or to unspike them and break them." On May 24th the sally was made. The combined force drove the foe out of their works, only to find that the Irish had withdrawn their guns up the hill. A charge of Irish horse then drove them in turn back to their lines.

On the 29th, as the feeding problem was getting serious, the women and children were evacuated from Bonratty in the *Roebuck* and the *Anne and Percy* and taken to Cork and Kinsale. Muskerry too had his problems, chiefly over supplies and pay. A prolonged siege was out of the question with an undisciplined force. A decision must be forced without delay. Muskerry was under the impression that Bonratty was well-provisioned and that the ships could continue to provide all necessities.

Though fighting had gone on almost continuously, the main attack had hardly begun. Sorties, with the object of destroying the Irish works, were finally checked by a gun which Muskerry placed in the lower part of his approaches. He now decided to make a diversion to his attack from the north by sending a party into the southern corcasse. He had observed that Penn had posted the *Trial* off the corcasse, between it and Quay Island and near the sluice. Penn had done so because Muskerry had placed two guns in a position enabling them to fire directly down the Orgarney, which, as Penn noted, "will much annoy us in our making up to the Castle." He had warned McAdam to ask for ammunition in good time "before the rebels blocked up the water passage to Bonratty, as was most probable they would." At the approach of Muskerry's party, the parliamentary troops guarding the sluice were seized with panic and took to their heels. At night, however, the invaders, seeing some lights moving towards them from the Castle and thinking they heard the sound of the dreaded horse, in their turn also panicked and fled. Penn instantly grasped the fact that the corcasse was the real key to Bonratty. He brought the *Green* frigate to lie off it as well as the *Trial*, and sent four guns, quaintly termed "murderers", from his own ship and from the *Increase* to Quay Island "to clear the flankers". This move apparently revealed to Muskerry the real key to the position, for he now concentrated upon the capture of the little castle, which would allow him to move into the corcasse.

By June 12th the Irish had drawn their lines so close that the problem of feeding the horses had become acute. They were moved to Quay Island, whence they could be ferried to any given spot. The

Charles (6), *Sampson* (20), *Roebuck* (10), and the *Truelove* (18)
now came in with a hundred soldiers, "good proper men", who were
sent up to Bonratty. The *Charles* was sent to join the *Green* frigate
"for the better stopping up of the passage." The *Roebuck* and the
Increase were sent to Kinsale with empty casks to fetch drink, as
only sixteen days' supply was left. Muskerry too was in great straits,
since he had no money left for pay and he knew the lack of it might
lead his men to disperse to their homes. Little did he know that
Bonratty was desperately short of food and munitions.

He must take the little castle, "as it much annoyed the Irish
in their trenches and retarded their approaches." He brought up
some big guns, sent from Limerick, to batter it. But the walls were
so thin that the shot passed through them without shattering the
fabric. The garrison after every shot were able to pour a volley of
bullets through the holes. The closing in of the Irish made Penn
anxious for the safety of Quay Island. He set to work with the seamen to build a line and work there, fearing an attack by the enemy's
horse and foot at low tide across the sand and rocky ground that
lay between the Island and the corcasse. "In extreme foul weather,
with much rain and dirt" he personally supervised the work.

On July 1st he was summoned by McAdam to a consultation as
he hourly expected another assault. Penn found a council of war, "in
which I desired not to interpose, as not willing to engage myself in
the shore-matters, otherwise than I might with freedom perform my
duty in my proper sphere." However, he joined them at dinner. As
they sat eating, the cannonade grew to such a pitch that McAdam left
to go to the little castle to see what damage had been done, and to
encourage his men by his presence. At this moment a gunner of a
field piece took a sighting shot which passed through an upper
window and killed McAdam. To Penn it must have seemed a shot
comparable in luck and effect to that which had sunk the *Duncannon.*
And it sealed the fate of Bonratty. From that moment the morale
of the garrison simply crumbled. Major Hooper, who took over
command, was described by Penn as "pusillanimous". He had
neither courage, nor the power of inspiring men. Trouble broke out
almost at once. Penn heard some of the soldiers grumbling about
some money McAdam had found in the Castle, demanding part of it

for their pay, and at once placed a guard over the room in which it was stored. The officers too began to quarrel and Penn had to order them to their posts. His chief anxiety was that some deserter, especially from among the Welsh, might carry the news of McAdam's death to the Irish.

The rot continued to spread. Early next morning Penn found some officers in McAdam's room, with eighteen bags of money and some plate in front of them, which they were about to divide. He begged them to leave enough for the soldiers' pay and for the future. "But", he commented, "what power my poor rhetoric to this purpose had, you may easily guess if ever you saw or heard it preached on a poor miser." He could make no impression on them. The *Charles* was sent off to Kinsale to ask Lord Broghill for help, while a boat, sent up to Bonratty with provisions, returned with the news that a Welsh deserter had betrayed the news of McAdam's death. The Irish, Penn was told, were calling out to the defense "to get a better commander."

On the 5th men were selected from the *Truelove* and the *Sampson* to relieve the seamen serving in Bonratty. This was done with some difficulty "which cannot be avoided when men are enforced to land service." Fierce fighting continued ashore. The Irish burst their way into the little castle, and though an instant counter-attack drove them out again, they were now within pistol-shot of the works.

Part of a house near the little castle was battered down. What was far more alarming was the fact that Muskerry had got a gun into the corcasse, "which flanks all our works and will thereby do us great damage." Muskerry had seen his opportunity to force a decision by a swift blow. Now was the critical moment, for he knew of the loss of morale caused by McAdam's death. He had faggots prepared so as to fill and cross the ditch and he got two small field-pieces down to the seashore "near the dam, to beat off the ship that rid there at anchor, with the intent to play on the back of those that should again attempt to recover that post." All was set for the final attack — for Muskerry it was either victory or retreat.

On the following day, the 10th, Penn went up to Bonratty. To his surprise and dismay there was no sign of the *Green* frigate or of the *Antelope* at their accustomed post off the corcasse. "I doubted

all was not well." He soon learned the reason: "coming up to the
ships, I understood the enemy had gotten the corcasse . . . for, having
beaten off the two ships, one being shot through the hull, the other
through the sail, and not being able to make good their riding, or
damnify the enemy, they were forced to quit the place, and anchor
higher among the rest of the ships."

With the first light of dawn, the field pieces had opened fire
and forced the two ships to slip their cables. At the same time the
Irish attacked from the hill, hurling their faggots into the ditch,
crossing it and storming into the little castle through a breach in
the wall. In an irresistible wave they pressed forward to take some
of the inner works. On they pushed to attack the half-moon at the
east end of the garden, only to be repulsed with some loss. Other
troops poured into the corcasse, now undefended by the ships, and
secured possession of it. The way to Bonratty Castle itself was open.

Muskerry, a good soldier, pressed home his successful attack.
At dawn the next day he launched another fierce assault. His troops
forced their way between the in and out guards. The morale of the
defense, already at a low ebb, crumbled. Filled with panic, the
troops still holding the corcasse fled from it across the sand and
rocky ground, "unworthily", as Penn wrote, "and made a confused
retreat to the Island, where I found many of them at my landing."
He instantly took command. He had the fugitives ferried over the
Orgarney to the easternmost corcasse, to keep open a line of retreat
for the troops now cut off in Bonratty. Within two hours that fell
also. Bonratty was completely isolated. Penn at once shipped the
women and children from Quay Island. He had some breastworks
built in view of an attack by enemy horse at low water. Two hot
skirmishes took place ashore. Then all was quiet, but what had
happened was unknown.

A strange silence ensued all that night in dramatic contrast to
the last few days. Not a gun nor a musket was heard. In the morning
an officer came from Bonratty to tell him the terms of surrender:
quarter, with the right to march out with full honors of war. Penn
stigmatized these as "so mean, and so far beneath the honour of a
soldier, which I should never have consented to." But he saw that
the officer had made up his mind and he sent him back to Hooper.

At six o'clock that evening fire was suddenly opened on the ships, which had to retire further down the Shannon. The miserable Hooper surrendered next day. The soldiers and seamen were embarked upon the ships, the guns and horses brought off, and the works on the Island destroyed. The squadron sailed for Kinsale.

Thus the expedition ended. The failure was due to the fact that the Orgarney was too narrow and the tide off the corcasse too shallow for the ships to be able to defend it. Relief must come from the land. Yet the expedition had come near to success. Had not a chance shot killed McAdam, a resolute and inspiring leader, the result might have been different. It was strange how ignorant each side was of the other's difficulties. Penn and McAdam had no idea that Muskerry's army was on the point of breaking up for want of pay, while Muskerry was under the impression that the garrison were amply supplied.

More than a naval squadron was needed to deal with the royalists forces in Ireland, or even to establish a naval base. An army, properly supplied and well-led was necessary. Still, the one lesson learned at Bonratty was to be put into good effect later on, when a force led by Cromwell, and supported by a fleet under Blake, was to demonstrate the value of a properly co-ordinated amphibious warfare. Only thus could the nest of privateers in Ireland be smoked out and ended.

At Kinsale it was agreed that Moulton and Crowther in the *Lion* (45) and the *Entrance* (40) should convoy ships between Ireland and England. The *Truelove* (22), *Blessing* (24), and the *Charles* (6) were to ply between the Shannon and Galway. The *Sampson* (20), *Peter* (10), and the *Discovery* (26) were to cruise between Kinsale and Land's End, while the *Green* frigate (6) lay off Youghal. The *Antelope* (36), *Trial*, and the *Fellowship* (28) were sent to Milford.[1]

Here Penn learned there had been a royalist rising. On February 11th Colonel Carne had swooped down on Cardiff with two thousand horse and captured the town, although not the Castle. Crowther came up from Penarth in the *Expedition* (18) on the 21st, anchoring off the town. He landed sixty seamen, who were driven at once into the Castle. To support them, Crowther sent boats, armed with small

guns, to lie inshore and keep up continual fire. Laugharne too
rushed up troops, who defeated and captured the Royalists, thus
raising the siege. Prompt naval action had held the rising in check
until the troops could arrive and once more South Wales was safe.[2]

In the west Fairfax had moved out of his winter quarters to
attack Dartmouth. He sent for Batten at Plymouth. Batten had left
five ships before Falmouth to prevent the escape of the Prince of
Wales. Now, since Plymouth had been relieved, he was able to go to
Fairfax's assistance. He sailed in the *St. Andrew* (45), taking with
him the *Constant Warwick* (30), *Expedition* (16), *Providence* (18),
and *Robert* (8), and six other vessels. On the 19th he anchored off
Dartmouth. A hundred seamen were landed to assist in an immediate
storm. As the approaches were very steep and the roads very slip-
pery, it was impossible to bring up the guns. Batten therefore
covered the water front, while, in pouring rain, the troops broke into
the defenses. The royalist guns were soon taken, and turned upon the
town. In a short time Dartmouth fell. A hundred guns were taken,
and two ships of twelve and ten cannon, one belonging to the Governor of Barnstaple and the other to Captain Johnson of Newcastle.
Purposely the royalist flag was left flying and a French ship fell into
the trap and sailed in. The crew managed to throw overboard a
packet of letters before being boarded, but these were recovered.
They were from the Queen, Jermyn, and others, and they revealed the
negotiations between the King and the Scots, which the Scottish
Commissioners in London had denied.[3]

The fall of Dartmouth was followed by that of Chester on
February 2nd. Twenty ships were taken in the Dee. Efforts had
been made to run in supplies from Conway, but Captain Stephen
Rich, in the *Rebecca* (22), patrolled the approaches, while three
small ships guarded the Dee to prevent them getting in. Colonel
Coote, conducting the siege, was, however, contemptuous of Rich's
efforts. He asked Brereton for something better "than a stinking
boat or two that are not able to do any good." Now only Conway
remained as a port for the unlikely arrival of troops from Ireland.[4]

Fairfax, after defeating Hopton at Torrington, advanced into
Cornwall, forcing the Prince of Wales to embark in the *Phoenix*,
on March 10th, and to sail from Land's End for the Scillies. On the

8th Fairfax had arrived at Launceston. Here he received letters, captured on an Irish ship at Padstow, from the Earl of Glamorgan, which reported that six thousand Irish troops were ready for transport to England, while another four thousand would soon be available. Conway was their only port of landing, but the Irish Guard gripped the seas too firmly for any ship to hope to reach it safely.[5]

Hopton gave up the hopeless struggle on March 10th. He surrendered and his army was disbanded. On the same day, St. Mawes Castle also yielded, giving Fairfax the eastern side of Falmouth harbor. Six days later the fort at St. Dennis surrendered, making the siege of Pendennis itself possible. John Arundell, the Governor, had posted the *Great George* (40) on the north side of the Castle, from which she was able to fire on two regiments advancing from Penny-come-quick and Arwenack towards Penryn. Fairfax returned to Exeter, which surrendered on April 13th, leaving Colonel Hammond to carry on the siege. Soon Barnstaple gave in, and St. Michael's Mount, thought to be impregnable, followed. All Cornwall, save Pendennis, was lost to the Royalists.[6]

Batten, who had been at Portland to receive the surrender of the Castle, now sailed for the Scillies with nine ships.[7] A trumpeter had already been sent by both Houses requesting the Prince of Wales to entrust himself to their care. This invitation, akin to that of the duck-loving Mrs. Bond, was not unnaturally declined.[8] The fate of the Prince looked grim when Batten arrived off the Islands on April 12th. Fortunately a violent storm scattered the squadron. Seizing his chance, the Prince embarked in the *Proud Black Eagle* (24), of four hundred tons, under Baldwin Wake. On the 16th she sailed for Jersey,[9] arriving the next day, about sunset. This so alarmed the parliamentary Governor, Colonel Russell, that he sent off an express to Batten asking for help. He also wrote to Warwick, begging for ships, since he feared an attack upon Guernsey. Nor were his fears allayed when a little later the *Doggerbank* and the *Eagle* came in with the Prince's retinue on board.[10]

After missing a royal prey for the third time, Batten returned to blockade Pendennis. The list of the Summer Guard, issued on April 16th, told him that forty-two warships, twenty-one merchant-

men, with another thirty-three in reserve, were to be set forth.*
Probably the assembly of privateer captains, driven from the Cornish
ports to the Channel Islands, had been taken into account. While the
Navy had been busy in the west, Bowden, the parliamentary captain
turned privateer, had impudently taken a ship off Dover, and carried
it back to Jersey.[11] Here now were gathered Captains Baldwin Wake,
Bowden, Baudains, Jones, Skinner, Jelf, Smith, Blaize, Piquet, Amy,
Vandersell, and others — unfortunately the names of their ships
are not stated. From Ireland Lord Digby arrived in the *St. Francis*,
followed by Lord Culpepper with two Dunkirk frigates. Had Russell
paused to think, he would have realized that, while he could not
attack the ships, sheltered as they were by the castles, the privateers
were not likely to risk their crews in an attack by land.

On May 12th Baldwin Wake, who was going to Guernsey to
replace old Sir Peter Osborne as the royalist Governor of Castle
Cornet, took with him two frigates and a supply ship. Unexpectedly
he ran into two parliamentary frigates engaged on convoy duty. They
swooped down eagerly upon him. He put about and was chased back
to Jersey, where he ran for shelter under Elizabeth Castle. Here they
dared not follow him and they therefore went on to St. Malo to pick
up their convoy.[12]

Next day Wake, in the *Proud Black Eagle*, with the three frigates
from Ireland, mounting some eighty guns, put off again. Suddenly
the wind fell calm. Such a dense fog descended that it was difficult
to steer. Equally suddenly the fog lifted, and a small shallop, cruising
between Herm and the Great Bank, saw them and opened fire. The
sound of the gunfire roused the crew of the ancient *Convertine* (40)
as she dozed on the Great Bank. The rising sun revealed the supply
ship beaching herself on the sands of Castle Cornet. The Guernsey
gunners opened fire on her. Then the fog came down again, and the
Convertine, now under sail, had to grope her way through the murk,
steering by the sound of the gunfire. She found herself in contact
with the four frigates, who poured in broadsides as they passed,
but her double bulwarks protected her and she answered with her
culverins. Under this heavy fire, the frigates hastily broke off the

*Appendix I

action. In the clearing fog the *Convertine* chased them to Sark. The last frigate, the *St. Francis,* only escaped her with great difficulty. Had the parliamentary frigates, which had gone to St. Malo, remained, Wake's little squadron might have been wiped out.[13]

As Pendennis was now in great straits, Captain Diamond, in the *Doggerbank,* was sent off on June 4th from Jersey with provisions. Bad weather drove him into Parraulx, in Brittany. Two frigates from Ireland, the *Warspite* and the *Increase* (14), learning of his arrival, made for the place. When the *Doggerbank* sighted them, she cut her cables, and made for the open sea. For three miles a fierce chase took place, each ship firing as fast as it could, until at last the *Doggerbank* was boarded and carried to England.[14]

In August another attempt was made to relieve Pendennis. Three small ships set out, but they found it impossible to break through the night guard. Batten had posted ten large boats, which continually patrolled before the harbor, and the three had to return.[15] Faced with starvation, Pendennis surrendered on the 15th. John Halstock, Batten's kindly surgeon, did his best for the sick and starving women and children.[16] The final conquest of the west was completed by Sir John Ayscue. On the 29th he anchored off the Scillies, with the *Expedition* (18) and the *Warwick* (20). On September 12th the Articles of Surrender were signed, and Colonel Fortescue's regiment was landed to garrison the Island. As Ayscue observed, it was now possible to protect the shipping coming up the Channel, "as it was cleansed from the King's men-of-war who, if they had well understood their advantage, might well have made that place a second Algiers."[17]

With the cessation of hostilities the naval warfare was replaced by a war of words. Hugh Peters, when he brought Fairfax's dispatch reporting the fall of Dartmouth, took the opportunity to lay before the Houses his scheme for the reform of the Navy. Though he may have had the success of the New Model Army in mind, his proposals really harked back to the methods which had bedevilled the Army, for he proposed a revolving Committee of the Admiralty, composed of "seven very able men", who were to deal with all marine matters including Admiralty Courts. They were to have efficient secretaries, with competent salaries. When the admirals of the fleet were in

London, they were to sit with the Committee as assistants. Ships were to be built "in the merchant way" in any dockyard, rather than at the government yards, which entailed feeding a thousand men daily. Corruption would be avoided as well. The building of ships was to be supervised frequently by the Committee's Surveyor and they were to be paid for on completion. Peters, who had lived in New England, believed ships might be built more cheaply in the yards there, from whence also masts and guns might be obtained. The captains should be in constant pay. Their accounts were to be sent to the Committee for audit when they were called for, while the men were to be paid every six months, when they came in with the Guards. Misbehavior by the captains was to be made "a very example". These measures, declared Peters, would save the cost of Commissioners, Victuallers, Pursers, Stewards, and of docks. Nor would it be necessary to press the seamen, "every Captain knowing how the get his own gang." Each captain thus would know his officers and men, "whereby he may give a better account than now, when ships are manned by strangers."[18]

Apart from the difficulty of finding "seven very able men", it is not easy to see what would have been gained. The existing Admiralty and Navy Commissioners were able and experienced men. Warwick still guided the Navy — though not in actual command of the fleet — he had kept the reins of control in his own hands, and with his strategic ability he had seen the war as a whole. Moreover, it was not likely that the admirals would often be in London, nor at the time when their advice would be needed. To abolish the state dockyards would probably have provoked riots among the vast numbers of dismissed officials and workers. It was doubtful if the building of ships in private yards would have led to better results. And it would have been almost impossible to supervise the building of ships in New England. The real remedy lay in the finding of a man like Samuel Pepys, at the time only thirteen years old.

To place the responsibility for rigging, victuals, and pay in the hands of the captain was to give him a task for which he was untrained and unfitted. Winnal, of the *Blessing*, had even starved his crew on the way back from Ireland, so that they had mutinied and brought away the ship.[19] The real fault lay in the fact that there were too few persons to check the ships' accounts, so that frequently a ship went out before the officials had completed their work — apart from the fact that there was often no money at hand to pay the crew. The suggestion that each captain should select his own crew, while it had the attraction of making a "happy ship", ignored the problem of an unpopular captain — and there were such. Further, it did not take into account the fact that many men preferred to serve in the merchantmen, where the pay was better and the risk less.

The scheme came to nothing, first because it meant a drastic administrative re-organization in the time of great uncertainty and secondly because there were a large number of vested interests involved. The Commons, many of whose members were stained with corruption, were not likely to want to deal with the problem.

The problem lay, not with the administration which, though understaffed, had wrought wonders in keeping the fleet at sea at all. It lay fairly and squarely upon the shoulders of Parliament, which had consistently ignored Warwick's repeated representations for money, supplies, and ships to enable the fleet to do its duty properly in face of immensely increased work. Parliament had been far more concerned with the Army, whose work it knew something about since it was near at hand, rather than with the Navy, and of this Parliament knew practically nothing. The Navy's work was, of necessity, almost unseen and unknown. The responsibility for providing the money was theirs and not that of the naval administrators.

Peters, however, was followed by Andrews Burrell, a well-known shipwright and a bitter rival of the Pett family. He attacked the Navy Commissioners in a pamphlet on May 18th, complaining that the ships were heavy and sluggish and could not carry out their duties. This was a hit at the Petts who had built many of them. Arms and ammunition for the King had been allowed to be landed — and Burrell made the wild assertion that not a single one of the King's vessels had been captured! The seamen, he declared, had been cheated of prize-money, captains who had done good service had received no recognition — he was unwise enough to instance Jordan, Gilson, and Mann, in their action with the *John*. On the other hand, captains who had misbehaved were continued in the service. Burrell went on to make great play with the building of the three new Fourth-Rates, the *Nonsuch*, the *Adventure*, and the *Assurance*.

Here lay the real crux of his complaint. He was disgruntled because only one of these vessels had been allotted to him, while the Petts had the other two. He demanded that he should build his ship without direction or supervision, and at his own price.[20]

On June 18th the Navy Commissioners replied.* They expressed themselves "confident that those aspersions and brain-sick notions, so plainly discovering his discontentedness and self-ends, will not get the least credits." Getting off to this good start, they answered Burrell point by point, blowing his contentions to the four winds. One hundred and ten merchant ships, unfortunately unnamed, had been made prize, and some returned to their rightful owners. Some captures of the King's ships were listed, though without date, by various captains. They went on to record the misdeeds of unsatisfactory captains, mentioning specially the three who had failed to take the *John*. The Captains of the *Cygnet* and the *Lucy* were recorded as having plundered four ships of Lynn, when the Earl of Manchester took the town. Phineas Pett, himself a Navy Commissioner, must have chuckled as he helped to demolish his rival.[21]

On August 4th the list of the Winter Guard was published.† Thirty-three warships and ten merchantmen were to go out. On October 5th a significant change was made. All commissioners were now to be in the name of the Parliament — the King's name being omitted. Batten was continued as Vice-Admiral, and Swanley was restored to his post as Admiral of the Irish Seas, though it was made clear that this was not to be interpreted as a reflection upon Moulton's conduct.

What of the King? Lord Jacob Ashley still had three thousand men, and Charles ordered him to cut his way through to Oxford. But on March 21st he was overwhelmed by Brereton, Birch, and Colonel Morgan, at Stow-on-the-Wold. The King then tried to negotiate with Parliament. He unsuccessfully proposed an Act of Oblivion, and the removal of sequestrations from his supporters' property. On April 27th he left Oxford in disguise, to entrust himself to the Scots, with whom he had also been in negotiation. He reached

*Appendix P
†Appendix J

Southwell, near Newark, on May 5th. "He fancied himself to be a
guest, but the days of his captivity had in fact begun." The Scots
took the King with them to Newcastle. Here, on July 23rd, Commissioners arrived from Lonon with propositions for "a safe and
grounded peace."

Now came an event that was to have momentous consequences.
Batten was sent to the Tyne in the *Leopard* (38). With him was
Gilson, in the *Constant Warwick* (30), and Coppin, in the *Greyhound*
(12).[22] They had been sent with a twofold purpose, to support the
Commissioners in their dealing with the Scots, and to prevent the
King either from escaping by sea or from being taken to Scotland.
With Batten came his chaplain, Samuel Kem, who was also to play
an important part in future events. Both were staunch Presbyterians
and both were soon to come into close contact with the Scots.

The negotiations, known as the Newcastle Propositions, dragged
on wearily. Parliament demanded that the King should take the
Covenent; that it should control the Militia and the Navy for twenty
years; that Presbyterianism should replace Anglicanism; and that
the Irish Cessation should be annulled and the war there carried on
in such manner as the Houses should agree.

The Scots, however, were suspicious about handing over the
control of the Army to Parliament alone, for then they would have
no say in the matter. They feared the aggressive leaders of the great
army, now under Independent control, with whom they were at logger-
heads theologically. Moreover, the possibility of a union of the King
with the Covenanters had been destroyed by the secret intrigues of
Charles, through Glamorgan, with the Irish Confederates. An Irish
Roman Catholic army was to have been brought over to destroy
Presbyterians and Independents alike and Charles was not to take
the Covenant.

Old Lord Ashley's words to his conquerors, after Stow-on-the-
Wold, "you have done your work, and you may go and play, unless
you fall out amongst yourselves", now sounded prophetic. For discontent was mounting in England. Rumors of mutiny increased and
mutiny in fact took place at York among the unpaid troops. The
Royalists could pluck up new heart. A plan was unfolded to the King
for a general royalist rising, to be led by the Prince of Wales. But

failure had disillusioned Charles.[23] On September 10th he wrote to the Prince of Orange asking him to send over a ship so that, if necessary, he could escape. On November 21st a Dutch ship of thirty-four guns came into the Tyne, under the pretext of careening. Not unnaturally she aroused suspicion, and the Governor of Tynemouth Castle was warned to be on his guard.[24] She was followed, on December 9th, by a Dunkirk warship. Neither of these two captains would allow anyone aboard without their express permission.[25] Rumor also spoke of the coming of other Dutch ships, fitted out by Prince Rupert. It was reported, too, that the Scots had agreed to hand over the King to Parliament in exchange for £400,000, the amount of their claim on England.

An escape by the King was attempted on Christmas Eve, but the plan miscarried.[26] Batten and his ships were ordered to keep station at Tynemouth, both to prevent a further escape and to watch the Dutch vessels. Batten thereupon sent the *Constant Warwick* and the *Greyhound* to ride as close as they could to the suspect ships.[27]

During the long months that Batten's vessels lay at Tynemouth, both he and Kem must have met the Scots in Newcastle many times. They had much in common. Both were ardent Presbyterians. Both were highly suspicious of the Independents, now rapidly rising to power. Both resented the arrogant claim of the Roundhead Army to be the sole victors in the Civil War. Cromwell's remark that he would willingly fight the Scot, should they try to enforce Presbyterianism, had sunk deep into the minds of the Scots, who resented the assumption that their army had done little to secure the victory. Moreover they knew at first hand the contribution the Navy had made to victory in the north. All these matters the Scots must have talked over with Batten and Kem.

It is only with assumptions of this kind in mind that the future revolt of the fleet can be explained, especially in view of Batten's secret correspondence with the Scots leaders later on. Both sets of men must have drawn fairly close together. Batten was also probably a disappointed and disgruntled man. Probably he had hoped and expected to be appointed Lord High Admiral, but instead he had been given command for six months only. He had played an active part in the work of the Navy and he was jealous for its good name.

To be told that the Army alone had won the victory aroused his resentment and anger.

The Scots were now faced with the problem, once the money came from Parliament, whether to take the King with them, or to leave him behind. Should they remain and risk a struggle or should the English come to take him by force? The King, however, still stoutly refused to take the Covenant, despite the entreaties of the Scots. The Estates in Edinburgh finally decided to leave him behind. In January the English Commissioners, who were to conduct Charles to Holmby House, arrived. On the 11th Kem preached before the King. His sermon was entitled "An olive branch found after a storm in the North Sea."[28] It was an appeal to the monarch to come to an agreed peace with Parliament, and it indicated the lines upon which he, and Batten too, were thinking. Batten said later on: "we fought all the time to fetch the King to his parliament."[29] Most men were weary of war and wished a lasting settlement, which would define both the powers and authority of the King and of Parliament. Englishmen are tenacious of their ancient institutions and a settlement without the King was to most of them unthinkable. The King, who had previously been addressed by Andrew Cant, a Scotch minister as "Thou enemy", and more condescendingly as "Thou piece of clay",[30] found Kem's sermon gave him much satisfaction. He expressed the wish to hear him again next Sunday. Kem, too, received much satisfaction and Charles must have appeared to him, and to Batten also, as a person of good sense, who was willing to listen to reason.

Meanwhile in Ireland Ormonde had offered to resign. He was determined not to submit to the rule of the Papal Nuncio. This, to his mind, spelt the setting up of Roman Catholicism, and the destruction of the Protestant Settlements. He was angered, too, at Glamorgan's secret negotiations, which had taken place behind his back. He offered, therefore, to place Dublin and the fortresses which still held out in the hands of Parliament. He stipulated, however, that the King must approve his action. Commissioners were sent to Dublin, but, since Charles withheld his consent, Ormonde would not accept their terms. They had to re-embark their troops and go to Carrickfergus.[31]

As a result of this incident the Admiralty Commissioners instructed Batten and Swanley to assist Inchiquin and Broghill. They were to pay special attention to the convoy of troops from Bristol, Chester, Liverpool, and Minehead. Swanley was also warned that the rebel frigates from Wexford and Waterford were increasing in numbers and strength and were doing much mischief to merchant shipping. He was to order Penn and Thomas, in the *Assurance* (32) and the *Nonsuch* (34), to ply about Land's End, Wexford, and Waterford to deal with them. Probably the loss of Dunkirk by the Spaniards to the French in October had driven some of the privateers from their base there to Ireland.[32]

These measures met with an immediate success. On December 30th, Jelf, a notorious Jersey privateer, had set out from Brittany and sailed over to the English coast. Here he sighted what appeared to be a merchantman. As he drew near her, he discovered to his consternation that she was a warship. She opened fire and Jelf's crew promptly mutinied. One of them cut the mainsail, which fell with such force that the ship lay at the mercy of the foe. She was captured and taken to London. Those of her crew who took the Covenant were sent to Ireland, while Jelf and the rest were imprisoned.[33]

At home the victors had split into two bitter groups. A struggle now began between the Presbyterians and the Independents at Westminster. The Presbyterians would allow no liberty but their own. They prescribed Anglicanism and they laid upon the beaten Royalists the burden of paying for the war by means of fines and the sequestration of their estates. They met the growing desire for freedom of conscience and of worship, which had grown up among the Bible-searching, hard-praying men of the New Model, by repression. By an Act of 1646, Unitarians and Free-Thinkers could be put to death. Baptists and Sectaries could be imprisoned for life. Laymen were forbidden to expound the Scriptures. Yet the growth of these opinions had largely been due to the haste with which the Presbyterian chaplains had left the army to secure the livings out of which the Anglicans had been turned. To the Independents, or Congregationalists as they may be termed, the Act was anathema. Not for such a conception had the men of the New Model fought.

Independency seemed hardly to have touched the fleet. Its crews were almost continually at sea and new ideas did not reach them. Political affairs and struggles were hardly known to them. They had been successfully led by admirals and captains whom they had learned to know and trust. Of the quarrels of the army leaders it neither knew nor cared, but they were most conscious of the many times they had been thrown in to pull the chestnuts out of the fire for the Army. Land service, as Penn had acutely noted, had become unpopular among the seamen, who felt they had to be used because the troops had failed. Herein perhaps lay the germ of the suspicion of the Army that was to break out in the fleet.

With the Civil War at an end, Parliament turned to the problem of reducing Ireland. It proposed to send over six regiments. But it forgot that the pay of the troops was heavily in arrears. Colonel Michael Jones, when he tried to embark his men at Chester, found that they would not move without pay. The soldiers already believed that the Presbyterians had actually connived at the flight of the King to the Scots so as to deprive them of the fruits of their victory. Now they suspected, not without good reason, that their opponents wished to remove part of the Army to Ireland so as to rid themselves of a possible rival to their own power. Only by a single vote was Holles' motion to send away the six regiments defeated. The struggle between the Army and the Presbyterians had begun. The struggle between Authority and the People, to which the war with the King had brought no solution, had now given place to a new and more dangerous conflict.

CHAPTER IX

1647

Batten is Replaced by Rainsborough

While the dark clouds of political dissent were gathering in England, the Navy was still actively engaged at sea. On December 14th 1646, Penn, in the *Assurance* (32), had chased the *Patrick* of Waterford. He captured her off the coast of Munster. Aboard her was a "person of quality", Juan de Urbino. Penn is said to have stripped him naked, placing him among the common mariners. Penn's brother, George, had suffered at the hands of the Spanish Inquisition, and this was his reprisal. The story seems unlikely, for, after an inquiry requested by the Spanish Ambassador, Urbino was set free. Indeed, Sir Abraham Williams is spoken of as having treated his captive with respect.[1]

Swanley then sent Penn to join Captain Thomas, of the *Nonsuch* (34), who had taken a prize near Waterford. Five frigates had come out and Thomas reported that if he had a consort he could have taken them all. On one of these ships the Papal Legate was reported to have embarked for Biscay. The rumor proved false, although it probably prompted Swanley's action. In these powerful newly-built Fourth-Rates, the captains, on February 4th, swooped down on four vessels, coming out of Waterford. All were captured.[2] On the 26th the Committee for Irish Affairs warned Swanley that a number of rebels "of quality" were about to embark in six ships to sail to France from Waterford. Their interception was a matter "of very great consequence." Penn and Thomas, therefore, were to ply at the mouth of Waterford to secure them. Swanley was directed to send them more ships if needed.[3] No record exists of the result. It is clear that the Irish Guard were making their presence felt off Ireland.

Events had been moving fast in the political arena. The Presby-

COLONEL THOMAS RAINSBOROUGH

terians proposed to disband part of the army, reducing it to ten thousand foot and one hundred horse. Of these four thousand two hundred were to be sent to Ireland. No officer was to be employed unless a Presbyterian, and no member of Parliament was to hold a commission. This clause was aimed at Cromwell. The burning question of the arrears of pay was not even mentioned — the soldiers were forbidden to petition either Parliament or their officers. Thus the Independents were given an opportunity, not indeed God-sent, but one born of stupidity and arrogance. With all hope of redress for their grievances denied to them, the troops began to turn their thoughts to active resistance. In their anger they were the readier to listen to the theories and teachings of the Independents and herein lies the clue to the events of 1647.

Chance now intervened to show the way the wind was blowing. In March a vessel sailed from Tower Wharf for the Downs, laden with supplies for the troops in Ireland. As her master was eager to be off, he decided not to wait for an escort, but to join a convoy at Portsmouth.[4] At the same time Captain Cannon, a chaplain turned privateer, set out from Jersey. Realizing his seamanship might not be as orthodox as his theology, he took with him a professional captain, one Chamberlain. Off the Sussex coast they snapped up the supply vessel and carried her back to Jersey. She proved to be one of the richest prizes any privateer had ever brought into the Island.[5] Her loss enraged the Commons. At the suggestion of Colonel Thomas Rainsborough, now serving in the Army, his regiment was ordered to Portsmouth. From here it was to sail to Jersey to capture Elizabeth Castle, with Rainsborough in command.[6]

Rainsborough came of a refugee family from Germany. He may have served with his father, William, in an expedition against the Barbary pirates in 1637. He had been Vice-Admiral to Lord Forbes in the Merchant Adventurers' futile expedition to Ireland in 1642. He had brought relief to Hull in the *Lion* in 1643, when he was captured. He was exchanged for Captain Kettleby, after which he joined the Army and served with distinction at Bristol. Many of the senior officers of his regiment had come from Massachusetts in the new world. From them he probably imbibed his ideas of freedom and independence, which developed into a fanatical republicanism, containing above all a passionate belief in the equality of all men. This earned for him the title of "Leveller". He saw life, it has been said, in terms of principles rather than of persons, and so in Parliament he had followers instead of intimates. He possessed unconsciously the maddening self-righteousness of the convinced reformer which may explain the complaint, made later on by the seamen, "of his unsufferable pride, ignorance and insolency." His fanaticism provoked the dislike of most people and the affection of none. To put it bluntly, he was an impossible person.

His plan for smoking out the privateers' nest in Jersey received a rough shock, for the soldiers, angry with the non-payment of their arrears, were suspicious of a move that would take them out of the way of redress. On May 28th they mutinied and set out to seize the artillery at Oxford. Rainsborough was sent off in pursuit. He caught up with them at Abingdon where, with great difficulty, he re-asserted his authority and prevented them from moving further.

Already there had arisen in the Army a body called the "Agitators", composed of two representatives from each regiment. Originally they were the result of a consultation by the officers to ascertain the views of the rank and file, and now they claimed to speak in the name of the whole Army. Cromwell was alive to the danger. He sought to solve the problem between military anarchy and parliamentary tyranny by a third course. The King, the fount of authority, and the Army, the weapon of power, should act together. Boldly, therefore, he sent off Cornet Joyce, first to seize the artillery at Oxford, then to secure the person of the King at Holmby and to remove him to Newmarket. Joyce did both. On June 4th he carried off Charles, a stroke revealing to the Presbyterians in the Commons the determined temper of the Army. Their own plan to win over the King was forestalled. They had been prepared to accept the King's offer to set up Presbyterianism for three years, provided he was not required to take the Covenant; in return Charles would grant them the control of the Militia for ten years. The Commons were about to raise their own army from the City Militia and to bring in a Scotch army to aid their own, but they were too late.

Amid this manoeuvring for position, the Navy carried on with its routine duties. In March the list of the Summer Guard was issued.

It was composed of forty-five warships, thirteen merchantmen, with six Second-Rates and twenty-six merchantmen in reserve.* Fifteen ships were allotted to the Downs, twelve to the Western Guard, sixteen to the Irish Guard, four to Guernsey, four to the north, and four for the fisheries. Obviously the intention was to deal with the privateers, while a stricter watch was to be kept on Jersey, owing to the presence of the Prince of Wales.[7]

The Western Guard was soon at work. On May 1st Richard Owen, in the *Henrietta Maria* (44), with Andrew Woodward in the *Roebuck* (6), met a fleet of Swedes. Five warships were escorting eleven merchantmen, laden with salt, homewards from Portugal. Owen ordered them to strike their topsails to acknowledge England's sovereignty of the seas. This they refused to do, saying they had their Queen's orders not to strike to anyone. Owen then called on two merchantmen to assist him, but in the meantime the Swedish Admiral had sailed off. Owen made after him, but, as he was too far ahead, Owen gave his Vice-Admiral a broadside. The Swede replied, putting Owen's tiller out of action. He was forced into Portsmouth for repairs, while the Swedes made for Dieppe. Owen at once sent off a frigate to Batten, lying in the Downs, reporting the action. He added that he had done "great execution on the Switzers."[8] Batten instantly sailed for Dieppe in the *St. Andrew* (45), with the *Garland* (40), *Convertine* (40), and the *Mary Rose* (26). About eight o'clock in the morning on May 3rd he found the Swedes off Boulogne. He summoned all their captains aboard, who repeated to him their Queen's orders. After a council of war, Batten decided to take their Vice-Admiral into the Downs and to let the rest go. But the warships followed him, declaring they dared not go home without their Vice-Admiral. Batten was now instructed to release him, although his and Owen's action was approved, "in regard of the maintenance of this Kingdom's Sovereignty at Sea."[9]

Rumor soon got busy with the affair. The Venetian Ambassador in Paris declared that angry letters had passed between Batten and the Governor of Boulogne. Batten had complained of the shelter given to the privateers in this port.[10] Parliament took up the com-

*Appendix K

plaint. As a result, Cardinal Mazarin, involved in war with Spain and fearing the power of the Parliament's fleet, issued an Edict on May 20th: all privateers were forbidden to enter French ports; all prizes were to be restored; no one was to buy the merchandise of such prizes; all privateers in French ports were to be confiscated. Mazarin went still further. He induced the Prince of Wales to revoke all letters of marque, and not to permit more to be issued.[11]

The news came like a death sentence to the privateers. Chamberlain, who had taken a prize into Boulogne, found the Edict staring him in the face. He could neither sell his prize nor pay his men. They promptly deserted to the parliamentary ships lying in wait outside the harbor. In the town he found Brown Bushell, Smith, and Johnson, all fellow captains. They drowned their sorrows in drink, reeled out, and drove the remnants of their crews to the ships. Somehow they dodged their way past the waiting ships, and got back to Jersey.[12]

Here they found Carteret's fleet of privateers coming into port, most of them with prizes. The climax came on June 13th, surely an unlucky day, when Gernet and Amy came in. Their ships were decorated with flags of all colors, taken from twelve merchantmen, which trailed in their wake. They could only lay up their ships, pay off their crews, and wait. As they declared their prizes had been taken before the Revocation, they were able to sell them and to live on the proceeds.[13]

The Western Guard had not been idle. On May 22nd Bedall in the *Adventure* (30), had fallen in with seven ships transporting Irish troops from Waterford to Dieppe for service in France. Off the Scillies he had boldly made his way into the little fleet and had cut out one, the *Patrick* of Waterford. He took her into Stokes Bay. Gilson too, in the *Constant Warwick* (30), had snapped up an Irish warship, and had taken her into the Thames.[14]

The Irish Guard had also continued its activities. On May 28th Penn was plying between Waterford and Wexford in the *Assurance* (32). Off the Salters he took a ship, going to Waterford to embark soldiers for France, and took her into Milford Haven. Here Swanley informed him he had been promoted to be Rear-Admiral. Swanley, in the *Lion* (45), sailed with Penn, with the *Satisfaction* (20) and

the *Globe* (24), to Greenold Bay, before Wexford. Here they found
the *Recovery* (20) and the *Increase* (14). As the *Assurance* was so
foul, Penn took her into Kinsale to clean. Back at Greenold Bay he
found that Swanley had left for Dublin. The *Hunter* now came in
with a prize, the *Orange Tree* of Brill, which Penn sent off to Bristol
with letters from Inchiquin. Swanley then came in again. He told
Penn that the blockade of Waterford and Wexford had compelled
the privateers to use Galway and Limerick instead. Penn, with his
knowledge of those waters, was to sail there. The Irish Guard was
making life difficult for the raiders.[15]

The political arena was becoming increasingly stormy. The
Presbyterians had been frightened into voting the payment of the
arrears due to the troops. Even so the Army refused to listen to
any proposals before they were laid before an Army Council and
they emphasized their demand by moving to Royston, nearer to
London. The Presbyterians took up the challenge by appointing a
Committee of Safety and by empowering the City to raise cavalry.

Nor did they forget the Navy. On July 12th, the Admiralty
Committee warned Batten "in these times of distemper, through want
of caution and vigilancy, neither the ships be surprised, nor the
mariners deceived upon any pretext whatever." They went on
piously to add a reminder: "we are confident that as Parliament
hath always had a special regard to the payment of the mariners
at a rate above that of former times, so they will continue faithful
to their commanders."[16] It was a wise precaution for, on the 21st,
the Agitators sent a letter from St. Albans, to which the Army had
advanced, to "all honest seamen of England" explaining their objects
and asking for the sailors support.[17]

This was followed by an Army "Declaration" which asked for
the dissolution of Parliament, the right of petition, and for religious
toleration. It was angrily rejected. Thereupon the Army brought
charges against eleven members of Parliament. The members were
accused of correspondence with the Queen, with attempting to bring
in the King on their own terms, with trying to raise forces for
another war, and of misrepresenting the Army. The eleven, among
whom were Sir William Waller, Sir Phillip Stapleton, and Colonel
Edward Massey, had all been deprived of their commands under the

Self-Denying Act. Naturally they resented this in view of their good service in the war and they were jealous of the New Model. They were probably in touch with the Earl of Lauderdale, acting as a go-between for the King, the Scots, and the Presbyterians. As all the Independents had been removed from the City Militia, an opportunity was given for a riot there in the King's favor, providing the Army an excellent excuse to march in to restore order. On August 14th it called for a purge of Parliament.

The eleven members saw the red light. On the 16th, five of them, including Waller and Stapleton, embarked for France armed with passes from the Speaker. Unfortunately they entrusted themselves to a certain rascal, Green. He sent them off under another captain and then, under the pretence that they had sailed without his authority, he obtained a warrant at Gravesend to detain them. He informed the inhabitants that they had gone away with sixteen chests of treasure. Soon a dogger boat, belonging to Roger Lamming, was manned by expectant volunteers. They chased the ship until they met the *Nicodemus*, which took over the pursuit and soon arrested her. She was taken to Batten, in the Downs in the *St. Andrew*. Batten sent for Green and Lamming. Next day at a council the passes were examined and the baggage searched. As all was in order, Batten allowed them, under an Admiralty order, to embark in the *Leopard* and to sail to St. Malo. Green and Lamming now arrived. In the presence of Kem, Batten told them they were knaves, Kem adding that they ought to be hanged.[18]

Now Batten was drawn into the political arena. Green, who had been dismissed for being on shore drinking instead of being at sea, got to work with Lamming. Soon a certain Andrew Gosfright came forward before the Mayor and Jurats of Sandwich stating that he had heard John Sprigham, chaplain of the *Providence*, accuse Batten. Sprigham avowed he had heard Batten declare that "the Army, notwithstanding they did hold the king in suspense, would in the end take off his head." But when Sprigham was examined he denied he had heard Batten use these words. Under pressure he admitted he had heard Batten say that he "feared the Army would not deal fairly with the King." He declared these words had been spoken in

the last six weeks, though curiously enough he could not recall
the time or the place.[19]

When this was reported to the Committee of Both Houses, now
largely Independent in character, they sent for Batten. In petty spite,
they subjected him to the indignity of coming up by land, instead
of, as Vice-Admiral, in his own ship. He was charged with allowing
the five members to go to France — which looks as if Green and
Lamming had been at work. To this was added, by "that false man,
Mr. Smith", secretary to the Navy Commissioners, the threat of
having another unspecified charge laid against him, if he did not
instantly resign.[20] The threat may have been based on Sprigham's
evidence. Batten promptly resigned, but for a reason unknown to the
committee of five who judged him. Batten, as a stout Presbyterian,
had been alarmed by the Army's action in seizing the King. He
feared the growing power of the Independents, especially in the
Army, and he had no wish to see a settlement determined by the
Army alone. He had determined that the weight of the Navy must
be thrown against this. Sprigham's words were probably true.[21]

In Scotland sympathy had veered to the King. The Hamiltons
had taken up his cause in earnest. They were thinking of an invasion
in the following year, for Lauderdale had been active. Batten had
offered to bring twenty-two ships to declare for the Scotch and
English Presbyterians, if they could be victualled elsewhere than
in England. He realized, however, that the Scots would not betray
themselves by allowing him to use their harbors. He hoped instead
they would exercise their influence so that he could procure the
provisions he needed in France.[22] The close relations he had established at Newcastle had revealed to him the minds of the Scots, and
now he was in full touch with them.

On October 8th the Houses voted that Colonel Rainsborough
should be appointed Vice-Admiral in Batten's place. The Independents wanted a man of their own in command of the fleet, instead
of a Presbyterian. Here was something for which Batten had not
bargained. He had hoped that by resignation he could still keep
secret his plan for using the Navy. His fury knew no bounds, for
Rainsborough was one of the men who had sat in judgment upon

him. And to be replaced by a Leveller! But the committee's action
went further: Batten must give up to Rainsborough the official resi-
dence at Deal, else he could still exercise his influence on the fleet.
Despite the illness of his wife, Batten was turned out, and took refuge
in a common alehouse. The action was an unwise one, for in Batten's
own words, "how this wrought upon my fellow seamen I hope I
shall all my life thankfully remember: they best knew what service
I had done, and now beheld mine and their own reward."[23] Loyalty
to a commander and a comrade has always been in the best tradition
of the Navy. Any suspicion of shabby or underhand treatment ever
arouses in the Englishman sympathy for the sufferer. Batten, however, was still continued as a Navy Commissioner, perhaps to soften
the blow, but more probably because it was considered that out of
actual command he would be comparatively harmless. Yet Batten
was a disgruntled and embittered man. He awaited his time, determined to regain the Navy, and he began to make his plans for
this purpose.

The Independents now split into two parties. One was practically republican. Under the leadership of Rainsborough, the group
were determined to rule by the sword and they aimed at the aboli-
tion of the monarchy. The other, led by Fairfax and Cromwell, still
wished for an understanding with the King, by which alone they
could hope for parliamentary support. There followed the great
debates of the Army in Putney church. Here Rainsborough put forward the Agreement of the People, by which a new form of Government was to be set up. There was to be a single chamber, elected
every two years by manhood suffrage, without any property qualifi-
cations. In Cromwell's view this would lead to nothing less than
anarchy.

Out of the debate emerges a clue that may point to one reason
why Rainsborough was appointed Vice-Admiral. "I am loth to leave
the Army, with whom I will live and die, insomuch that rather than
I will lose this regiment of mine, Parliament shall exclude me the
house or imprison me. For truly while I am employed abroad I will
not be undone at home."[24] He was suspicious that his opponents had
seized on the fact that he was practically the only Independent with
experience of command at sea. He judged that they had made this

an excuse to remove him from the command of his regiment, for at sea he would be unable to spread his Leveller opinions among the Army.

But he saw himself outnumbered. To prevent the defeat of the Agreement, he proposed it should be considered at a rendezvous of the whole Army. In addition he suggested that all negotiations with the King should cease — which Cromwell opposed. The simpler Levellers suggested the liquidation of Cromwell by shooting and of the King by knocking on the head.

Cromwell became alarmed. He had heard the fanatic, Harrison, declare that the King "was a man of Blood" and that they must now prosecute him. Cromwell, well acquainted with the secrets of the Levellers, may have suspected that Rainsborough intended to kidnap the King from Hampton Court or that Charles might be assassinated. He was determined to prevent this. His cousin Whalley had charge of Charles and was warned, possibly by Cromwell, that "there are rumours of some intended attempt upon the King's person. Therefore, I pray you, have a care on your guard." Whalley showed the King the letter and Charles, already warned by the Royalists of danger, escaped from Hampton Court on November 11th.

The news threw all parties into consternation. No one knew where the King had gone. Immediate orders were sent to the Winter Guard, consisting of twenty-five warships,* to be on the watch. Crowther and Penn were instructed to stop and search all vessels: if the King was aboard he was to be detained.[25] An embargo stopped all ships in southern ports from sailing, an act forcing Charles, hiding at Titchfield, to give himself up to Colonel Hammond, Governor of the Isle of Wight, since the ship, for which Charles was waiting, could not sail from Southampton.

By now the struggle no longer centered in the control of the King's person, but in that of the Army. At the rendezvous at Corkbush Field, near Ware, on November 15th, Rainsborough was present, although without his regiment. In defiance of orders, two Leveller regiments appeared with copies of the Agreement stuck in their hats. Rainsborough now went up to Fairfax and sought to present him

*Appendix L

with a copy of the Agreement. Fairfax brushed him aside and rode
up to Harrison's regiment, telling them to remove the papers from
their hats, which they did. Lilburne's men, however, continued defiantly to wear them. Cromwell instantly rode along their ranks,
ordering them to obey. They refused. With drawn sword he charged
into their ranks alone. The grim resolution upon his face, with the
sudden boldness of his action, struck fear into the troopers. Discipline re-asserted itself, as the frightened men tore the papers from
their hats and begged for mercy. The ring-leaders were arrested
and three sentenced to death by an impromptu court martial. The
leaders were ordered to cast lots and the losers were shot on the field.
Cromwell and Fairfax had asserted themselves as masters of the
Army. Fairfax at once reported to the Houses Rainsborough's attempt at mutiny. On the 16th the Lords resolved "that Colonel Rainsborough, who is named in the General's letter to have been active
with others at Ware, may not be suffered to go to sea, till this matter
be fully examined".[26] On December 9th the Commons, by three
votes, agreed he was not to command the fleet.

By now a royalist tide was running strong in the land, and
especially in London. The King had accepted the Scots terms, by
which Presbyterianism was to be established for three years, though
no one was to be compelled to take the Covenant. All Independent
and other religious sects were to be suppressed. The Army leaders
saw that if the King and the Scots were to be opposed, it could only
be in the name of the existing Parliament. But the Army must be
united. At a great prayer meeting at Windsor, Rainsborough abandoned mutiny, which had so dismally failed him. He confessed to
a "deep sense he had of the late distempers and miscarriages in
which he had been engaged, and his resolution to avoid such errors
for the future".[27] He might almost have been a repentant Communist
speaking. Fairfax, requested by the meeting to pardon him, accepted
these assurances. He wrote at once on the 23rd to the Commons,
requesting that Rainsborough should be sent to take command of the
fleet. He emphasized his request by adding ::I understand, by persons
well affected to your service, that there is some want of good guards
about the Isle of Wight, though there be now more than ordinary
need thereof thereabouts." Then he continued significantly: "indeed

the whole business of your sea service seems to be elsewhere in too loose a posture, considering the state of affairs."[28]

The Lords, however, despite Fairfax's letter of re-assurance, held to their former refusal, "conceiving it of the most dangerous consequence, that a person who hath had such a character from the General and the Army should be employed in a place of so great trust and importance to the Kingdom." The Commons contemptuously ignored this refusal, on January 1st, instructing Rainsborough to take command of the ships guarding the Solent. For the King had tried to escape. The ship he had expected had arrived at Southampton and was waiting, both for him and for a fair wind. Charles had got ready, when he noticed to his horror that the wind had changed and was now blowing from the north — the passage down the Medina and up Southampton Water was impossible.

Hammond was now warned by Cromwell that Carteret had sent three boats from Jersey, with a bark from Guernsey, to rescue the King. Cromwell gave instructions to order the parliamentary ships to keep a strict lookout for them, especially as they pretended to be French vessels.[29]

Amid these happenings the Irish Guard had been active. Crowther had persuaded Thomas Bushell to surrender Lundy Island, off the north Devon coast, by allowing him to retain all his property. Lundy rose sheer out of the sea, so that it was impossible to bombard, while to have stormed it would have been equally difficult, and it had no safe anchorage, so that it was useless to privateers. These facts influenced Crowther in making a bargain agreeable to both parties.[30] A small squadron, under Reeve William, had been sent to deal with the privateers, operating from Galway and Limerick. It was made up of the *Increase* (14), the *Mermaid*, and the *Charles*. The *Charles* was wrecked on the Clare coast, and the *Cat* was taken up in her stead. She boldly made her way into the Shannon, where she captured the *St. John the Baptist* and the *Middleburg*. Since she had no commission, the Admiralty Commissioners laid it down that she was covered by the squadron's general one, which allowed her to keep her prizes.[31]

In Jersey, however, a new prosperity unexpectedly seemed to open for the privateers, a golden dawn after darkness. The Prince

of Wales had rescinded his edict against letters of marque some-
time about the middle of August. Everything sprang to life. The
ruffling captains supervised the fitting out of their laid-up ships;
guns and ammunition were hurried aboard; the paid-off crews came
flocking to the vessels eager for fresh adventure and for prize money.
The captains boldly resolved to try and cut out one of the parliamentary frigates moored on the Great Bank, off Guernsey. Amy
was in command, with Chamberlain as his lieutenant, while other
captains acted as officers. The crew was made up of seventy resolute
men, armed with muskets, pistols, cutlasses, and boarding pikes.
The galley itself mounted five guns. Sailing north-east they arrived
off Castle Cornet at nightfall. Here they saw an enemy frigate of
forty guns, which they dared not tackle. As they went back to Jersey,
they sighted at daybreak a small frigate, which they recognized as
the *Hart*, of ten guns, anchored under shelter of the Island. Here
was their prey and they bore down on her. The frigate, however,
weighed and came to meet them, with most of her crew concealed
below decks. Broadsides were exchanged, in which the low-built
galley got the worst of it, for her crew were exposed to the full fire
of the *Hart*. Amy therefore decided to try and lure the *Hart* on the
Paternosters, a rock reef. The *Hart* followed after him; but she had
shifted all her guns to starboard, so that as she came abreast she
poured in a broadside. Amy returned it and a running fight ensued
along the westward coast of Jersey. Here the Captain of the *Hart*,
who feared to risk his ship among the hidden rocks, broke off the
action and returned to Guernsey.[32]

More and more captains poured into Jersey, as the French
ports were still closed to them. Captain Gernet brought in a new fast-
sailing vessel. His partner was an ex-chemist, who had sold off all
his medicines, bottles, and gallipots, and who had sunk his capital
in this privateering venture.[33] Loud were the outcries of the merchants about the damage inflicted by these "Jersey pirates", for
the removal of Batten had made things easier for the privateers.
Fairfax must have had this in mind when he wrote "the business
of your sea service seems to be elsewhere in too loose a posture."

The year had ended on an uncertain note for the Navy. It did
not know yet who was to command it, except that the proposed Vice-

Admiral was a Leveller and an Independent, who had left the Navy
for the Army. It was suspicious of him, since Rainsborough seemed
to supplant a seaman who had served with ability through the whole
war. The Navy resented, too, the manner in which Batten had been
treated. Nor had Batten forgotten it and his thoughts began to turn
to the King. He recalled his meetings with the Scots at Newcastle.
Now that they had agreed with King, Batten decided to continue his
correspondence with them. There was a cauldron on the boil, which
boded ill for the Independents.

CHAPTER X

1648
The Revolt of the Fleet

Rainsborough had been instructed by the Admirality Committee to enquire carefully into the behavior of his captains. If he had good reason to suspect any of them, he was to put their charge into other hands.[1] This order practically turned him into a political commissar, engaged in smelling out the slightest odor of disaffection, a task requiring the exercise of unlimited patience and tact. But these were qualities in which the new Vice-Admiral was notoriously deficient. Already he was unpopular with the officers and seamen, who resented him for being foisted upon them.

He began work at once, urging the need for getting the Summer Guard to sea as soon as possible, since the Irish privateers were increasing in numbers and boldness. They were now operating as a combined fleet, under Ormonde's orders, instead of as isolated units. One had taken four ships near Plymouth. A Dover ship, one of his victims, had made a great fight, and had only surrendered after many men had been killed and the Master's legs blown off. The same night two more privateers had come up, with three prizes they had taken. Rumor spoke of two more squadrons, one of five ships and two more of two ships, all active in the Channel. United they could deal with any single parliamentary frigate they might meet. To deal with them, Rainsborough proposed to have two squadrons constantly plying in the Channel, one westwards as far as Land's End and the other eastwards as far as Dover. But to carry out this plan more ships were needed. He ended with an unsuccessful request to have Kem, the Minister at Deal, removed. But Kem was allowed to remain, a decision which was to have disastrous consequences.[2]

The Solent was well guarded. Although Carteret had sent a

SIR WILLIAM BATTEN

vessel to Cowes to rescue the King, all it could do was to smuggle in a letter to him and to carry back the reply to Hyde.[3] Charles was now trying to bring to his aid the Presbyterians, the Scots, and the Royalists. The Leveller threat to property had turned many of the Presbyterian gentry and the City merchants into Royalists. The wilder utterances of the more extreme sects seemed to point to anarchy in religious life as well. The country stood in fact upon the brink of a royalist revival.

By this time the Independents had decided that it was useless to try to come to terms with the King. They knew what they had fought for and they were determined to bring it about. Early in January a Vote of No Addresses to the King was carried in the Commons and this was followed by the dissolution of the Committee of Both Kingdoms. In its place a new Committee was created, taking its name from its meeting place at Derby House. It was composed of the English members of the old Committee, with three Independents replacing the three Presbyterians who had died. By this stroke the Scottish Commissioners were dismissed from connection with the government of England and on the 24th they left London.

Once back in Edinburgh they bent their efforts to win the nation to the King's cause. They secured the support of Hamilton and his party, despite the opposition of the Marquis of Argyle. With the aid of the nobles, Hamilton secured a majority in the Scottish Parliament and slowly the nation drifted towards war with England.

The seething discontent first broke out in South Wales. The local forces were ordered to disband, upon the receipt of two months pay, with bonds for the rest of their service. All accounts must be audited. Poyer, in command at Pembroke, was then accused by the local committee of the misappropriation of public money. He promptly refused, not once but twice, to hand over Pembroke Castle to Colonel Fleming, who had been sent to replace him.[4] Poyer, quarrelsome by nature, now decided he might as well be hung for a sheep as for a lamb. He started to fortify the Castle and to collect to himself the troops who were discontented with the meager financial terms of disbandment.

The local committee took alarm at the possibility of a new Civil War, especially as Milford Haven lay open to any outside help that might come to Poyer's support.[5] Additional troops were thus ordered to join Fleming and Rainsborough was instructed to send a ship to ride in the Haven, as near to Pembroke Castle as possible. If necessary, it was to land battering pieces to help Fleming.[6] By now some of Laugharne's troops, which had also refused to disband, joined Poyer and he felt strong enough to open fire on Fleming's quarters. The first shot in the new Civil War had been fired.

The *Expedition* (18) now arrived and two whole-culverins were landed, which Fleming hoped "would be a great terror to them." But his report ended on an ominous note: he feared that the garrison at Tenby might also join the revolt.[7] His fears were justified. On March 16th the garrison mutinied, shipping themselves in boats and lighters to Pembroke Castle, which they entered through one of the waterside postern gates. With this accession of strength, Poyer made a sally on the 23rd. Though he was driven back, some revolted troops, coming from Glamorgan, fell unexpectedly upon Fleming's rear and overwhelmed him. He just managed to escape to the *Expedition*, but his culverins were captured. This success emboldened Poyer to declare openly for the King.[8] It was plain that a dangerous royalist movement had developed and that, unless speedily checked, it might well spread throughout South Wales. Fairfax instantly ordered Colonel Horton to march against Poyer. On April 1st Crowther was ordered to sail from Ireland with his squadron to Tenby, there to act in conjunction with Horton.[9]

Crowther's hands, however, were already tied. Inchiquin had again changed sides, having declared for the King on April 13th.[10] His sympathies naturally lay with the large landowners. The Vote of No Addresses had also convinced him that this defiance was aimed not only at the King, but at his own class as well. Thus, when Colonel Barry arrived at Cork with troops sent from France by Ormonde, he welcomed him with open arms. Crowther had no choice but to blockade the Irish ports. To complicate matters still further Penn, his Rear-Admiral, was under suspicion, as he was known to be on intimate terms with Inchiquin. Penn was arrested and sent to London. However, he was soon set at liberty and given back his ship. Nevertheless, the matter rankled and the authorities had to write to reassure him that they were convinced of his loyalty.[11]

In this alarming situation Rainsborough, on the 25th, proposed that nine ships should be sent to guard Milford Haven, with another nine for Ireland.[12] But worse news came. The revolt had spread to the north when, on April 28th, Sir Marmaduke Langdale, with a party from Scotland, had surprised Berwick-upon-Tweed. Captain Ball, in the newly built Fourth-Rate *Adventure* (32) was, however, off the town. He light-heartedly "tossed niney-four cannon balls" into it, driving the Royalists from their works.[13] Sir Arthur Heselrige asked for ships to reinforce Ball and to prevent the damaged sea wall from being rebuilt. Fairfax was ordered north with all speed.[14] Additionally, the ubiquitous Brown Bushell seems to have been operating as a privateer of Newcastle, for Captain Lawson of the *Covenant* (12) was ordered to apprehend him "as he was about to seize upon our merchants' goods for the use of the King of Scotland."[15] Lawson was successful and Brown Bushell was executed on March 29th 1651, on the charge of betraying Scarborough Castle.[16]

On May 11th Crowther wrote from Penarth to say he had to abandon the blockade of Kinsdale, since he only had with him his own ship and another frigate, the *John*. He had, as ordered, sent the rest to Tenby. He was thus too weak "to risk meeting the enemy's men of war, which are rife." He had sent the frigate to Bristol for repair, while his own ship, the *Bonaventure*, was very foul and unserviceable. Anxiously he asked for news of the Summer Irish Guard, "the long retarding of which may prove of sad consequence if the enemy's assistance, daily expected by sea, should fall in ere we have force enough to oppose them."[17]

On May 17th the list of the Summer Guard was issued. It comprised thirty-nine warships,* including the new Fourth-Rates of five hundred and fifty to six hundred and fifty tons, and of thirty-two guns, the *Nonsuch*, *Adventure*, and *Assurance*, built in 1646, and the *Elizabeth*, *Phoenix*, and *Dragon*, built in 1647. Nineteen ships were allotted to the Irish Guard, of which nine were to guard Milford Haven and to ply about Land's End.[18]

This strengthened force indicated the increasing danger of the royalist revolts. Horton, who had retired to Brecon, now ad-

*Appendix M

vanced to secure Carmarthen, held by Colonel Rice Powell. He had demanded an agreement with the King in order that the privileges of Parliament, the laws and liberties of the people, and the Protestant religion, might be preserved.[19] Horton soon found himself held up by Powell's troops, posted on the top of a hill, which could not be stormed. So he sent Fleming, with a small troop of horse, to secure a ford on the far side of the Welsh, so as to enter Carmarthen from this direction. Unfortunately Fleming ran into an ambush, in which he was killed and his men taken prisoner. This disaster forced Horton again to retire to Brecon on April 27th, in order to replenish his ammunition, but the move left the way open to Swansea and Cardiff.[20]

Laugharne, who had now joined in the revolt, though for what reasons it seems impossible to discover, at once marched into Glamorgan. He was decisively defeated by Horton at St. Fagans, near Cardiff, on May 8th and fled to Tenby. Swansea and Cardiff were safe again.[21] Horton instantly pushed his horse on to try and rush Tenby, but it was too strong for them and Horton had to bring up his foot. The *Bonaventure* (36) and the *Expedition* (16) came in to blockade the town from the sea.[22]

The alarmed authorities meanwhile had sent Cromwell from Windsor to march into South Wales to check the spread of the disorder. By May 11th he was at Chepstow. On the 24th he wrote to say that since Horton had affairs well in hand, he himself was moving on Pembroke.[23] Tenby surrendered on June 1st and Horton joined Cromwell. The latter's guns, however, had been lost in a ship that had sunk in the Severn, near Berkeley. Though they were recovered, contrary winds prevented their arrival. Therefore Hugh Peters, Cromwell's chaplain, went to the Haven and brought back two demi-culverins and two drakes from the *Lion*. Their arrival settled Pembroke's fate, and it fell on the 11th.[24] Seapower, with its mobility of artillery, had enabled the Army to capture the centers of revolt in time to prevent it spreading further. Had it not done so, there was a possible, though highly unlikely, chance of a landing of Irish troops in the Haven.

Before Cromwell had left Windsor a great meeting of the Army officers and the Agitators took place to consider the situation created by the new Civil War. These rugged soldiers, nurtured on the Old

Testament, professed to see in their failure to win the King to the path of peace, a sign of divine wrath. Here was their sin. They resolved it was their duty "to call Charles Stuart, that man of blood, to an account for the blood he had shed, against the Lord's cause and people." Once again the soldier saints in high exaltation rode forth to war. And with them rode Cromwell.

There was much with which to contend. There were riots at Norwich. The Thanksgiving services in London for the victory at St. Fagans, were practically empty, the mobs instead shouting for the King. A petition from Surrey led to the crowds being cleared from Westminster Hall by the soldiers. Kent, too, waited for a hoped-for invasion by the Scots. With Fairfax and Cromwell absent, London was expected to declare for Charles.

Nor did the Royalists neglect the Navy. Here their agents had been at work for some time. They could report on April 25th "it is certain that all the Navy is discontented and wavering."[25] Special attention had been paid to Batten. At the Hoop Tavern, in Leadenhall Street, he met and plotted with these agents to bring about a revolt in the fleet.[26] A secret movement was organized in the ships themselves. With his intimate knowledge of the men and officers, Batten was able to select officers capable of leadership when the moment arrived, among them Lendal, Lisle, and Mitchell, of his old flagship, the *Reformation*. On shore at Deal, his former chaplain, Kem, now minister of the church there, was the probable go-between for Batten and the leaders aboard. The object of the movement was to remove Rainsborough from command, which it was hoped would lead to Batten's recall. To this end a subtle propaganda was instilled into the minds of the ordinary seamen. Rainsborough was represented as a man of destructive principles in religion and policy, an enemy of peace and of the kingdom which the seamen had sworn to uphold with their lives and fortunes. Had not the power and affairs of the Navy been placed in the hands of those who were enemies to king and kingdom, even of the monarchy itself? Had not the King's name been left out of the Commissions, leaving only that of the Army and the Parliament? Had not land-commanders been given ships? And was there not a scheme to introduce land-soldiers into every ship, to overawe the seamen, contrary to the ancient customs of the sea?

There was no talk of a revolt — the seeds of discontent and suspicion were sown quietly.[27] But these ideas the seamen imbibed as their own, as doubtless they drank deep of free beer, plentifully supplied by the agents, in the taverns at Deal, Portsmouth, and elsewhere.

Batten too was active. On April 13th he had gone to Bristol where the *Constant Warwick* had cone in to revictual. She brought in a prize she had captured off Ireland. Batten, as part-owner of the ship, had come to arrange for the sale of the prize. He took the opportunity to spread his propaganda among the crew before the ship sailed for London and his efforts were shortly to bear fruit.[28]

Unrest had also been simmering in Kent for some time. On May 10th certain persons, charged with disturbances on the previous Christmas, had the bill against them thrown out by the grand jury at Canterbury. The jury went further, presenting a petition, similar to those of Essex and Surrey. They asked that the King should be allowed to treat in person with both Houses; that Fairfax's Army should be disbanded, with all arrears of pay made up; that the known laws of the kingdom should be continued; and that the privileges of Parliament and the liberty of the subject should be preserved. With the fleet in the Downs, the unrest was bound to be known to the seamen. Here was the Royalists' opportunity. When the moment was ripe they could get rid of Rainsborough and replace him by Batten. Kem probably arranged with Lendal to come aboard at the right time for the ships to revolt, for, on May 23rd, an unknown agent wrote: "I have laboured to put the present fleet now at sea under the command of Captain Batten, who is a person of most clear affections to your instant endeavours. . . . I have treated freely with him, and find he will most willingly undertake it, if a fleet of twenty ships, men of war, can be hired or borrowed for some short time, that he may appear in a condition to protect himself and his friends." Many of the seamen had promised to bring their ships when Batten desired it, nor would the captains dare to oppose it, when the seamen knew that Batten was engaged. The agent promised that he could "furnish some shipping here, and some from abroad", while Batten hoped that his friends would provide a month's provisions and that the Scots would invite him to their harbors to victual. Then he proposed to go to the Isle of Wight to rescue the King.[29]

The answer was to be sent, with any letters for Batten, to Lady Carlisle: "from that hand Captain Batten will esteem highly of it." For Lady Carlisle knew of the scheme. Yet she was a dangerous woman, an inveterate intriguer, with a delight in gossip. She is said to have let out Charles's plan to seize the five members, while she was known to have intrigued with the eleven members at her Whitehall lodgings. She was the medium between the King and the Earl of Lauderdale, a woman more dangerous to her friends than to her foes.

But the agent's vague plan for borrowing a fleet was not to be needed, since a chance spark set ablaze the inflammable material. On May 20th Rainsborough reported that the night before a large fleet had come in from the westward. A man in mean dress had landed. Lendal pretended to recognize him as the Prince of Wales and sent him for safety to Sandwich. Here some of the *Providence's* crew, "touched by his beggarly condition had given him money, and when he gave himself out to be the Prince of Wales they had joined him." Half the *Providence's* crew, with some of the officers, followed suit. They took him to the Bell Tavern, where the populace received him with great enthusiasm and transport of joy. The man, however, was an imposter, named Cornelius Evans. Yet the news spread like wildfire. Sandwich, Rochester, and Faversham were seized for the King, and the gentry placed themselves as commissioners at the head of the revolt.[30]

This alarming news shook Derby House into swift action. They ordered Rainsborough to seize the imposter and to send him to London. If the Mayor refused to give him up, musketeers were to take him by force. Rainsborough was to drive out the royalist garrison in Sandwich and take the town, if it could be done with safety. He was also to re-inspect a ship, lying about Queensborough, which they suspected of being involved in an attempt to rescue the King, timed, they thought, for the 24th or 25th.[31]

On the 25th Rainsborough replied with still more alarming news: the distemper had spread to the fleet. Though somewhat allayed, it must be speedily suppressed. "That which is the greatest motive to the seamen is that these parts are wholly for the King." He was about to send "two mistrusted ships", the *Providence* (22) and the *Convertine* (42), to the northward, "if they will be commanded." In view of what had happened the remark was ominous. He concluded that "a line or two from your Lordships might be of great encouragement to many among us."[32] Then for the moment the trouble seemed to abate, for the two ships sailed. Two centers of disaffection had been safely removed. At a council of war, on the 26th, called to discuss the situation, all the captains, save Nixon of the *Roebuck* (14), were present. They declared their intention to live and die for the Parliament. Confident that he could safely leave the fleet in their charge, Rainsborough went ashore to inspect the defenses of Deal Castle.

Meanwhile the royalist Commissioners had dealt with Evans. They had decided not to trust such an obvious imposter. As they entered the Bell, Evans appeared, waving a plumed hat and shouting, "raise the town, stand to me, seamen." The Commissioners cleverly pacified the mob by placing musketeers before the Tavern, as if to protect Evans. But the seamen took him out by the back door, sending him by boat to Thanet. Here eventually he was arrested by the Parliamentarians, and sent from Canterbury to London, where he was imprisoned in Newgate. From here he mysteriously escaped very shortly. On the night before Rainsborough went ashore Kem visited the royalist Commissioners, telling them he had repented of his former errors, and had resolved to join the King's side. He offered to take a copy of their Petition to every ship in the fleet. This they gladly accepted. Kem's chance had come at last. Next day, with a party of horsemen, he rode past Rainsborough who defiantly waved his sword at them from the roof of Deal Castle. Kem, with some Commissioners, rowed out to the fleet, where the seamen received them with enthusiasm, declared for the King, accepted the Petition, and placed between decks any officers or men who would not join them. They were rewarded with a distribution of money.

The wild outburst of cheering which ran from ship to ship alarmed Rainsborough. He instantly took boat and rowed out to the *Reformation*. The crew told him that "he had nothing to do with them, nor should he be admitted to the fleet which had declared for the King — whom they would liberate from the Isle of Wight." They added that "he had been a kind and good-natured commander to them", and that "they had no designs on his person or his goods."

When he asked for a pinnace to take him to London, Lendal told him "we cannot spare the least vessel in the Downs: they are all engaged on a better service. There is a Dutch flyboat — you can book a passage in her for London for sixpence."[33] But Captain Penrose, of the *Satisfaction* (20) told a different and probably truer story: the crew told Rainsborough they would obey him no longer and that he would come aboard at his peril; he might go in the boat he was in, which, "after many threats and uncivil passages", Rainsborough had to do.[34]

Lendal now summoned the captains aboard. Some of them went, but Penrose refused on the ground that as no Vice-Admiral was aboard, there was no power to call a council. Forty men, with drawn swords, were sent to fetch him. But Penrose still refused, believing that his own crew would stand by him. To his dismay they all shouted to him, "go, go." And Penrose had to yield.

He told Lendal he would not sign the Kentish Petition. Then, with great courage, he asked the *Reformation's* crew if they cast off their allegiance to Parliament. To this they significantly answered that they stood for King and Parliament. Penrose then tried to side-step Lendal by suggesting they should choose some honorable person for Vice-Admiral, whereupon they shouted, "a Warwick, a Warwick." This must have disconcerted Lendal, for it was quite unexpected. Moreover it appeared to deal a death-blow to Batten's plot. Penrose improved his position by suggesting he should take letters to the Speaker, telling him of their proceedings and promising that if Warwick were sent to them, they would obey him. This they agreed to do. They even took an oath that, when Penrose left, they would not make choice of any one else.[35]

In their Declaration, taken by Penrose, the seamen stated they conceived Rainsborough to be a "person not well affected to the King, Parliament, and Kingdom." They had joined the Kentish gentlemen, because they approved of the objects of their Petition.[36]

It seems that political motives, cleverly mixed up with the personal dislike of Rainsborough, had brought about the mutiny, for the seamen spoke of the "insufferable pride, ignorance, and insolency of the Vice-Admiral that alienated the hearts of the seamen." The word insufferable is now what most people felt about Rainsborough. Penrose, it is clear, saw that he would have to go. Though no mention was made of pay, it seems probable that as the Army's wages were months in arrear, the Navy, out of the way and unseen, was even worse off in this respect.

The wretched Rainsborough, meanwhile, had arrived at Landguard Fort, opposite Harwich, on the 27th. From here he wrote a letter, in a shaky hand, clearly showing his agitation. He disclosed that the *Reformation* (46), *Swallow* (36), *Hind* (16), *Satisfaction* (20), *Roebuck* (14), and the *Pelican* (12), had all mutinied and imprisoned their officers. His own Lieutenant, Lisle, was one of the ringleaders, while only four men on the flagship had stood firm. He begged that orders should be sent to Hull, Newcastle, and the northern and western ports to guard against betrayal. They were to detain the fleet if it should arrive, though how this was to be done he did not say. He had come to Harwich, since he had sent the *Tiger* (32) there some days before the trouble started. To his dismay he had found the *Providence* (22) there also. He had boarded them both, "to try if it be possible to gain them, either by fair means or threats", but without success. He feared that Sandown and Walmer Castles, which he had manned with seamen, part of whom had revolted, were lost, together with Deal Castle.[37]

When this further news reached London, on the 28th, the Parliament was filled with consternation, as it was so completely unexpected. Its implications were only too evident: the King might be snatched out of their grasp; foreign aid might be brought in; the Irish troops might be brought over to join the revolt; and a blockade of London might bring ruin to the City, while the monied merchants, already fearful of the Levellers, might refuse to find more money and go over to the King. Upon them Parliament depended financially. The regaining of the Navy was vital to the resolute, bold, and determined men of the Army. Without it their victories would be worthless and perhaps lost. They were men of practical common sense and they acted swiftly. They swallowed the bitter pill that, in spite of warning, they had made a bad choice in Rainsborough. Clearly only Warwick could regain the fleet. Thus they re-appointed him Lord High Admiral. Yet even he had been suspected in the previous summer of royalist proclivities. But they had no other choice. He was given authority to treat with the mutineers and to grant indemnities if he thought fit.[38]

Meanwhile, Lendal, Lisle, Kem, and the Kentish Committee had been frantically working to undo the mischief to their plan unconsciously caused by Penrose. Warwick must on no account be allowed aboard his flagship. He had sailed on the 30th in the *Nicodemus* (10). Off the North Foreland he was saluted by the *Hind* (17), by which he understood that the fleet was willing to receive him. At the same time he observed uneasily that the flag still flew in the *Reformation's* maintop, notwithstanding his approach. Captains Penrose and Harris put off from the *Hind* to board him, followed by another boat, containing the two Bargraves and Hammond, of the Kentish Committee, with Lendal and two officers of the *Reformation*, and the ubiquitous Kem. The Captains told him that up to the night before the seamen had been prepared to obey him. Then the Bargraves and Hammond had boarded the *Reformation*, "and infused such desperate principles into the seamen that most of them had deserted their previous resolutions." They had resolved not to admit Warwick, unless he engaged with the Kentish Gentlemen. The conspirators had been successful.

The Bargraves and Hammond then arrived and told Warwick that before he could go aboard he must sign the Petition. This Warwick refused to do, saying he had been sent to take command of the fleet and that his business was with the seamen alone. He could take no notice of anything they might propose, but if they put it in writing, he would submit it to the Houses. To this they answered that they could not do so without the authority of the committee.

Kem and the officers then came in, and Warwick peremptorily announced he had come to take charge of the fleet, with power to indemnify such of the mariners as should submit to his authority. They answered they had joined with the Kentish gentry in their Petition. They re-asserted its main points and repeated that Warwick must agree to them if he wished to board his flagship.

Warwick replied that the Petition was outside his authority. It was a matter for Parliament alone. His concern was with the fleet and seamen and he intended to go aboard his flagship to take charge of the fleet. The deputation said they would take his answer back to the *Reformation* and bring back a reply. They asked that Penrose should go with them, that he "might testify to their carriage in that business." Soon they returned, accompanied by Hammond and the elder Bargrave. Their attitude was not promising, for they insisted upon an agreement between Warwick and the Kentish gentry. Penrose then drew Warwick aside, warning him of the distemper aboard the flagship. Only the efforts of the Gunner had prevented a proposal to shoot at his flag. Indeed, the younger Bargrave was still aboard, encouraging disobedience by promises and threats.

Hammond then tried to persuade Warwick to go to Rochester, under a safe conduct, to meet the committee. Possibly he hoped that they might win him over to them. Warwick sternly answered he had no authority to do this and he abruptly refused. Matters now took an ugly turn on the *Nicodemus,* for the crew had learned of the *Reformation's* answer. In their anger they refused to keep Warwick aboard. They objected to his wearing his flag at the maintop and they refused to let him sail in the *Nicodemus.* Instead they told him he must sail in the *Rebecca* (22), or else they would put him ashore to return by land. Warwick's three years of absence from personal command had lost him the magic of intimate touch with the seamen. But he still stoutly stood his ground. He pointed out that they themselves had invited him to take command and had agreed to let him return in the *Nicodemus,* if agreement could not be reached. After much angry discussion, egged on by Bargrave, Hammond had to admit the justice of Warwick's contention. He prevailed on the seamen to let Warwick sail, though they demanded that the *Nicodemus* must return. Warwick flatly refused, whereupon, much to his relief, the deputation left.

Warwick now called a council of war with Captains Moulton and Pacey, of the *Nicodemus.* They resolved that everything possible had been done and that it was not safe, in view of the temper of the men, for Warwick to remain in the Downs. He must sail at once and report to Parliament. This he did, directing the *Rebecca* to follow and so she cut her cables and left, before the mutineers could prevent her sailing. It was decided to go to the Thames, in case the crew spread the disaffection to the ships in the north or east. Near the Hope, Warwick got the cheering news that Fairfax, who had been recalled from his northern march, had taken Maidstone. He sent this information to Mitchell, boatswain of the *Reformation*, warning him that unless the ship was delivered back to him, misery and ruin would fall on the crew. There would be no indemnity for them. It was but a Partian shot, for the mutineers were jubilant at their repulse of Warwick. Already they had gone too far in their revolt to draw back at the mere threat of possible consequences.[39]

But Warwick was an anxious man. He had failed to regain the fleet. By this time, too, he knew that his brother, Henry Rich, Earl of Holland, had been appointed Commander in Chief of the army about to be raised by the Royalists — a suggestion to the court at St. Germains by Lady Carlisle. Holland had at once appointed George Goring, now Earl of Norwich, to the command of the forces in Kent. Warwick was confronted, not only with his own failure, but also with the unpleasant fact that his brother was in command of the royalist troops, operating against the Parliament.

CHAPTER XI

1648
Warwick and the Revolted Fleet

Warwick's failure had created a serious situation. Though he had acted with courage and firmness he could not have felt confident. How would the Houses regard his efforts? How would they deal with him? The mutineers had treated him as they had treated Rainsborough. Now they had seized the Castles at Deal, Sandown, and Walmer, essential for the safety of the fleet lying in the Downs. Dover Castle too was besieged and how any support from the sea could reach it was difficult to imagine. How far would the revolt spread? Poyer had been shot at Covent Garden on April 25th, and Powell and Laugharne had been imprisoned. But their fate had not deterred royalists revolts in other parts. What would the ships at Portsmouth do? Would the Irish Guard be affected? Time alone could answer these questions, which must have passed through Warwick's anxious mind, as the *Nicodemus* bore him back to London.

The Houses, however, still retained their confidence in Warwick, despite his failure. Who else indeed could they be sure of to replace him? There was no one. The Lord Mayor and Common Council of the City, on June 1st, petitioned that "Captain Batten might be restored to the place of Vice-Admiral," but to no avail. Cheering news, however, came from Peter Pett, in charge of the dockyard at Chatham. He had undergone a trying and exciting time. The Rochester Committee had tried to get him and the dockyard hands to sign their Petition, which he had refused to allow. The Committee then seized Upnor Castle, manned it with musketeers, and searched all vessels moving in the Medway. So, on May 24th, Pett sent the *Fellowship* (28) to Gillingham for safety. On the 26th the Committee countered by sending a warrant to her Captain, Jervoise, to search

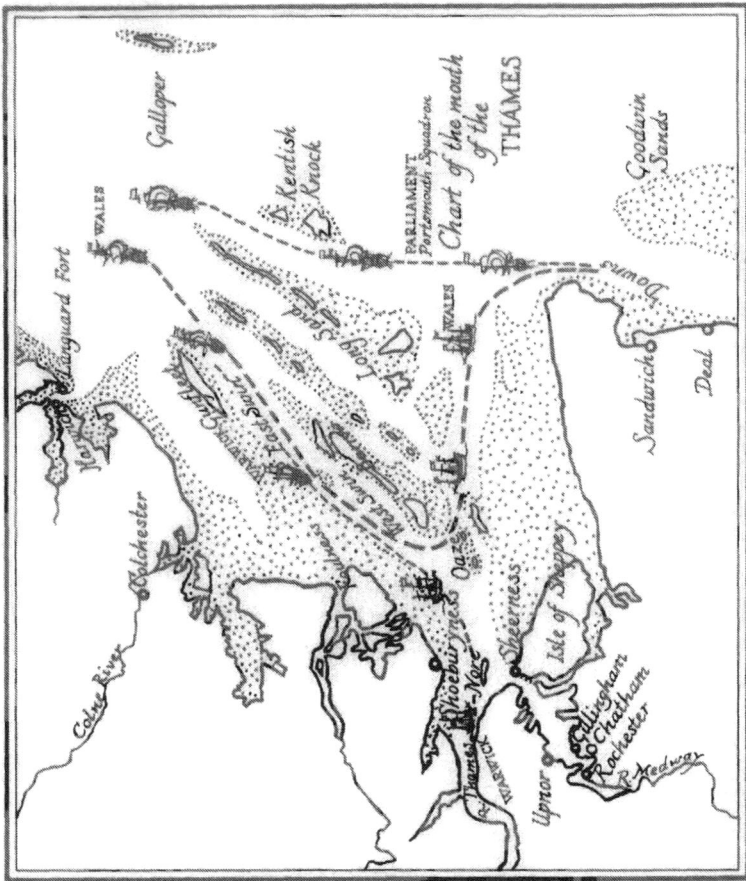

THE MOUTH OF THE THAMES

her. Next day they took her to Upnor, removing her powder and shot. Then they ordered her gunner, Pratt, to fetch forty barrels of powder from the *Sovereign* (90) and the *Prince* (70). Pett refused to permit this. Next day a company of musketeers, guided by Dirkin, one of the principal gunners of the Navy, arrived before the dock. Pett promptly shut the gates, stood his men to arms, and spoke to Dirkin out of the window. When Dirkin produced his warrant, Pett "blushed at the impudency and insolency of this order" and refused to obey. As Dirkin was unable to enter the dockyard itself, he seized the two ships and sent twenty-five barrels of their powder to the mutineers.[1]

But the defeat of the Royalists at Maidstone on June 1st alarmed the Committee, especially as the Earl of Norwich had retreated across the Thames. They sent Captain Bonner and Mr. Morland to order Jervoise to bring away the *Fellowship*. Pett forestalled them by arming a boat with musketeers and seizing her. He arrested the three men and next day completed his task by securing the *Sovereign* and the *Prince*. Pett's courage and resolution "with those few forces and men we had" saved the situation at Chatham, for the loss of the two most powerful ships in the Navy would have been an overwhelming addition to the revolted fleet. Some of its officers grew anxious about their position. Pett caustically describes them: "some of our Samaritan officers and common men became Jews, and would join us." But he dealt firmly with them, "because I found by experience their unparalleled perfidiousness to the Parliament, divers of them having been the chief actors in this rebellion." He listed them and then he ordered the Clerk of the Cheque to suspend the victuals and wages, till they could clear themselves, of all he found guilty. He ended by suggesting to the Admiralty Commissioners "whether it would not be a thing very fit to purge the Navy of such ill members."[2]

Soon Colonel Rich recaptured Canterbury, relieving Dover Castle. He then invested the three Castles at Deal, so that Fairfax was free to leave Kent. Essex needed him badly, since on June 4th the County Committe had met at Chelmsford to arrest the royalist leaders within the county. Instead the mob carried them off as prisoners. In alarm the Houses offered an indemnity to all Essex men, if they would liberate the prisoners. To prevent their release the Earl of Norwich hurried to Chelmsford and raised a royalist force. They established themselves at Colchester, with the object of pushing on into Norfolk and Suffolk, where more Royalists awaited them. But Fairfax had already crossed the Thames and on June 12th he was only a mile and a half outside Colchester. He began the siege at once.

The defeat at Maidstone had also alarmed the mutineers in the fleet. Now, as they could not hope for much support in Kent, the question of supplies became acute. It was necessary to find a new base. So on June 4th they sailed for Yarmouth with the *Reformation* (46), *Swallow* (36), *Satisfaction* (20), *Hind* (16), *Roebuck* (14), and *Pelican* (12). Here they found that the Parliamentarians held the town too strongly for them to excite a rising. There was nothing for it but to return to the Downs, where they anchored again on the 7th. Neither the Channel Islands nor the Scillies could provision them, and they were probably uncertain of Scotland or Holland.[3]

Just after they left Yarmouth, Captain Coppin of the *Greyhound* (12) came in from the north. When his crew, mostly Deal men, learned of the mutiny, they compelled him to sail for the Downs. "So I perceiving this complied with them; and coming aboard of her that wears the flag, God directed me so, that I seemed to join with them in their horrid designs, till such time that it pleased God to work my deliverance out of their hands. Then after much merriment at the Castle I went aboard." Here Coppin found that most of his men had gone ashore to their homes. After consulting with the master and the officers, he resolved to run for Harwich, in spite of having only thirty-six men to work the ship. About 5 p.m. he set sail, whereupon the *Warwick* (22) and the *Pelican* (14) cut their cables and pursued him. He escaped safely to Harwich, where he found the *Providence* (22), the *Tiger* (32), and the *Adventure* (30). Coppin added that Lendal had told him that the mutineers intended to sink colliers in the Medway to prevent ships coming out of the river. They obviously feared the *Sovereign* and the *Prince*. But the presence of the *Warwick* (22), *Antelope* (36), *Crescent* (14) and the *Convertine* (40) among the mutineers shows that the revolt was still spreading. The *Convertine* had arrived in the

Thames to pay off. Her crew mutined, put their officers ashore, and joined the revolters. Coppin's escape, however, had the effect of bringing the *Warwick* (22) into the Thames, where she returned to duty.[4]

On June 3rd Warwick went to Portsmouth, as he was very anxious about the situation there. Batten was ordered to go with him, but failed to do so.[5] Writing on the 5th, Warwick reported that things were well in hand. As the ships' companies had declared themselves loyal to him, he suggested an indemnity might be granted to the Kentish gentlemen, as he had heard they were aboard the ships in the Downs. Otherwise he feared they might urge the mutineers to hold out to the last, to save themselves. If such an indemnity were granted, it must be on the condition that the ships were handed over to him. He concluded by saying he had heard the revolted ships intended to go to Holland. Confident and re-assured, he returned to London on the 10th.[6]

At this point it is useful to view the position of Warwick's ships. Between the Medway and Greenhithe were the *St. George* (50), *Unicorn* (50), *Fellowship* (28), *Nicodemus* (10), *Greyhound* (12), *Hector* (22), and *Adventure* (30). At Harwich, blockading Colchester were the *Tiger* (32), *Warwick* (22), *Providence* (22), *Dolphin*, and *Hunter* (6). The loyalty of the *Tiger, Warwick* and *Providence*, however, was very doubtful. At Portsmouth were the *Nonsuch* (32), *Phoenix* (32), *Mary Rose* (20), and the *Robert* (12). The *Bonaventure* (36), *Garland* (40), *Lion* (40), and the *John* (28) were expected to come in there shortly.[7]

For the moment the mutineers appeared to be in a strong position. They had ten ships, including some of the strongest, and they were strategically placed between Warwick's divided forces in the Thames and at Portsmouth. But they had no definite leadership or plan. Their only sources of supply were the three Castles at Deal. Since these were now invested, it was uncertain how long they could hold out. So, on the 10th, the fleet left the Downs and sailed for Helvoetsluys in Holland, where they intended to place themselves under the command of the Prince of Wales.[8] He had embarked at Calais on July 9th, in a Dutch ship. Among the nobles with him was Prince Rupert. There may have been a skirmish as they came out, for the Admiralty Committee wrote to Captain Pearce, of the *Hector*, "We have not forgotten the service you performed on the coast of France in maintaining a fight with two frigates of the enemies."[9]

At a council of war, Warwick and his captains resolved to assemble as great a fleet as Parliament should think fit to reduce the rebels. A gratuity was to be offered to such officers and men as should volunteer for service.[10] There was urgent need, for disconcerting news was coming from Portsmouth. The loyalty of some of the ships there was so doubtful that it was proposed to remove their sails to prevent them being taken to sea.[11]

Batten had made a secret visit to Portsmouth, as an extract shows: "as soon as Batten knows where the ships are, he will go to them, and is assured that the ships that are at Portsmouth will follow him." Batten had reported that "he had much ado to make the sailors quiet for the time he was at Portsmouth, but thought it best to do nothing till the ships were all ready." This letter from an unknown agent was dated June 24th.[12] Batten was angry at the failure of the plan to replace him in command of the fleet, and he was clearly determined to take any ships he could over to the Prince: "I had resolved no longer to serve those persons who (as His Majesty himself told them) do change their principles with their successes. And to deal clearly with the world, I engaged myself to the Prince of Wales, though this, I presume was then unknown to Derby House and the Headquarters."[13]

But was this unknown? On June 21st Mr. Hinckman and Mr. Phipps were ordered to attend the Committee of Both Houses "to testify what they can say against Captain Batten" — who was known to have been in Portsmouth and who was suspected of sending armed men to join the rising in Essex.[14] Lady Carlisle had written a letter on behalf of Batten to the Prince of Wales on the 14th.[15] Had she been gossiping? On July 4th "the whole business of fact concerning Captain Batten was reported to the Houses", and he was summoned to appear on the 8th and 18th. But he did not appear.[16]

Batten had realized that he was in a dangerous position and that he was suspected. He determined to join the Prince, since his plans had failed. After hiding himself in his house at Limehouse, he took with him Captain Elias Jordan and boarded the *Constant*

Warwick, at Leigh, near Southend, on her way to London. Captain Dare, her Captain, reported that Batten, "by his malignancy had poisoned the company and had carried the ship to the Prince's fleet." This happened somewhere between July 14th and 18th. For on the latter date the Prince wrote to thank the officers and men of the ship for bringing her over to him.[17]

At Helvoetsluys the Prince rewarded Batten with a knighthood. He was made Rear-Admiral, with Lord Willoughby of Parham, who also had changed sides, as Vice-Admiral, the Prince assuming chief command. On the 17th the Fleet sailed for the Downs, but contrary winds forced it into Yarmouth. On the way they captured a London ship, laden with cloth, sailing for Rotterdam. The town authorities in alarm, sent a deputation aboard, but the Prince reassured them by declaring he had no designs on the place. He asked them to supply him with fresh meat and other necessities, since he wanted to sail with the first favorable wind. As he paid for the supplies, the City Fathers raised no objection and on the afternoon of the 24th he sailed. With him were the *Convertine, Swallow, Antelope,* and the *Reformation.* The *Constant Warwick, Satisfaction, Crescent, Hind, Roebuck,* and *Pelican* were still revictualling in Holland.[18]

Warwick was having no easy time. On July 10th news came that the seamen and watermen, under color of petitioning Parliament, intended to come up the river in armed pinnaces and long-boats to create disturbances in the City.[19] The Lord Mayor and the Masters of the Watermen's Company were ordered to prevent this invasion. Thus on the 19th Captain Brandley, of the *Tenth Whelp* (14), was sent down to Erith to prevent the masters and seamen from going in barges to the Downs. He was to seize their arms, and to send up the men in custody.[20]

Good news, however, came from Fairfax and Rainsborough, who had joined him. Mersea Island had been seized to prevent all approach up the Colne from the sea. Three ships, laden with provisions for Colchester, had been driven back by two ships, which had come from Harwich.[21] Walmer Castle had been taken, though the other two Castles at Deal still held out. More troublesome news came from Portsmouth. The crews of the *John* (28) and the *Garland* (40) had refused to leave their ships until they were paid, and the only remedy for this sit-down strike was to pay them off. The crews of the *Tiger* (32), *Providence* (22), *Warwick* (22), *Dolphin,* and the *Hunter* (6), which were blockading the Colne, were in such a doubtful temper that Warwick reported he dared not send them to sea.[22] On July 22nd Moulton wrote from Bristol to say that the men of the *Dragon* (32) were in a state of mutiny.[23] It was an alarming state of affairs.

Further complications hampered Warwick. There were complaints of the poor state of the victuals. More serious was the lack of seamen, for more than half the ships were without a full crew. He suggested that men should be taken from forty colliers which had come into the Thames, invoking the aid of Trinity House, "in regard of the influence they have over the seamen." Above all he complained of the lack of frequent information of the proceedings of the revolted fleet and he asked for ketches to be taken up for this purpose.[24]

He had good reason to be worried, for the Prince was back in the Downs. Here he was joined by the ships from Holland with the exception of the *Roebuck* and the *Constant Warwick*.[25] On the way from Yarmouth the *Blackmoor Lady* (18) had been captured, with the *Guinea* (24), which were added to the fleet.[26] The *Constant Dacre,* a small frigate, however, had run ashore near Margate, and had been captured by parliamentary troops.[27] One may wonder why the Prince did not attack the small squadron off Harwich. In view of the temper of their crews they probably would have joined him, without firing a shot. This the Prince naturally could not know. He had only four ships with him and he dared not risk an action which might have resulted in the loss of vessels — he must keep his fleet in being at all costs.

Warwick's main problem, from his strategic position at the mouth of the Thames, was to divine which spot the royalist fleet might threaten. There were various rumors. Scarborough, Yarmouth, Hull, might be attacked, or an attempt even made to rescue the King from the Isle of Wight. Warwick's position enabled him to defend London, his main concern, and also to move to any threatened spot. His authority had been strengthened by allowing him to pardon such mutineers as might surrender within twenty days. Above all he was given power to fight, should he think it necessary.[28] On August 5th, Derby House suddenly awoke to the fact that Batten's clerk, Jorey, was still working in the Navy Office. There was a real risk that he was, or might be, passing on valuable news about naval preparations to the revolted fleet. He was forbidden to continue. It was specially necessary to conceal the weakness of Warwick's forces and the unreliability of some of the crews — men had been dismissed from the flagship, *St. George,* and from the *Fellowship.*[29]

The wisdom of Jorey's dismissal was justified when, on August 10th, Batten came into the Downs with the *Constant Warwick,* the *Roebuck,* and a Scots ship with the Earl of Lauderdale aboard. With him came Dutch soldiers, who were landed near Sandown Castle.[30] They were instantly charged by a strong body of horse and foot, who drove them back to their boats in confusion, with the loss of twenty men killed.[31] On the 14th a stronger force of eight hundred well-armed men were landed silently at night to relieve Deal and Sandown Castles. They got ashore without detection, and tried to work their way round behind the leaguer investing Deal. Then suddenly their lighted match was seen, as they approached through the darkness. Colonel Rich ordered one hundred horse and three hundred foot to charge, who bore down in a headlong fury. The thunder of the hooves and the flash of steel in the eerie darkness was too much for the advancing troops. They broke and fled. Many were killed and a hundred were captured. Lendal himself had led the seamen, "who were most for action before they came ashore, but in the time of service failed their leader."[32] This failure, with the fall of Deal Castle, made a return to Holland to get provisions inevitable.

Derby House now grew restive. On August 24th they wrote to Warwick reporting that "the ships in the Downs are in great disorder, and they lately have taken. several alarms, which instead of uniting them for resistance have increased their confusion, they expecting to have carried their business without fighting." They went on pointedly: "we conceive you would find no great difficulty with them, and are very sorry that you have not been before this time at sea." Time was passing; victuals were being consumed which they did not know how to replace; and the reputation of the Navy was being lost. They ended bluntly: "the ships in the Downs are but eleven, as we are informed. We desire your Lordship to take the first opportunity to go to sea, and proceed against the revolted ships and such as adhere to them, according to your commission and instructions."[33] But, before Warwick could comply, he was to find himself confronted by the royalist fleet instead.

The Prince had his troubles too. More serious than the shortage of supplies was the temper of the seamen, who were openly grumbling and discontented. Merchantmen, coming out of the Thames, had been captured and, to keep the good will of the owners, many of the vessels had been allowed to be ransomed. This was a bitter grievance to the seamen, who had hoped for prize-money. In their anger they laid the blame upon Batten and Jordan, declaring "they had spent their time in making bargains with the merchants to discharge these ships", and implying that they had put the money into their own pockets. Nor were they alone in their opinion. "This displeased many among us, made the sailors more insolent that they upbraided them to their faces with treason and corruption." It is clear that discipline already was hard to maintain and that Batten and Jordan had lost the respect of their men. With the loss of respect went the loss of authority and morale.

A great division of opinion arose as to the best course to take. The Prince, in view of both the shortage of provisions and the unlikelihood of obtaining support on land, had determined to sail for Holland to revictual. Batten wished to take the fleet to Scotland, others to go to the Isle of Wight to rescue the King. The seamen were firmly for going to the Thames to seize the colliers returning to London and then sink them in the narrowest part of the river, below Tilbury Hope. This would prevent Warwick from coming out to join the expected squadron from Portsmouth.[34]

On the 28th the Prince gave orders to sail for Holland. As soon as this was known the seamen decided otherwise. Four of the principal ships promptly steered for the Thames. Their crews wanted to be English sailors of an English King, not to threaten England from a base in a foreign country. They would rather, they declared, live on half rations than go back to Holland without striking a blow. Here was an opportunity which might never recur.[35] A swift decision had to be made. The Prince anchored and called a council of war. There was no course to take other than that upon which the seamen had already decided. The officers and men were asked to take a Covenant not to deliver up the Prince; but the seamen declared they had taken too many already, and that they were loyal to their Prince.[36]

Since Colchester had fallen on the 27th, the five ships blockading the Colne were free to join Warwick. They could not have come at a more opportune moment, for the two rival fleets were now roughly equal in strength:

WARWICK	Rate	Guns		ROYALISTS	Rate	Guns
St. George	2	50		Reformation	2	45
Unicorn	2	50		Swallow	3	36
Adventure	4	30		Antelope	3	36
Tiger	4	32		Convertine	3	40
Providence	4	22		Constant Warwick		30
Fellowship	4	28		Satisfaction	5	20
Hector	5	22		Roebuck	6	14
Warwick	5	22		Hind	6	17
Tenth Whelp	5	14		Pelican	6	12
Recovery	5	20		Crescent	6	14
Greyhound	6	12		Guinea		30
Nicodemus	6	10		Blackmoor Lady		18
Hunter	6	6		Love		
Dolphin	6			Five other ships		
Dogger boat						312
		318				

PORTSMOUTH	Rate	Guns
Lion	2	45
Nonsuch	4	32
Phoenix	4	32
Mary Rose	4	28
Weymouth	6	12
Hart	6	10
Robert	6	12
Lily	6	8
Dove	6	8
Three Ketches		
		187

When Warwick learned that Royalists were off the mouth of the Thames, he sailed down the river on the ebb-tide, anchoring west of Shoeburyness. Soon the enemy were sighted approaching, so Warwick weighed and worked towards the Oaze Shoal to gain the wind. At the sight of his fleet, cleared for action, the royalist seamen begged the Prince to go below. He firmly refused to do so, telling them his honor was more to him than his safety. Then, with the true instinct of a leader, he took up a screwed gun and said: "I am confident with this piece to-day to shoot Warwick through the head, if he dares in person to appear in the fight." Any doubts the seamen had of the Prince were now laid to rest. They were filled with resolution as they recognized that, young though he might be, he was a man who would lead them.[37] Night now began to draw on, and both fleets anchored within uneasy sight of each other.

A royalist account says the Prince had eleven fighting ships and some merchantmen "which pretended to fight for us." The council had discharged five among some cloth ships and others, "which had one hundred and twenty guns, more for honour than for use." This meant that the guns were used merely for saluting purposes. Both ships and guns would have been useless in action. Lord Willoughby, the royalist Vice-Admiral, with "stout Jordan" as his captain, anchored a mile ahead of the main body and within a mile and a half of Warwick.[38] At 8 p.m. the Prince summoned Warwick to strike his flag and to surrender his fleet, upon a promise of general pardon. Warwick replied that he had been appointed by both Houses and that he would continue to fly his flag, "notwithstanding the opposition of any person whatsoever." He then called a council of war, at which it was decided that each ship should weigh and keep the wind and, if attacked, each ship should aid the other: action was to be avoided until the arrival of the Portsmouth squadron, now hourly expected, for Warwick would then be superior in ships and gun-power.[39]

Next morning, on the 30th, for the first time in English history, two fleets of Englishmen stood ready to battle with each other. As the flood-tide swept up, each fleet weighed and tried to gain the wind. Warwick, however, held on to it, and for some hours the contest of seamanship continued. Warwick expected battle at any moment. Anxiously he maintained his declining action, eagerly scanning the horizon for the hoped-for Portsmouth ships. Like Jellicoe, centuries later, he was the one man who could lose the war, or the results of it, in a single action. If he was defeated, London might declare for the Royalists. The Portsmouth squadron might be defeated, might flee for safety, or even join the Prince, and the command of the sea would pass to the Royalists. The Irish Army might be transported to England and the Civil War might begin again.

His decision to decline action was the right one. Yet in itself it might contain the seeds of disaster, for his crews were disaffected — to what extent he could not tell. Such inaction might lead them to go over to the Prince. This possibility Derby House had ignored when they had ordered Warwick to attack in the Downs. Suddenly a violent storm blew up at four in the afternoon, the wind shifting from SSW to NNW. Both fleets were forced to anchor, Warwick off Shoeburyness, and the Prince some three miles to seaward. Once again night came down on the two fleets.[40]

If the intervention of the elements came like a decree of Providence in Warwick's favor, for the Royalists it brought the ruin of all their hopes. For them immediate victory was essential: Warwick must be brought to action and defeated. The storm had snatched this away from them. Their provisions and their drink were completely exhausted. Early next day at a council of war Warwick decided to abide by his policy. Should the Royalists retreat, however, he would keep close touch with them, so as to be able to support the Portsmouth squadron, if it arrived. At all costs he must keep his fleet in being. His decision was also based on the danger that if the great ships engaged, they might be forced on the sand shoals, both his own vessels and those of the foe, "whereby the strength of the Navy would be much impaired."[41]

Still there was no sign of the Portsmouth ships. Then, about 10 a.m., the royalist Vice-Admiral started to weigh anchor. Was he going to attack? To Warwick's infinite relief he withdrew down the Swin, followed by the rest of his fleet. Warwick followed at a distance, using his smaller ships to keep in close contact with the retreating vessels. Slowly throughout the day the enemy worked their way seawards. At 6 p.m. Ball in the *Adventure*, fired a gun. It was a signal that he had sighted a fleet ahead of the Royalists. This must be the Portsmouth squadron. Warwick crowded on all sail — here was the opportunity for which he had waited — the Royalists would be caught between two fires. But Warwick was doomed to bitter disappointment. The distant ships were merely a fleet of colliers.[42]

Warwick anchored in the middle of the Gunfleet, about a league and a half short of the Royalists. Then he heard a gunshot in their fleet and he saw them begin to haul up their sails. To his mind this meant that they were anchoring for the night. But after darkness fell, the Royalists sailed. Suddenly Pattison, master of the *Reformation*, saw a light. The Prince, Rupert, and the seamen eagerly clustered around him. They all agreed that it must be the Portsmouth ships. Rupert at once persuaded the Prince of Wales to steer for them. But Batten, who had come up on deck, declared firmly they were only colliers, and induced the Prince to resume his former course.[43] The *Swallow* and two or three more ships nevertheless stood with the approaching vessels. The Prince sent a ketch to warn them that if they fell amongst these ships they were to say they were merchantmen and then sail after the Vice-Admiral, who carried three great lights at his stern. But the ketch could not find the *Swallow* and her escorts in the darkness. At 9 p.m. they discovered they were in the midst of the Portsmouth squadron. The Royalists, although it was pitch dark, were able to identify each ship. They hailed one. She answered she was the *Mary Rose* (28), of the parliamentry fleet, and that they were waiting for a tide to carry them into the Thames. The *Swallow* (36) and her consorts were about to run her aboard. The wind, however, thrust them away on to another frigate of twelve guns. In the confusion someone raised a cry, "fire a gun to give our Admiral notice." Two shots were fired, which "hurt the enemy frigate." But now the *Swallow's* Captain realized it was hopeless to engage so many vessels and he persuaded his crew to break off the action.

The writer of the account adds, however, that they might have boarded the frigate and carried her off, for the *Mary Rose's* crew had told them the ship was ill-manned. The lights of the Royalists' Admiral had caused them such alarm that there was not a single candle alight in any ship. The writer comments: "how great an opportunity was missed, had the Prince gone to them, we had had them without a blow, and by consequence entrapped Warwick the next day."[44]

Yet in the opinion of others, "the presence of the Prince was not to be adventured in a dark sea-fight, especially as another enemy fleet being, for ought we could certainly know, within hearing." This is probably the truer view.[45] It might have been possible to overcome the Portsmouth squadron, but the noise of the gunfire must have attracted Warwick's notice and he was not the man to lie idle at such a moment. Unless the squadron could have been overcome instantly, the Prince would have been caught between two fires. Moreover, naval tactics at this period did not provide for night fighting. In the last resource the lack of water and provisions must have compelled the Royalists to yield in any long battle. Warwick had preserved his fleet in being, as he was bound to do. But so also had the Royalists. They had failed to destroy him, but Warwick also had failed to win back the revolted fleet. It continued to constitute a potential danger to Parliament's control of the sea, to the safety of the merchant shipping, and to Parliament's prestige at home and abroad.

The second Civil War practically ended with the defeat by Cromwell of the invading Scots at Preston, on August 17th. With the exception of South Wales, Kent, Essex, and Nottingham, the country had remained quiet. Sir Marmaduke Langdale's rising in Yorkshire ended with the Scots defeat at Preston. An attempt by some sailors to seize Portsmouth had been detected before they could act. The people were weary of war and wished peace. However much they sympathized with the sufferings of the King, they were not prepared to fight to redress them. Even if Warwick had been defeated it is difficult to see how the Royalists, leaderless and without cohesion, could have been victorious. They would have had little chance against the dour, determined, disciplined troops, led by the resolute and experienced generals. It now remained for Warwick to prove himself by securing the revolted fleet once more for the service of Parliament.

CHAPTER XII

1648

Warwick Fails and Is Replaced

Bad weather kept Warwick at anchor until September 2nd, when he picked up the Portsmouth squadron and proceeded to Aldeburgh. From here he sailed to the Downs, where his arrival brought about the surrender of Sandown Castle on the fifth.[1]

News now came that the Prince had anchored at Helvoetslyus on September 2nd. His presence there, to the minds of Derby House, called for instant action.[2] They urged Warwick to sail for Goree or Helvoetslyus, at the mouth of the Maas, before the Prince could strengthen himself. At the same time they instructed their agent in Holland, Doctor Isaac Dorislaus, to prevent the sale of captured cargoes — the Prince had taken several merchantmen.[3] But Warwick's task was difficult. Apart from fitting out his ships, he was conscious that he no longer possessed the same hold over his men as of old. The sense of failure depressed him. The probable fate of his brother, the Earl of Holland, must have troubled him, since it could not fail to make him personally suspect too. Such conditions did not make for decisive leadership.

Alarming news came from the Scilly Islands. On August 6th the inhabitants had captured the Governor and his officers as they left church. In their absence St. Mary's Castle had already been seized. Orders were sent to Sir Hardress Waller, Governor of Plymouth, to deal with the matter, but as no naval forces were available to cover a military landing, nothing could be done.[4] The elated Scillians sent to ask the Prince for help. Captain Skinner, in the *Crescent* (14), was sent off with provisions.[5]

Should the Prince make his base there, as Skinner's presence seemed to indicate, the shipping trade would be endangered, and

THE *Constant Reformation*

not the least, the communications with Bristol, the neighboring ports, and above all with Ireland. In conjunction with the Channel Islands the shipping in the Channel itself would be imperiled. From Dorislaus came another rumor: the revolted fleet might be going to Scotland.[6] Once again Derby House urged Warwick to sail for Goree, although they left him free to do as he thought best. To their minds too much time had gone by. It was vital to deal with the Prince's fleet.[7]

At last, on the 17th, Warwick sailed for Goree in the *St. George* (50). His Vice-Admiral was Richard Haddock in the *Unicorn* (50), with Sir George Ayscue in the *Lion* (40) as Rear-Admiral. With them went the *Phoenix* (32), *Nonsuch* (32), *Adventure* (32), *Tiger* (32), *Mary Rose* (26), *Providence* (22), *Fellowship* (28), *Hector* (22), *Warwick* (22), *Recovery* (20), *Greyhound* (12), *Tenth Whelp* (14), *Nicodemus* (10), *Hunter* (10), *Dolphin*, and three ketches.[8]

They arrived off Goree on the 19th, whereupon Warwick held a council of war. Alexander Bence, an Admiralty Commissioner (was he sent as a political commissar to watch Warwick?), moved earnestly "to go into the river." This was agreed. The fleet then anchored four miles from the revolted fleet. The decision was fortunate, for a great tempest of wind and rain sprang up, so that, in Bence's words, "had we rid without we had all been dispersed, if not lost."[9] That night Warwick sent in a summons to the Prince to surrender his fleet, but the Prince had left for the Hague. Not until the 24th did his answer arrive, demanding the surrender of Warwick's ships. It is devoutly to be hoped that Warwick did not know that the Prince was suffering from small-pox, when he read the letter. Although it was a delicate diplomatic situation, action was essential and a *fait accompli* would probably have solved the matter to the relief of all concerned, even the Dutch. Certainly the resolute men in power in England would not have paused for such diplomatic niceties. More precious time had been lost. It seems strange that no time limit was fixed for the Prince's answer. Already that curious inertia which characterized Warwick's actions had begun. The opportunity to seize the enemy's fleet had passed. On the 22nd, a Committee of the Estates of Holland came aboard to proclaim Dutch neutrality, demanding from Warwick a promise not to commit any hostile act in their harbors. He replied he had no such intention: he was entrusted by Parliament to reduce the Kingdom's fleet to their obedience; if affronted, however, he would defend himself.[10] This practically bound him to a passive role.

The revolted fleet was not Warwick's only worry. He had been asked by Derby House to send ships to act in consort with Cromwell's troops at Newcastle and to protect the Channel shipping, since Cromwell was about to march in pursuit of the defeated Scots army. But even Warwick could not conjure up ships from the vasty deep. To him the Channel was the more pressing problem. For, on the 21st, he ordered the *Elizabeth* (32), under Captain Reeve, with Joseph Jordan in the *Expedition* (18) and Wheeler in the *Cygnet* (10), to ply between Land's End and Scilly. They were to take good care not to go within range of the guns at St. Mary's Castle. Then they were to ply as far as Weymouth. As news had come that some of the smaller vessels of the revolted fleet had gone to Guernsey, Wheeler and Jordan were to sail there. If they could, they were to surprise these ships or drive them away. Wheeler was then to put into St. Malo, to see if any ships required convoy. Then he was to rejoin Reeve and Jordan in the Channel.[11]

On the 25th a fresh complication occurred. Tromp arrived at Goree with sixteen ships to protect Dutch neutrality. To make his intention unmistakeably clear, he anchored between the rival fleets. He passed by Warwick without saluting him, but dipped his sails and fired five guns to the royalist Admiral. This left no doubt about where Dutch sympathies lay. On the same day Strickland, Parliament's Envoy to Holland, sent news to England that the Royalists were preparing five ships to oppose Warwick. They had planted many of the ships' guns ashore and had quartered soldiers to defend the ships.[12]

On the 30th Derby House replied to both Strickland and Dorislaus. They complained the Dutch had not only allowed supplies to go to the Prince, but had also allowed him to plant guns ashore. The Dutch had even given him carriages to mount his guns, "to the great danger of our fleet, which carriages, we conceive, are had from some of the people under the State's obedience. All respect is shown to the revolters' ships by the States, but they do not the like to ours. Besides which they suffer formed companies to march to their assistance, and fire-ships to be provided against our fleet." The Envoys were instructed to make representations to this effect to the Dutch Government.[13]

To Warwick Derby House wrote more sharply. Nothing had been done against the enemy, "which we thought might best have been done at your first approach, before time had been given them to consult for their defence." Derby House continued even more plainly: "we conceive to lie there upon the bare defence and to do nothing, unless provoked, will not reduce the revolted ships." They observed that it was possible that the enemy, lying in security to refit and supply, would be able to come out, if Warwick had to retire. They suggested, though they left it to Warwick's discretion to do what he thought best, another course of action. If he could not find an opportunity to attack, "it might be more honourable to return to the Downs, than to be forced to do so, either by the increased force of the enemy, or through lack of victuals." Short of actual recall they could not have expressed their disapproval of Warwick's inaction more severely.[14] The letter made Warwick and his captains uneasy and uncomfortable. Among themselves they spoke of "Greenheaded seamen and ignorant landsmen." This may have been aimed at Bence, who probably had expressed his disapproval of the inaction from the first. But how could Warwick attack when he did not know the posture of the foe? Guns too were ashore. If they had been clapped aboard, the foe might have cut their cables and forced them ashore, or even have blown them up.[15] "Methinks they did protest too much."

Before Warwick received his superiors' letter, he had written on October 2nd saying that he was in urgent need of victuals. Some of his ships were nearly out of supplies. From "these parts" he could only obtain seven days' supply for the whole fleet. He asked for six weeks' provisions for two thousand men to be sent as speedily as possible, which would enable him, if any of the revolted ships got out, to send vessels after them to capture them. He asked for bills of exchange to be sent to Holland, "to content such of the seamen as shall earnestly press for money", for he feared "the want thereof may otherwise hazard a distemper in some of them."[16]

But if Warwick was uncertain of the temper of his men, the situation in the royalist fleet was hardly more satisfactory. Sir Francis Doddington, writing to Sir Edward Hyde, declared the appearance of Warwick's fleet had filled them with alarm. They were in no condition to resist any attack. Already aboard the *Hind* there was disorder. Quarrels and dissensions were rampant. At the end of October Willoughby was dismissed, and Prince Rupert took his place as Admiral. Batten and Jordan were still unpopular with the seamen, Batten indeed having retired to the Hague. He had refused to go aboard Rupert's ship "because of malice against him" and Jordan was sent in his place. But he too soon joined Batten.[17] These changes of command were to the royalist advantage, since as a leader Rupert was worth the other three together, and more.

In the meanwhile the *Crescent* had reached Scilly on October 13th. She returned safely to Jersey with the ex-governor, Buller, on board, with some of his officers. The captives were handed over to Sir George Carteret and imprisoned in Elizabeth Castle. On November 11th the *Crescent* again sailed with supplies for Scilly. On her return she sighted a ship, which she took to be a Londoner, returning from Spain. She gave chase, rapidly gaining upon her. Then, to Skinner's astonishment and horror, she suddenly threw off the covers concealing her guns and opened fire. He had run into the *Elizabeth* (32), which had deliberately lured her within range. Against such overwhelming odds Skinner had no option but to surrender and the *Crescent* was taken into Plymouth, where Skinner was imprisoned. After a short while, he managed to escape and to find refuge with friends at Topsham. On February 7th, 1649, he got back to Jersey.[18]

This heartening little success in the Channel was followed by dramatic events at Helvoetslyus. The withdrawal of Batten and Jordan led to the secession of the *Constant Warwick*, late in the evening of November 5th. Probably Batten, as part owner, had arranged this unexpected event, which at last roused Warwick to action. On the 8th he moved in and anchored by Tromp. The Dutch Admiral had sent off eight of his sixteen vessels, possibly because some of his captains had not remained neutral, but more probably because Warwick's inaction did not justify his keeping so many

ships, so expensive to maintain.[19] Some of Warwick's ships now
closed with the Royalists, with the result that the *Hind* (17) surrendered the same night. Next day Warwick was encouraged to
move further in still. But Tromp did the same. Rupert thereupon
slipped his cables and retreated up the harbor with the *Reformation,
Antelope, Convertine, Swallow, Satisfaction, Love, Roebuck, Guinea,*
and the *Blackmoor Lady*.[20]

Everything now depended upon which fleet could gain the
Sluice, or narrow entrance to the inner harbor, the strategic point
and the key to the operations. As the *Reformation* lay nearest to
the Sluice, Warwick sent the *Tenth Whelp* to forestall her by getting
in first. Both ships made for the Sluice with all the speed they could
muster. The *Tenth Whelp*, a smaller and faster vessel, got ahead.
Captain Allen of the *Guinea* was on shore. He gave the impression
he was a friend, by calling to the crew to throw him a rope so he
could make her fast. Instead a boat brought it to him and then,
as she was putting off, he let go and the *Whelp* fell back.[21] Another
account says that George Rosewell of the *Love* cut the *Whelp's* cables
from the shore. A report from the parliamentary side, which sounds
as if it was written by Bence, tells a different story. "They all hastened
to gain the Sluice, which we might have prevented, had there not been
slackness in some. We had one frigate in their Admiral's way, and
lay before the Sluice's mouth. Where our Vice-Admiral [Haddock]
might have been also, if ordered, and then the valiant Prince would
not have run his head into that hole, as presently afterwards he did,
by carrying a hawser on shore, and the Guinea frigate also. The
rest being at an anchor as near the pier as they could get."[22]

What does emerge is that the *Reformation* got into the Sluice
first, despite the efforts to stop her. During the night the cables of
the *Swallow, Guinea,* and *Blackmoor Lady* were cut, and they were
all hauled into the Sluice. Still outside were the *Antelope, Convertine, Satisfaction,* and the *Love*. Early next morning the *Love* also
cut her cables and ran for the Sluice, but one of Warwick's ships
laid her across her hawse, forcing her to anchor. Though some of
the soldiers aboard, who had been recruited in Holland, shouted
for her to fire, the *Love* surrendered instead. Warwick now ordered
ships to secure the *Satisfaction*. By night her captain had agreed to

surrender, provided such persons as wished to go ashore could do so with their baggage. To this Warwick agreed, and once more the *Satisfaction* was his. That night the harassed Royalists succeeded in hauling in the *Antelope,* leaving the *Convertine* still outside. Of the rest of the royalist fleet, the *Crescent* had been captured while the *Pelican* simply vanished. Warwick, reporting his success, wrote that he intended to remain a few days longer, "to pursue some opportunity and then would come home, since I fear the great ships will be damaged if they lie long aground."[23]

An effort was made to capture the *Convertine,* but Rupert had secretly filled her with officers, who lay hidden upon their stomachs, with only stones and pikes to defend themselves. However, a boy in maintop of the attacking frigate saw them, and they "quitted that design, the frigate sheering off again." Eventually the *Convertine* got in.[24] In order to protect the inner harbor she was moored "lying athwart, with her starboard side to the enemy." Batteries, armed with guns from the ships, were erected, and both they and the *Convertine* were defended by three hundred Dutch soldiers. A double purpose was served. Rupert's seamen, many of whom were anxious to respond to Warwick's invitation to desert, were thus prevented from doing so, although some made their way overland to join the parliamentary fleet.[25]

With the rival ships so close to one another many disturbances took place ashore. The Royalists complained that Warwick sent his seamen ashore to mingle with their old companions, "to work upon and corrupt many of the seamen that it appeared afterwards that many were debauched; some whereof went on board his ships, others stayed to do mischief." Warwick also experienced the same trouble. "Some of the *Falcon's* company, whereof seven being ashore, only three returned, the other four engaged with the revolters." Drunken brawls and quarrels marked the meetings of the rival crews ashore.[26]

On November 15th Derby House wrote to thank Warwick for his success. They hoped he would be able to finish his work before the winter. As some of the revolted ships had come in, they suggested he would be able to spare some of his vessels, for they were daily receiving complaints of the infesting of the western seas by

Irish privateers. They asked with good reason for ships from the Winter Guard both to deal with them and to reduce Scilly. On September 30th Colonel Heane, Governor of Weymouth, had complained, "the seas are pestered with Irish men-of-war, no less than thirty in a fleet." The Isle of Portland had been beset by them. If he had not had men ready, it would have been taken. The Island was so convenient for the privateers that it would have been a miracle if any ships passed safely either east or westwards.[27]

Derby House now reeled under a great and unexpected shock, for, on November 21st, Warwick sailed for England, arriving two days later. He justified his action by pointing out the danger of being frozen in — the fleet would thus be immobile and in danger of capture by the soldiers. He had been denied the safety of the inner harbor, his provisions were running short, and none could be obtained in Holland. He concluded rather strangely: "the mariners, by conversing with the revolters, might have been drawn into distempers: whereof there was some experience in some of the *Falcon's* company." Derby House perhaps might have considered this a somewhat feeble excuse for ceasing to blockade a weakened enemy.[28]

Bence wrote from the Downs on November 23rd, severely criticizing Warwick's action. He mentioned the Admiral's fear of ice and of the lack of victuals and added the significant sentence: "for these reasons and some others best known to himself, he did resolve, with these ships undisposed of, to go into the Downs." Obviously he thought Warwick's reasons futile and he was thoroughly dissatisfied with his return home. Bence, however, was an Admiralty Commissioner, with little experience at sea. The danger from ice and the lack of supplies were real. Yet surely frigates might have been left on watch to warn Warwick, should Rupert attempt to sail.[29]

Derby House reacted with surprising mildness. On the 27th they asked Warwick to send ships to Plymouth to protect shipping against the privateers.[30] On December 1st they warned him that Rupert's fleet was expected to go to Ireland. He was to see that all places where water or supplies could be obtained should be guarded and that all ships should be warned. Such victuals as he needed to enable him to pursue the Royalists would be instantly sent. They concluded with

the information that they had just learned that Rupert would sail
on December 9th[31]

On the day before they wrote, Warwick held a council, at
which Captains Haddock, Moulton, Penrose, and Harrison were
present. All were clearly aware that they needed to justify their
coming home. They asserted that it was impossible to get into the
Sluice for safety against the ice, for Tromp had not only taken in
his warships there, but any Dutch vessels that were in the harbor.
Even had they been able to go in, they were afraid that their own
men might be corrupted by the revolters. Since no provisions could
be obtained, even from England, they had sailed for home.

The condition of the fleet was serious. Most of the ships were
foul from long service. Stores of every kind were needed — the
vessels in the Downs had only three weeks victuals left, which were
defective and stinking, so that the seamen were sick. For this reason
the council feared they might even refuse to take in fresh supplies.
Pay was lacking and winter clothing needed. The upper decks of
some of the ships leaked and let in water. Accordingly the captains
asked for four months pay for two thousand men, for sweet and
well-conditioned victuals, and for one thousand four hundred men
to be sent them at once. They recommended that a gratuity be paid
the seamen for their services in the past expedition, adding that "the
same is humbly expected by them, and their disappointment may be
of very prejudicial consequence."

Of the Winter Guard of thirty-two ships,* six were in the
Downs, three at the Isle of Wight, ten in the west, two on the north
coast, eight refitting in the Thames or at Portsmouth, and the *Lion*
and the *Fellowship* would have to be laid up. They proposed to send
the *Falcon* from the Downs to warn shipping of the expected coming
out of Rupert and to advise them to keep together for safety. The
Phoenix, Nonsuch, Tiger, Dragon, Providence, and *Weymouth* were
to be recalled from the west to strengthen Warwick's ships in the
Downs, leaving the *Assurance, Elizabeth, Expedition,* and *Cygnet* to
guard the west.

*Appendix N

They ended on a pessimistic note. They would do their best, but unless pay, the gratuity, and good victuals were sent, "little or nothing can be expected from the ships here, for the prevention of the revolters designs."[32] To this despondent letter Derby House did not reply, since its last meeting took place on December 19th. On On February 7th, 1649, the Committe was dissolved.

Warwick now had with him the *St. George* (50), *Unicorn* (50), *Mary Rose* (38), *Phoenix* (32), *Nonsuch* (32), *Tiger* (32), *Dragon* (32), *Providence* (22), *Greyhound* (8), and *Weymouth* (12). Rupert's fleet had been reduced to seven warships, with five other ships, probably of no strength. But Warwick did nothing. Even if blockade were impossible, surely frigates might have been kept on watch. An inertia seemed to possess Warwick and his captains. The driving force to tackle the urgent work at hand was nowhere evident. If such had been apparent at Goree, it was even more so now in the Downs. Authorities in London were conscious of it, for criticism was being freely expressed, not only by Bence.

Walter Strickland, writing from the Hague in January, 1649, spoke plainly. "The Prince's men bring in our merchants like slaves and captives: a few ships staying here had in a short time undone them for ever." He criticized Warwick personally and directly. "I know not what fate hath accompanied our resolutions at sea, but certainly the worst hath ever been followed, or else a company of fellows, destitute of all things, could not have undone us, by wanting all things when we wanted nothing. . . . I hope things will be better carried. Their consciences ought to check them, whose doing nothing hath brought many to beggary. It is no great joy to see our merchants beggared, and Batten, that arch traitor, in a way of reconciliation. He made a fleet revolt, and must be saved for part of a ship. Truly, sir, we are too willing to save enemies and lose our friends.[33]

The last remark obviously referred to the *Constant Warwick*, of which both Batten and Warwick were part owners. Batten and Jordan had returned to England, availing themselves of Warwick's amnesty. Strickland clearly attributed Batten's pardon to the fact that he brought back the *Constant Warwick*, the price Warwick was willing to pay for his interest in the ship.

If there was inertia on Warwick's part, there was energy in

Rupert's actions. He too had his problems. How might he best use his small fleet? The failure of the royalist risings in England had placed the Independents firmly in power and a new base must be sought elsewhere. Not much longer could Rupert rely upon the benevolent neutrality of the Dutch. His obvious base was Ireland, where he decided to take his ships. But there was much to do: men and money were lacking; discipline was at a low level. The manner in which Rupert tackled these problems was illustrated by the episode of the *Antelope*, whose crew disobeyed an order to help rig the flagship. Rupert at once boarded the *Antelope*, where he found the men sullenly gathered together in a body. It was a moment for instant action. Rupert advanced fiercely upon them, sprang at the ringleader, lifted him up by his waist, held him over the ship's side, and swore to drop him into the sea if the mutiny did not instantly cease. The suddenness and surprise of this action wrought such terror upon the rest of the crew that they forthwith returned to duty.[34]

Money was furnished by the Queen of Bohemia, Rupert's mother, and by the sale of the *Antelope's* guns, as she was unseaworthy. Despite the ice, or because there was little or none at all, raiders were sent out. Since there were no ships to stop them, prizes were taken. The *Thomas*, the *William and Margaret*, the *Susan*, and the *Elizabeth and May* were all snapped up, brought in, and sold. In January Rupert was able to send out six small vessels on a raiding expedition, which had a prosperous time.[35] The *Roebuck* brought in a collier, with three hundred pounds aboard. The *Charles*, the *Guinea* renamed, secured the *Exchange* of Ipswich, which was renamed the *James* and added to fleet. The *Thomas* too took another vessel. And still Warwick remained inactive in the Downs.[36]

On January 1st Rupert sailed for Ireland with the following ships:

Constant Reformation (45)	Prince Rupert, Admiral
Convertine (40)	Prince Maurice, Vice-Admiral
Swallow (36)	Sir John Mennes, Rear-Admiral
Charles (40)	Captain Allen
Thomas (24)	Captain Barnaby Burley
James (29)	Captain Braithwaite
Elizabeth hoy	

The *Antelope* was left behind, and was eventually destroyed by Captain Richard Badiley of the *Happy Entrance*. At the end of June, 1649, his boats crept into the harbor by night and burned her.[37] The *Roebuck* (30) and the *Blackmoor Lady* (18) were at sea, with orders to join Rupert off the Scillies.[38]

In company with Rupert were three Dutch East-Indiamen. His fleet thus appeared to be made up of nine ships — one of the Dutchmen was of a thousand tons. Captain Moulton, lying in the Downs in the *St. George* (50), with the *Happy Entrance* (40), *Constant Warwick* (22), and the *Satisfaction* (20), was not prepared to face the odds of nine to four. He made no attempt to stop Rupert.[39] He may have been right, yet it seems incredible that, with a Winter Guard of thirty-two ships, Rupert should have been allowed to sail without any attempt to bring him to action. It may well have been that some ships were in dock after long service at sea. Warwick, too, may have been forced by political clamor to disperse his ships to protect the trade routes, but this he had resolutely refused to do in time past. Now he seems to have become a different man, with the sense of failure looming over him. Had he become sensitive to criticism? Did the inertia which possessed him lead him to take the easy and popular course? In the old days he would have never have concentrated upon the minor danger at the expense of the major one.

After the execution of the King on January 30, 1649, on February 23 the new Council of State dismissed Warwick from his post as Lord High Admiral. The trial of his brother for armed rebellion was pending and Warwick could not be continued in charge of the fleet. Vigorous men and vigorous measures would be needed to deal with the danger from Rupert. Warwick's recent actions and administration had given no sign of vigor. On the contrary, his policy of masterly inactivity, though preserving the fleet in being, had practically blunted the Navy as a fighting force. A blight had settled upon the fleet. The Independents were men of action — action had won them their victories — and they had looked in vain for such in Warwick. And so Edward Popham, Robert Blake, and Richard Deane were appointed as "Commissioners to command the fleet at sea" in his stead.

Thus Warwick passes sadly and somewhat ingloriously from the scene. He vanishes almost unknown from naval history. Yet he deserves to be remembered. Without him Parliament could not have won their victory. He gave the struggle an essential cohesion and unity by sea which was lacking in the military command. He had secured the fleet for Parliament. He had been a first-rate administrator, with an eye for detail both in material and personnel. He had been a sailor's admiral, with a hold on their affection and trust, which he had lost only at the end of his career. His strategic ability had given Parliament the comand of the sea. His instinct for the important focal points had secured Hull and the North Sea. His western squadron had secured Plymouth and the Channel approaches. His possession of Milford Haven had prevented the landing of Irish troops there as well as holding the royalist troops in South Wales in check. From this base he had neutralized the capture of Bristol, while the Irish Guard had been able to operate against Ireland and the privateers. From the Downs he had controlled the Channel, and so had prevented any possibility of foreign intervention. By sending a squadron to Carrickfergus he had enabled the Liverpool ships to stop the transport of the troops from Ireland to England.

All this he had done with a minimum of ships. He had achieved so much because he had firmly kept the reins of control in his own hands. By envisaging the war as a whole he had coordinated the work of his squadrons, so that they acted as a whole and never became independent units. Thus he was able to plan and direct the naval operations. He was strong enough to resist the clamors of the merchants to disperse his ships in a wild chase after the privateers. He never sacrificed his major objectives to minor ones. As far as he was able, he protected the merchant shipping by the means of convoys.

Through the constant patrolling of his squadrons he had prevented troops and munitions from reaching the King in any large numbers. His control of the outer lines of communication had enabled his amphibious force, accustomed to operate at long distances from their bases, to compensate for the unwillingness of the soldiers to move outside their own counties — an enormously important fact during the Civil War. The Navy could swiftly bring supplies, land troops and seamen to fight, and disembark cannon, and these could be rapidly brought into action. Thus hard-pressed places and troops in widely scattered spots, adjacent to the seaboard, could be supported. Above all, they were thereby bound into the pattern of the war.

Warwick had the ability to select good commanders, perhaps the real test of a leader. They were men who could take responsibility. They could make decisions for themselves, as the circumstances of the struggle made necessary, acting as they had to far away from their central command. Moreover, he could see clearly the limitations of his ships. He had learned that they could not relieve besieged forces, though they could support them, and so he insisted that relief must in the end come by land. To realize limitations is once again the mark of a real leader.

Despite the neglect of Parliament to furnish him with ships, supplies, victuals, and money Warwick had held tenaciously to his purpose. Thereby he had assured himself of the loyalty and trust of his seamen. Magnificently they responded to his leadership. The swift action of his ships had done much to prevent the spread of the royalist reaction in the Second Civil War. Though he failed to regain the revolted ships, he had boldly faced their leaders in the Downs with firmness and courage. Then by a declining action he had preserved London, saving the remainder of the fleet. He had faced the revolted fleet, not knowing how far he could rely upon the men in his own ships. This again required courage, and Warwick was not found wanting. Yet more than courage was needed. Determined and instant action was necessary. If an attack upon the revolted fleet in the Downs was impossible, surely an immediate action on arrival at Goree should have been launched. Lack of determination and resolution begat inertia. Not only was Rupert's fleet not destroyed, but it was allowed freedom to raid and to escape. Warwick was no longer the Warwick of old.

Yet the sense of failure and the lack of confidence in his men which blighted his final command must not be allowed to detract from his overall achievement. To the great leaders, such as Fairfax and Cromwell, who justly won fame, Warwick's name must be added. He and his squadrons did much to ensure the victory of Parliament.

Nevertheless, his name has vanished into obscurity and his fleet has been forgotten. To understand the greatness of Warwick as an Admiral, and to realize the important part his ships played, is surely to view the Civil War in a truer proportion and perspective.

Appendices
Ship Lists

A. SUMMER GUARD 1642 [Penn 1. 22]

Ship	Rate		Commander	Lieutenant	Men	Tons
James	2		Earl of Warwick, Admiral	Slingsby	260	875
St. George	2		Sir John Mennes R. A.	William Smith	260	792
Rainbow	2		William Batten V. A.	Lutten	260	721
Reformation	2		Sir David Murray	Stansby	260	732
Victory	2		Captain Fogge	Fogge	240	742
Henrietta						
Maria	2	"	Hatch	Watts	250	793
Unicorn	2	"	Trenchfield	Somerton	260	769
Charles	2	"	Swanley	Darey	250	810
Vanguard	2	"	Blith	Blith	250	751
Entrance	3	"	Owen	Bowen	160	767
Garland	3	"	Slingsby	Walters	170	767
Lion	3	"	Prysse	Hill	170	602
Antelope	3	"	Burley	Willby	160	512
Mary Rose	4	"	Fox		100	321
Expedition	4	"	Wake		100	301
Greyhound	6	"	Wheeler		50	126

MERCHANT SHIPS

Ship	Rate		Commander	Lieutenant	Men	Tons
Martin	Capt.		George Martin	Hackinger	210	700
Sampson	"		Ashley	Andrew	130	600
Caesar	"		Joseph Jordan	Norton	180	600
London	"		John Stephens	Pomeroy	180	600
Unicorn	"		Edward Johnson		143	475
Mayflower	"		Peter Andrews		121	450
Bonaventure	"		George Swanley		120	400
Prosperous	"		William Driver		120	400
Hercules	"		Moyer		150	350
Paragon	"		Leonard Harris		150	350
Hopeful Luke	"		Lee		105	350
Golden Angel	"		Walker		105	350
Exchange	"		Lucas		89	325
Maidenhead	"		Lewton		90	300
Providence	"		William Swanley		81	271
Jocelyn	"		Partridge		60	200

HIS MAJESTY'S SHIPS FOR THE IRISH SEA

Ship	Rate		Commander	Lieutenant	Men	Tons
Swallow	3	Capt.	Thomas Kettleby		150	360
Bonaventure	3	"	Henry Stradling		160	557

MERCHANT SHIPS

Ship	Rate		Commander	Lieutenant	Men	Tons
Discovery	Capt.		John Brokhaven		144	380
Ruth	"		Robert Constable		120	400
Employment	"		Thomas Ashley		132	440
Peter	"		Peter Strong		81	270
Pennington	"		Elias Jordan		36	235
Fellowship	"		Thomas Colle		87	290
Mary	"		William Chapel		30	103
John	"		John Thomas		15	50

B. WINTER GUARD 1642 [Lords Journals 5. 379]

King's Ships	Rate	Commander	Men
Henrietta Maria	2	Earl of Warwick, Admiral	250
Rainbow	2	Capt. William Batten V.A.	240
Happy Entrance	3		160
Expedition	4		100
Providence	4		100
Greyhound	6		50

MERCHANT SHIPS

Maidenhead			85
Providence			81
Jocelyn			59

MERCHANT PINNACES

Mary			15
William and John			12
Neptune of Weymouth			12

IRISH COAST FOR LIKE SERVICE

KING'S SHIPS

Charles, Admiral	2		250
Lion	3		170

KING'S PINNACES

Crescent	6		50
Lily	6		35
Swan	6		20
Hart	6		40

MR. THOMPSON

Employment			120
Ruth			120
Discionary			120
Peter			81
Pennington			46

AT BRISTOL

King's Ships	Rate	Commander	Men
Fellowship			90
Mary			30
Little Mary			30

MERCHANT PINNACES

Mary			42
Charity			36
Richarden			30
Elizabeth			24

MERCHANT SHIPS TO BE ADDED TO THE IRISH GUARD

Zante Merchant	390
Good Hope	390
Achilles	260
George Bonaventure	242
Mary Bonaventure	240
Hopewell	200
Katherine	200
Pennington	135
Dolphin	100
Peter	150

C. Summer Guard 1643 [Penn 1. 66]

Ship	Rate	Commander	Men	Guns
Prince Royal	1	Earl of Warwick, Admiral		
		Richard Blyth, Captain	500	70
St. Andrew	2	William Batten V. A	260	45
St. George	2	Richard Owen R A.	260	46
Swiftsure	2	Robert Moulton	260	48
James	2	Henry Bethell	260	50
Rainbow	2	Peter Andrews	240	42
Victory	2	Nathaniel Goodlad	260	46
Charles	2	Tristram Stevens	350	46
Convertine	3	John Stansby	200	42
Antelope	3	Richard Haddock	160	36
Entrance	3	John Bowen	160	40
Leopard	3	Ben Crandley	160	38
Swallow	3	Thomas Rainsborough	150	34
Dreadnought	3	William Somaster	140	40
Mary Rose	4	Richard Blyth, junior	100	38
Eighth Whelp	5	William Thomas	60	18
Tenth Whelp	5	R. Hill	60	14
Greyhound	6	Abraham Wheeler	50	18
Nicodemus	6	J. Wood	45	10
Hart	6	Batts	40	12
Hind	6	Robert Bramble	70	10
Fortune Pink	6	Richard Billiard	14	8

"These two small vessels and the four ketches are to attend the Fleet."

Notterdam		Peter White	20	6
Revenge		John Mildmay	12	4
Prosperous		Richard Thompson		
Anne		Matthew Berry		
Hopewell		Christopher Berry		
Load's Boat at Dover.				

MERCHANT SHIPS

Ship	Commander	Tons	Men	Guns
Martin	George Martin	532	159	36
Hopeful Luke	Robert Lea	355	106	26
Maidenhead	James Lutton	285	85	20
Anne and Jonas	Thomas Jonas	300	90	22

Ship	Rate	Commander	Tons	Men	Guns
Hercules		Lawrence Moyer	468	135	28
Mayflower		Joseph Piggott	405	121	28
Scipio		Thomas Evans	425	127	28
Leopard		Thomas Clark	362	108	22
Friendship		Joseph Blake	366	109	24
Speedwell		Benjamin Peters	383	115	26
Providence		William Swanley	270	81	20
John and Barbary		Jo. Barker	283	84	20
Golden Lion		Lodwick Dick	450	135	30
Exchange		John Rochester	326	97	24
Golden Angel		Richard Lucas	431	102	26
Blessing		Thomas Shaftoe	200	60	18
Prosperous		William Driver	435	130	28
Elizabeth and Anne		William Coppin	88	28	18
George of Dover		George Bowden	121	36	12
Blessing		Thomas Ashmore	350	105	26
James Youghal		Thomas Morgan	100	40	8
Charity		Ralph Dansk	120	36	6
Jocelyn		John Stansby	196	59	12

COLLIER SHIPS

Ship	Rate	Commander	Tons	Men	Guns
Recovery		James North	360	70	11
Edward and Elizabeth		Edward Leigh	350	80	14
Dragon		James Peacocke	260	60	6
Hector		James Bedall	360	70	20

FIRE SHIPS

Ship	Rate	Commander	Tons	Men	Guns
Swan		Robert Hudson	200	12	
Sarah		Lambart Pitches	250	14	
Andrew and John		Thomas Croft	220	13	
Lyon of London		James Flowes	220	12	

HIS MAJESTY'S SHIPS OF THE IRISH GUARD

Ship	Rate	Commander	Tons	Guns
Bonaventure	3	Richard Swanley, Admiral	170	36
Lion	3	William Smith V. A.	170	42
Expedition	4	Joseph Jordan R. A.	100	15
Providence	4	William Brook	100	16
Crescent	6	Thomas Plunket	50	12
Lily	6	John Lambart	35	10
Star	6	Thomas Cook	60	12
Cygnet	6	J. Weils	70	14

MERCHANT SHIPS

Ship	Rate	Commander	Tons	Men	Guns
Employment		Thomas Ashley	132	30	
Ruth		Robert Constable	120	24	
Peter		Peter Strong	81	14	

TEN MERCHANT SHIPS ON THE COAST OF IRELAND

Ship	Tons	Men
Zante Merchant	390	117
Goodhope	390	117
Achilles	260	78
George Bonaventure	242	72
Mary Bonaventure	240	72
Hopewell	220	66
Katherine	200	60
Pennington	135	40
Dolphin	100	30
Peter	150	45

D.   WINTER GUARD 1643

No full list seems to exist.   Rawlinson A. 223. 75 states that twenty-two men-of-war and twenty-four merchantmen were to be set out.   The Lords Journals, Volume 5, page 332, gives their stations. Rawlinson A. 223. II gives the following merchantmen:

Leopard
Friendship
Speedwell
Providence
Blessing
Jocelyn
Elizabeth and Anne
George
James
Prosperous
Blessing
Ann and Joyce
Lucy
Adventure

E.   SUMMER GUARD 1644 [E. 669, F. 1. 16]

Ship	Rate	Commander	Tons	Men	Guns
James	2	Richard Blith, Warwick Admiral	857	260	50
Reformation	2	William Batten V. A.	742	250	46
Garland	3	Richard Owen R. A.	567	170	40
Bonaventure	3	Henry Bethell	557	170	36
Antelope	3	Edward Hall	512	160	36
Dreadnought	3	John Bowen	552	140	34
Lion	3	Robert Moulton	600	170	40
Entrance	3	Ben Crandley	539	160	38
Leopard	3	Richard Swanley	520	160	38
Swallow	3	William Smith	500	150	36
Mary Rose	4	William Somaster	521	100	28
Expedition	4	Joseph Jordan	260	100	18
Providence	4	John Stansby	260	100	18
John	4	Richard Haddock	400	110	28
Fellowship	4	William Penn	300	110	28
Globe	4	Richard Willoughby	300	100	24
Hector	5	John Stansby	300	70	20
Sampson	5	David Brown	300	70	20
Cygnet	5	J. Whetstone	160	70	18
Warwick	5	William Thomas	200	80	22
Star	5	Robert Constable	130	60	16
Hind	5	Thomas Pilgrim	100	70	13
8th Whelp	5	John Carse	200	60	16
Crescent	6	Peter White	140	50	14
Greyhound	6	Abraham Wheeler	120	58	12
Lily	6	John Lambart	80	45	8
Hart	6	Roger Beere	80	40	8
Nicodemus	6	Thomas Pacey	80	45	8
Warwick Hoy	6	Edward Peach	60	30	6
Spy	6	William Hazard	40	20	6

MERCHANT SHIPS

Ship	Commander	Tons	Men	Guns
Mayflower	William Cock	405	121	28
Jeremy	Augustine Bright	274	82	22
Employment	Thomas Ashley	440	132	30
Swan	Thomas Grimes	302	90	24
Honour	Edmund Seaman	359	108	26
Peregrine	Peter Tatum	247	74	20
Marmaduke	John Walter	415	124	26
Ark	John Lockier	150	60	14
Providence	Roger Mostin	180	54	16
Golden Lion	Lewis Dick (Lodwick Dick)	450	135	30

Ship	Commander	Tons	Men	Guns
Elizabeth and Anne	John Coppin	88	40	12
Lucy	John Willis	160	25	12
Fairchild	John Westfield	120	36	10
Benediction	George Tito	120	25	8
Seaflower	James Grand	70	12	4
Jocelyn	Robert Clarke	196	59	12
Anne and Joyce	Thomas Jones	300	90	20
Paramour	Thomas Middleton	430	129	28
Covenant	John Lawson	140	42	12
Green Dragon	Francis Green	300	70	22
Jane and Elizabeth		130	25	8
Hector	Thomas Bedall	300	80	22

"Six small pinnaces with six guns apiece, to attend the Fleet. The names of such Merchant Ships as are to be set forth by the way of reprisal, and victualled at the charge of the State."

Ship	Commander	Tons	Men
Hopeful Mary	Edward Bason	203	81
Mary Hope	William Burr	30	12
Rebecca	Stephen Rich	255	102
William	Leonard Bates	101	80
Hart Frigate	Eustace Smith	41	16
Grace	Crook	84	25
Seaventure	Gater Jailour	38	15
Thomas	Rand Harle	54	22
William and Sarah		50	20
Constant Good Hope		199	80
Blessing	Thomas Giner	37	14
Isabel and Margaret	Richard Brook	50	20
Spy	John Ball	96	36
Mary	Tracy Cater	180	72
Achilless		250	100
Magdalen		200	70
Lorne		150	60
Marigold		150	60
Lion		360	144
Scout Frigate		120	40
Matthew	James Morvell	80	
Adventure	John Purvis	180	70
Blessing	Francis Ashmore	350	140
Seahorse	Joseph Ashmore	77	30
Friendship	Rand Harle	166	64

F.   WINTER GUARD 1644 [Rawlinson 223. 18]

Ship	Rate	Ship	Rate
Reformation	2	Star	6
Leopard	3	Hind	6
Swallow	3	Crescent	6
Expedition	4	Lily	6
Providence	4	Jeremy	
Fellowship	4	Mayflower	
John	4	Hector	
Globe	4	Green Dragon	
Sampson	5	George Bonaventure	
Hector Prize	5	Magdalen	
8th Whelp	5	Gillyflower	
Greyhound	6	Anne and Elizabeth	
Cygnet	6	Lucy	
Warwick	6	Jocelyn	

G. SUMMER GUARD 1645 [Rawlinson C. 406, collated with Penn 1. 111, Rushworth 7. 144, and E. 699, F. 9. 36]

Ship	Rate	Commander
VICE ADMIRAL'S SQUADRON		
St. Andrew	2	William Batten
James	2	Richard Blith
Antelope	3	Edward Hall
Swallow	3	William Soamaster
Providence	4	John Stansby
Mary Rose	4	Phineas Pett
Warwick	6	William Thomas
Robert	6	William Rew
Cygnet	6	John Mann
Truelove		Gervase Coachman
Providence of Poole		
2 Ketches		
REAR-ADMIRAL'S SQUADRON		
Garland	3	Richard Owen
Leopard	3	Thomas Bowen
Sampson	5	Thomas Pilgrim
Hind	5	Anthony Young
Greyhound	6	John Coppin
Nicodemus	6	Thomas Pacey
Seaflower		
A Ketch		
NORTH SQUADRON		
Bonaventure	3	Henry Bethell
John	4	William Swanley
Covenant		John Lawson
Constant Warwick		John Gilson
Expedition	4	Joseph Jordan
Crescent	6	J. Edwin
Star	5	Robert Constable
A Ketch		
ENTERTAINED FOR PARTICULAR SERVICE		
Arke		John Lockier
Hector		Thomas Bedall

Ship	Rate	Commander
Adventure		Thomas Welch
Anne and Elizabeth		Robert Sparks
Merchant's Delight		Thomas Wills
Elizabeth		J. Bowman

IRISH SQUADRON

Lion	3	Richard Swanley
Entrance	3	William Smith
Globe	4	Richard Willoughby
Anne and Joyce		Thomas Jones
Rebecca		Stephen Rich
Magdalen		J. Hosier
Duncannon		Samuel Howett
Dainty Pink		
Green Frigate		Thomas Farmer
Charles		Robert Clark
Mary and Ann		Peter Wappal
Mayflower		Roger Phillips
Nicholas		Richard Bray
Anne Percy		Thomas Smith
Defiance		William Brooks
Spy		Andrew Davis
2 Shallops		

SCOTCH SQUADRON

Hector	5	Edmund Elliott
Lucy		Elias Jordan
George Bonaventure		John Crampe
A Fourth to be taken up.		
Fellowship	4	William Penn
8th Whelp	5	John Kearse
Jocelyn		Robert Clarke
2 small pinnaces to complete	8	

GUERNSEY SQUADRON

Dove	6	William Hazard
Welcome Pink	6	John Green
Lily	6	John Lambart

H. Winter Guard 1645 [Lords Journals 7. 594]

Ship	Rate	Commander	Ship	Rate	Commander
Lion	3	Robert Moulton	Sampson	5	Tho. Pilgrim
Leopard	3	John Bowen	Hind	5	
Entrance	3	John Crowther	Cygnet	6	
Swallow	3	Will. Soamaster	Star	5	Robert Constable
Fellowship	4	Will. Penn	Greyhound	6	John Coppin
John	4	Will. Swanley	Crescent	6	John Edwin
Globe	4	Robert Willoughby	Robert	6	Will. Rew
Providence	4	John Stansby	Welcome	6	John Green
Expedition	4	Joseph Jordan	Lily	6	John Lambart
Warwick	5	Will. Thomas	Dove	6	Will. Hazard
Hector	5	Will. Elliott	Richard and William		

MERCHANT SHIPS

Constant Warwick	John Gilson	Jocelyn	Robert Clarke
Mayflower	Roger Phillips	Lucy	Elias Drew
Anne and Percy	Thomas Smith	Rebecca	Stephen Rich
Covenant	John Lawson	Kentish	John Mildmay
George Bonaventure	John Crampe	Charles	Thomas Farmer
Anne and Joyce	Thomas Jones	Nicholas	Richard Bray

Rawlinson C. 223. 34 adds:

    Morecock
    Truelove
    Harry
    Ark
    Cavendish (Brown Bushell's prize, renamed Weymouth.)

I. Summer Guard 1646 [E. 669, F. 9. 88; stations on March 3rd from Rawlinson A. 223, F. 15]

Rate	Ship	Station	Commander
2	St. Andrew	Chatham	William Batten V. A.
2	Rainbow	Chatham	Thomas Trenchfield R. A.
2	James	Chatham	Richard Blith Senior
2	Charles	Chatham	Richard Swanley
2	Victory	Chatham	Ben. Crandley
2	Unicorn		Peter Andrews
3	Lion	Ireland	Robert Moulton, Admiral
3	Leopard	Downs	Henry Bethell
3	Garland	Chatham	John Bowen
3	Swallow	Dry Dock	William Soamaster
3	Entrance	Ireland	John Crowther V. A.
3	Bonaventure	Chatham	Walter Maynard
3	Antelope	Chatham	Edward Hall
3	Convertine	Chatham	John Mann
4	Expedition	West	Sir George Ayscue
4	Providence	Dry Dock	John Stansby
4	John	West	William Swanley
4	Fellowship	Ireland	William Penn R. A.
4	Globe	Ireland	Richard Willoughby
4	Mary Rose	Dry Dock	Phineas Pett
5	Warwick	Dry Dock	James Peacocke
5	Hector	North	Edward Elliott
5	Cygnet	North	William Peake
5	Sampson	North	John Pilgrim
5	Crescent	Chatham	John Edwin
5	Hind	West	Anthony Young
5	Swan	Ireland	Robert Clarke
5	Star	West	Robert Constable
5	10th Whelp	Ireland	William Lawrence
6	Greyhound		John Coppin
6	Roebuck	Downs	Andrew Woodward
6	Kentish	Downs	John Mildmay
6	Welcome	Guernsey	John Green
6	Robert	Downs	William Rew
6	Increase	Chatham	Robert Moulton Junior
6	Trial	Ireland	Brown
6	Royalist	North East	Owen Cox
6	Nicodemus	Chatham	Thomas Pacey
6	Charles	Ireland	Robert Clarke

Rate	Ship	Station	Commander
6	Green Frigate	Ireland	Thomas Farmer
6	Weymouth	Downs	John Pierce
6	Lily	Guernsey	John Lambart
6	Dove	Guernsey	William Hazard
6	Hunter		Joseph Bransby

MERCHANT SHIPS

Ship	Station	Commander
Constant Warwick	At Sea	John Gilson
Truelove	West	Gervase Coachman
President	Thames	Peter Whitty
Harry	North East	John Elison
Defiance	West	John Whitty
Samuel	Bristol	Matthew Wood
Jocelyn	Chester	James Moulton
Lucy	Portsmouth or West	Elias Drew
Magdalen	Thames	John Hosier
Ark	Portsmouth or West	Robert Bramble
Moorcock	North East	Robert Phillpott
Messenger	North East	Ben Trenyman
Hopewell	Sussex Coast	Francis Ceeley
Hector	Thames	Henry Parkhurst
Blessing	Thames	Thomas Winnal
Sampson	Thames	John Lyne
Rebecca	Chester	Stephen Rich
Anne & Percy		Thomas Smith
Delight		Thomas Leman
Exchange		Thomas Cheney
Discovery		Thomas Plunkett

"Merchant Ships ordered to be graved and fitted for sea, for the better defence of the Kingdom upon any emergent occasion":

Ship	Commander
London	John Stevens
Freeman	Jacob Hyde
Society	Nicholas Hurlston
Experience	John Swanley
Angel	Thomas Perry
Scipio	Thomas Ewen
Aleppo Merchant	John Millet
Falcon	Thomas Harman
Employment	Thomas Ashley

Ship	Station	Commander
Charles		William Weldy
Harry Bonaventure		George Swanley
Concord		John Bullard
George		William White
Defence		John Bostocke
Thomas & Francis		Elias Henderson
Crescent		Michael Phillips
John & Mary		Ambrose Chappell
James		John Limbery
Jeremy		John Moore
Ark		John Maylin
Lewis		John Barker
Edward		Thomas Day
Mayflower		Thomas Bett
Anne		William Badiley
Hector		Richard Fernes
John		Thomas Flute
Adventure		Richard Wyard
William & John		Sidrack Blake
Achilles		Michael Shatten
Giles		Henry Toope
Peter Bonaventure		Peter Lunt
Lisbon Merchant		Roger Garland
Dolphin		John Wall

J. WINTER GUARD 1646 [Lords Journals 8. 459]

Rate	Ship	Commander
3	Leopard	William Batten V. A.
3	Lion	Richard Swanley, Irish Admiral
3	Entrance	John Crowther, Irish V. A.
3	Swallow	William Soamaster
4	Mary Rose	Phineas Pett
4	Expedition	Sir George Ayscue
4	Providence	John Stansby
4	John	William Swanley
4	Warwick	James Peacocke
4	Globe	Richard Willoughby
4	Adventure*	Thomas Bedall
4	Nonsuch*	William Thomas
4	Assurance*	William Penn
5	Hector	Edward Elliott
5	Crescent	John Edwin
5	Swan	Robert Clerke
5	Tenth Whelp	William Lawrence
5	Cygnet	Abraham Wheeler
5	President	John Pilgrim
5	Hind	Arthur Young
5	Star	Robert Constable
6	Greyhound	John Coppin
6	Roebuck	Andrew Woodward
6	Dove	William Hazard
6	Kentish	John Mildmay
6	Robert	William Rew
6	Welcome	John Greene
6	Weymouth	John Pearce
6	Hart	John Bowen
6	Increase	Robert Moulton
6	Trial	Brown
6	Mary Galliott	Brandley
6	Peter	

*   Built this year

William and John)	
Charles)	Packet Boats
Three Swans)	

MERCHANT SHIPS

Ship		Commander
Constant Warwick		John Gilson
Discovery		John Wills
Samuel		Matthew Woods
Rebecca		Stephen Rich
Charles		Robert Clarke
Green Frigate)	Packet Boats on the	Thomas Farmer
Roebuck)	Coast of Ireland	William Liston

K. SUMMER GUARD 1647 [Penn 1. 236; E. 669, F. 4. 16]

Rate	Ship	Commander
	FOR THE DOWNS	
2	St. Andrew	William Batten V. A.
3	Entrance	John Bowen
3	Leopard	Ben. Crandley
3	Convertine	John Mann
4	Mary Rose	Phineas Pett
4	Providence	John Stansby
4	Fellowship	Jonas Reeve
6	Greyhound	John Coppin
6	Robert	William Rew
6	Roebuck	Andrew Woodward
6	Nicodemus	Thomas Pacey
6	Priam Ketch	Roger Laming
	Constant Warwick	John Gilson
	Jeremy	John More
	William Ketch	
	WESTERN GUARD	
2	Henrietta Maria	Richard Owen R. A.
3	Garland	Henry Bethell
3	Antelope	Sir George Ayscue
3	Swallow	William Soamaster
4	Adventure	Thomas Bedall
5	Hector	Edward Elliott
6	Peter	Henry Gervoise or John Mildmay
6	Crescent	John Edwin
6	Hart	John Bowen
6	Weymouth	John Pearce
6	Humber Ketch	Robert Nixon
	Roebuck Merchant	Edward West
	GUERNSEY	
6	Welcome	John Greene
6	Dove Pink	William Nixon
6	Lily	John Lambart
	William and Daniel	Thomas Clarke

IRISH GUARD

Rate	Ship	Commander
3	Lion	Richard Swanley V. A.
3	Bonaventure	John Crowther R. A.
4	Nonsuch	William Thomas
4	Assurance	William Penn
4	John	William Swanley
5	Recovery	Robert Dare
5	Satisfaction	Robert Moulton, Junior
5	Tenth Whelp	
6	Increase	William Ledgard
5	Star	John Lockier
5	Swan	Robert Clarke
	Discovery	John Wills
	Samuel	Matthew Wood
	Truelove	Jervis Coachman
	Anne and Joyce	Thomas Jones
	Anne and Percy	William Handcock

FOR THE NORTH

Ship	Rate	Commander
Warwick	5	James Peacocke
Pelican	6	Owen Cox
Hind	6	Anthony Young
Peregrine		Ben. Trenyman

IRISH FISHING GUARD

Magdalen		John Hosier
Blessing		Thomas Winnal

NORTH SEA FISHING GUARD

President	5	John Pilgrim
Cygnet	5	Abraham Wheeler

Also included but without station named

Expedition	4	Joseph Jordan
Globe	4	Richard Willoughby
Welcome Pink	6	John Green

MERCHANT SHIPS (13 in all)

Ship	Rate	Commander
Sampson		John Lyne

"Six Second Rate Ships ordered to be graved, and fit to be sent forth on any emergency, in case Parliament shall give order in that behalf."

Triumph	Robert Moston
Rainbow	Bryan Harrison
Unicorn	Peter Andrews
Victory	Nathaniel Goodlad
Swiftsure	Thomas Davis
Charles	Thomas Maynard

400 TO 200 TONS

Society	Nicholas Hurleston
Rainbow	Elias Jordan
Newfoundland Merchant	William Pees
William and Thomas	Thomas Porter
Paramour	Thomas Middleton
Civil Society	John Shaw
Thomas Bonaventure	George Hughes
Greenfield	Henry Powell
Merchant	Nehemiah Bourne
London Merchant	Anthony Newport
Mayflower	Thomas Bell
Beaver	Edward Coyte
Four Sisters	Roger Harman
Confidence	Charles Thorogood
Hector	Samuel Stanton
Giles	Henry Toop
Content	Godfrey Jones
Elizabeth	William Stag
James	Edward Button
John Adventure	Eustace Smith
George Bonaventure	John Cramp
Elizabeth	John Durson
Loyalty	William Coppin
Mayflower	John Cole
Exeter Merchant	Edward Belitha
Benjamin	George Clerkson

L. WINTER GUARD 1647 [Penn 1. 252; Lords Journals 9. 409]

Rate	Ship	Commander
3	Leopard	Thomas Rainsborough V. A.
4	Nonsuch	Richard Willoughby
4	Adventure	Thomas Bedall
4	Fellowship	Henry Jervoise
4	Mary Rose	Thomas Harrison
5	Hector	Francis Penrose
5	Warwick	Richard Ferne
5	Tenth Whelp	William Brandley
6	Greyhound	John Coppin
6	Hart	John Bowden
4	Phoenix (building at Woolwich)	Phineas Pett
	A Ketch	

IRISH SQUADRON

3	Bonaventure	John Crowther V. A.
4	Assurance	William Penn R. A.
4	Providence	John Mildmay
4	Expedition	Joseph Jordan
4	Dragon	Anthony Young
4	Elizabeth (building at Deptford)	Jonas Reeve
5	President	John Pilgrim
5	Swan	Robert Clarke
5	Star	John Taylor
6	Increase	William Legard

NORTH COAST

4	Tiger (building at Deptford)	James Peacocke
6	Pelican	Owen Cox

GUERNSEY

6	Weymouth	John Pearce
6	Robert	William Rew
	2 Ketches	

M.   SUMMER GUARD 1648 [Lords Journals 10. 36, 235]

Rate	Ship	Commander
2	Reformation	Thomas Rainsborough V. A.
3	Garland	Henry Bethell R. A.
3	Convertine	Thomas Mann
3	Swallow	Leonard Harris
3	Antelope	Edward Hall
4	Tiger	James Peacocke
4	Phoenix	Owen Cox
4	Adventure	Andrew Ball
4	Mary Rose	Thomas Harrison
4	Providence	John Mildmay
4	Fellowship	Henry Jervoise
5	Hind	Charles Saltenstall
5	Warwick	William Gregory
5	Tenth Whelp	William Brandley
6	Crescent	John Edwin
6	Greyhound	John Coppin
6	Hart	John Bowen
6	Nicodemus	Thomas Pacey
6	Roebuck	Robert Nixon
6	Lily	John Lambart
6	Robert	William Jennings
6	Dove	Jacob Reynolds
6	Hunter	William Warren

IRISH GUARD

Rate	Ship	Commander
3	Bonaventure	John Crowther V. A.
4	Assurance	William Penn R. A.
4	Dragon	Anthony Young
4	Elizabeth	Jonas Reeve
4	Nonsuch	Richard Willoughby
5	Hector	John Pearce
5	Star	John Taylor
5	Satisfaction	Francis Penrose
5	President	John Pilgrim
5	Swan	Robert Clark
5	Recovery	Peter Squibb
6	Weymouth	John Bowen

Guard of Milford, and to ply about Land's End

Rate	Ship	Commander
3	Lion	Sir George Ayscue
4	John	Edward Miott
4	Expedition	Joseph Jordan
5	Cygnet	Abraham Wheeler

O. Royalist Ships

Ships with the Catholic Confederacy's Commission [H. M. C. Ormonde I. 121]

Ship	Commander
St. Francis (Admiral)	Captain Nicholas Holt
Mary of Antrim	" William O'Donavon
Mary of the Isles	" Handemarche
St. Michael	" Booth
Mary and John	" John Rollestar
Cock or Santa Theresa	" Peter Deferterne
St. Peter (possibly the San Pietro)	" John Constant
Lord Crafford's Frigate	" Michael Casey
Cupido	" Manuel Buckson
St. Cornelius	" Francis Oliver
John Talbot and Michael Stafford's frigate	" D'Arcey

Ships under Haesdonck's Commission [Clarendon S. P. 1913]

Ship	Tons	Guns	Commander
Kings Arms and Sun of England	220	22	Capt. Lawrence Johnson
The Spread Eagle	240	22	" Daniel Van Voolen
The Flower de Luce	220	22	" Jacot Bollaert
The Henrietta Maria	60	16	" Eustathius Haling
The Star	80	16	" Adrian Van Dieman, alias de Sivert
The Neptune	60	14	" Giles Barthen
The Gennet	100	7	" William Sadlington
The Salvator, a little frigate, 2 brass guns			" Peter Clinkaert, now at Scarborough
The Salvator, a galliot		4	" Elias Ladone, lately taken by the Hollanders
The Adventure	140	12	" Francis Fawether
The Ferdinando	180	18	

Ships under Crisp's Commission [Compiled from Clarendon S. P. 2070; I. 6. & 7]

Patrick	Capt. Simon Peterson
Hare (wrecked off Brittany)	" Paul Roche
St. George	" George Bowden
St. George of Darmouth	" John Smith

N.   WINTER GUARD 1648 [Add. MSS. 9304, 22]

Rate	Ship	Commander
2	St. George	Lord Warwick, Lord High Admiral
		Robert Moulton, Captain
2	Unicorn	Richard Haddock V. A.
3	Leopard	
3	Bonaventure	
4	Nonsuch	Richard Willoughby
4	Adventure	Andrew Ball
4	Elizabeth	Jonas Reeve
4	Tiger	James Peacocke
4	Phoenix	John Bowen
4	Providence	John Mildmay
4	Expedition	Joseph Jordan
4	Assurance	
4	Dragon	
4	Mary Rose	James Harrison
4	Fellowship	Francis Penrose
5	Tenth Whelp	William Brandley
5	Star	
5	Swan	
5	Cygnet	Abraham Wheeler
5	Satisfaction	
6	Falcon	
6	Crescent	
6	Hunter	
6	Weymouth	
6	Hart	
6	Truelove	
6	Eagle	
6	Samuel	
6	Fly	
6	Scout	
6	Robert	William Jennings
6	Dove	Jacob Reynolds
	3 Ketches	

Ship	Commander
St. George of Falmouth	Capt. Thomas Amy
Green Knight	" Richard Teale
King David	" Jacques Carol
Phoenix	" Allen
Dragon (taken Fowey)	" Blake

Twenty nameless ships are listed, also four set out by Lord Jermyn. Crisp lost seven ships. One of 400 tons taken at Saltash; another lost between Falmouth and Weymouth; four at the loss of Weymouth.

Baldwin Wake

The Black Proud Eagle
Eagle

P. SHIPS CAPTURED BY THE PARLIAMENT FLEET [E. 340.
    31; Rawlinson A. 223, F. 36, 1645; PRO Audit
    Declared Accounts; AOI 1812/443 A]

1642	Swallow and Bonaventure taken by Batten's squadron.
1643	Providence taken by Mayflower.
	Fortune (Robert) taken by the Swallow.
	Mayflower by Eighth Whelp and Charity.
	Fellowship and Hart taken by Swallow and Robert.
	Crisp's frigate sunk by Providence.
1644	Dragon taken by Providence.
	Fortune of Dunkirk sunk by Providence.
	Globe and Providence taken by Irish Guard at Pill.
1645	Cavendish (Weymouth) taken by Eighth Whelp and Robert.
	Roebuck of Dunkirk taken by Mary Rose.
	Constant by Greyhound.
	Salvator taken by John.
	Black Horse with two Scarborough Warships by Hector.
	Jennet of Dunkirk taken by Providence.
	Royalist by Constant Warwick.

Welcome   )
Trial   )
Charles   )   Taken by Irish Guard.
Peter   )
William and John)

Kentish
Swan taken by Jocelyn.
Endeavour taken by St. Andrew.
Hector
Dover
Gift of Topsham.
Hunter

1646	Duncannon handed over by Lord Esmond.
	Doggerbank taken by Increase and Warspite.
	Great George taken at Pendennis.
1647	Truelove. Priam. Orange Tree. St. Patrick.
1648	Crescent taken by Elizabeth.

Constant Dacre
Angel (Dolphin)
Constant Warwick)
Hind   )   Taken by Warwick's Squadron
Love   )
Satisfaction   )

"There are numerous unnamed ships taken besides."

Key to the References

Abbott	Abbott, W. C. *Writings and Speeches of Oliver Cromwell*. Cambridge, Massachusetts, 4 volumes, 1937.
Add. MSS.	Additional Manuscripts, British Museum.
Arch.	Peacock, Edward. "Notes on the Life of Thomas Rainsborough". *Archaelogia*, volume 46. London, 1876.
Arch. Camb.	*Archealogia Cambrensis*, volume 22. Cardiff, 1876.
Ael.	*Archealogia Aeliana*, volume 28. Newcastle-upon-Tyne, 1867.
A.S.G.	Archief Staten General, 5739. Hague.
Bagwell	Bagwell, Richard. *Ireland Under the Stuarts*, volume 2. London, 1909.
Bayley	Bayley, A. R. *The Great Civil War in Dorset*. Taunton, 1910.
Bellum	*Bellum Civile*, edited by C. E. H. Charwych-Healey. Somerset Records Society, volume 18. London, 1902.
Cal. S.P.D.	*Calendar of the State Papers Domestic of the Reign of Charles I*. London, 5 volumes, 1887-93.
Cal.-Clar. S.P.	*Calendar of the Clarendon State Papers*, edited by by O. Ogle and W. H. Bliss. Oxford, 1872.
Cal. S.P. Ven.	*Calendar of the State Papers Venetian*, edited by O. Ogle and W. H. Bliss. Oxford, 1869.
C.A.M.	*Calendar of the Proceedings of the Committee for Advancing Money*. London, 3 volumes, 1892.

Carte	Carte, Thomas. *Life of James Butler, Duke of Ormonde.* Oxford, 6 volumes, 1842.
Carte's Letters	Carte, Thomas. *A Collection of Original Letters . . . among the Duke of Ormonde's Papers.* London, 2 volumes, 1739.
Carter	Carter, Matthew. *Expedition to Kent, Essex, and Colchester in 1648.* London, 1650.
Cary	Cary, Henry. *Memorials of the Great Civil War in England.* London, 2 volumes, 1842.
Chester	Morris, Canon R. H. *Siege of Chester.* Chester, 1926.
Chev.	*Journal de Jean Chevalier.* Societe Jersiase. Jersey, 2 volumes, 1906.
C.J.	*Commons Journals*
Clarke	*Clarke Papers,* edited by C. H. Firth. London, 4 volumes, 1894.
Coate	Coate, Mary. *Cornwall in the Great Civil War.* Oxford, 1933.
E.	Thomason Tracts in the British Museum
E.H.R.	*English Historical Review.*
Gardiner	Gardiner, S. R. *History of England, 1603-1642.* London, 10 volumes, 1884. Gardiner, S. R. *History of the Great Civil War.* London, 4 volumes, 1893.
G.C.W.	Burne, A. H., and Young, P. *The Great Civil War.* London, 1959.
Gilbert	Gilbert, J. *History of the Irish Confederacy and the War in Ireland.* London, 6 volumes, 1888.
Hamilton	*Hamilton Papers,* edited by C. H. Firth. London, 1880.
Harl MSS.	Harleian Manuscripts, British Museum.

H.M.C.	Historical Manuscripts Commission.
Hoskins	Hoskins, S. E. *Charles II in the Channel Islands.* London, 2 volumes, 1854.
Irish Sword	*The Irish Sword* (Journal of the Military History Society of Ireland), Dublin, 1952— .
K.P.	Wedgwood, C. V. *The King's Peace.* London, 1955.
K.W.	Wedgwood, C. V. *The King's War.* London, 1958.
Lewis	Lewis, Michael. *The Navy of Britain.* London, 1945.
L.J.	*Lords Journals.*
Macray	Edward, Earl of Clarendon. *History of the Great Rebellion,* edited by W. D. Macray. Oxford, 6 volumes, 1888.
MacNeill	*Tanner Letters, relating to Ireland,* edited by Charles MacNeill. Dublin, 1943.
Main.	*Life and Times of Sir Henry Mainwaring,* edited by G. E. Mainwaring. London, 2 volumes, 1920-21.
M.M.	*The Mariner's Mirror.* London, 1911-.
Oliver	Oliver, S. P. *Pendennis and St. Maurs.* Truro, 1875.
Oman	Oman, C. *Henrieta Maria.* London, 1936.
Opp.	Oppenheim, M. *History of the Administration of the Royal Navy.* London, 1896.
Penn	Penn, Granville. *Memorials of Sir William Penn.* London, 1833.
Pepysian	Pepysian Manuscripts, Magdalen College, Cambridge.
Petworth MSS.	Leconfield Manuscripts, Petworth.
Phillips	Phillips, J. R. *Civil War in Wales and the Marches.* London, 2 volumes, 1878.

Port.   *The Manuscripts of His Grace the Duke of Portland*
                 (H.M.C., 13th Rpt, App, pt. i), vol. 1. London,
                 1891.

Raw.   Rawlinson Manuscripts, Bodleian Library.

Rinuccini   Rinuccini, G. B. *Embassy in Ireland,* translated by
                 Anne Hutton. London, 1875.

Rushworth   Rushworth, John. *Historical Collections.* London,
                 8 volumes, 1721.

S.P.D.   State Papers Domestic. Record Office. London.

Spalding   Spalding, T. A. *Life and Times of Richard Badiley.*
                 London, 1899.

Sprigge   Sprigge, Joshua. *Anglia Rediviva.* London, 1647.

Stirling   Stirling, A. W. M. *The Hothams of Hull.* London,
                 2 volumes, 1918.

Tanner   Tanner Manuscripts, Bodleian Library.

Tupper   Tupper, F. B. *History of Guernsey.* London, 1876.

Vicars 1, 2, 3   Vicars, John. *Parliamentary Chronicle.* London,
                 1646. (1) "God in the Mount", (2) "God in
                 the Ark", (3) "The Burning Bush Not Con-
                 sumed".

War.   Warburton, Eliot. *Memoirs of Prince Rupert and
                 the Cavaliers.* London, 3 volumes, 1849.

Whitelock   Whitelock, Bulstrode. *Memorials of English Affairs.*
                 Oxford, 4 volumes, 1855.

Notes

PREFACE

1. G.C.W. 9
2. G.C.W. 76
3. G.C.W. 76
4. G.C.W. 99

CHAPTER I

1. Penn 1. 17
2. K.P. 125
3. K.P. 276
4. K.P. 290
5. Gardiner 10. 60-62
6. K.P. 329-331
7. Petworth MSS. 40
8. Opp. 216
9. Opp. 237
10. Opp. 235
11. Lewis 291
12. L.J. 4. 526
13. Gardiner 10. 108

CHAPTER 2

1. Hoskins 1. 181
2. Gardiner 10. 153
3. Stirling 1. 40
4. G.C.W. 15; E.H.R. Vol. 38
5. Letters Hen. Mar. 52
6. C.J. 2. 532
7. C.J. 2. 542
8. L.J. 5. 20. 26. 70. 215
9. L.J. 5. 182. 189
10. Macray 6. 39-44
11. L.J. 5. 178-180; Penn. 1. 41
12. L.J. 5. 174
13. L.J. 5. 169. 174. 185
14. L.J. 5. 189. 510
15. L.J. 5. 199. 356

16. L.J. 5. 206. 217; E. 112. 19
17. L.J. 5. 119; E. 202. 17
18. War. 1. 160
19. L.J. 238. 240. 253
20. Port. I. 54; E. 118. 22;
    E.112. 8
21. Vicars. 1. 160
22. Port. I. 54
23. L.J. 5. 314. 315
24. Cal. Clar. S.P. 1. 1618
25. Carte. 2. 325; Gilbert. 2. 55
26. E. 118. 45. 37; E. 40. 35. 37;
    E. 119. 24
27. Coate 35
28. Rush. 5. 69
29. L.J. 5. 417; E. 118. 10
30. L.J. 5. 396
31. L.J. 5. 407
32. L.J. 5. 496; E. 219. 16;
    E. 244. 25

CHAPTER 3

1. Bod. Lib. C. 14. Lich. 47
2. Cal. S.P.D. 1643. 447
3. Bellum 31
4. E. 246. 37
5. L.J. 5. 552
6. Bod-Lib. Rat. C. 29;
    Oman. 129
7. Rush. 5. 61; E.H.R. 1917;
    E. 95. 9
8. K.W. 160; E. 128. 4;
    Cal. S.P.D. 1643. 376
9. Coate 57;
    Cal. S.P. Ven. 1643. 256
10. E. 56. 1
11. Tanner 62. 160
12. Stirling 1.77; E. 629. 16
13. Vicars 1. 368
14. Vicars 1. 371
15. E. 59. 17

16. Penn 1. 69;
    Cal. S.P. Ven. 1643. 298;
    Macray. 3. 159; E. 62. 9;
    E. 64. 11
17. K.W. 241
18. Gilbert 1.151; Bagwell 2. 43
19. Penn 1. 83
20. E. 65. 29
21. Port. I. 130; E. 67. 3
22. Vicars 2. 21
23. Port. I. 129
24. Port. I. 138
25. Cal. Clar. S.P. 1. 1665;
    Carte 5. 442
26. Carte 5. 449
27. Vicars 2. 62; E. 74. 20
28. Port. I. 153; Carte. 5. 505
29. Port. I. 157; L.J. 5. 13
30. Carte 5. 527
31. Port I. 156
32. Carte 5. 514
33. Hoskins 1. 144
34. E. 74. 20; E. 76. 11
35. Port. I. 150
36. L.J. 5. 313
37. H.M.C. 15th Rept. App. 7. 67
38. Cal. S.P. Ven. 1643. 25. 34
39. Port. I. 131
40. L.J. 5. 330

CHAPTER 4

1. Port. I. 167
2. Ael. 26. 84
3. Carte 6. 55
4. Phillips 1. 204
5. E. 42. 12
6. E. 42. 12
7. E. 3. 12; E. 42. 17. 19
8. Chev. 1. 122;
   Hoskins 1. 194. 200;
   Vicars 2. 181
9. L.J. 6. 419
10. Bayley. 131
11. Bayley 149; E. 51. 9
12. Bayley 151
13. Bayley 157
14. Bayley 158-160; E. 51. 9

15. Bayley 163; E. 50. 23;
    S.P. Dom. 514. 544
16. Bayley 167
17. Cap. S.P.D. 1644. 181. 190. 204
18. Cal. S.P.D. 1644. 251;
    Vicars 2. 251

CHAPTER 5

1. Vicars 2. 224;
   E. 25. 2. 61. 25
2. Cal. S.P.D. 1644. 203;
   Tanner 61. 28
3. L.J. 6. 603
4. Carte 6. 83
5. Cal. S.P.D. 1644. 251
6. Cal. S.P.D. 1644. 356; E. 2. 29
7. Cal-S.P.D. 1644. 552. 555. 557
8. Cal. S.P.D. 1644. 389. 436
9. E. 10. 6
10. Cal. S.P.D. 1644. 359
11. Port. I. 196; E. 10. 6;
    L.J. 6. 617
12. Whitelocke 1. 317
13. E. 7. 10
14. Cal. S.P.D. 1644. 557
15. Gilbert 4. 244
16. Bagwell 2. 48
17. Irish Sword 2. 5. 17
18. E. 25. 1
19. Gilbert 4. 45
20. Gilbert 4. 116; E. 251
21. Ael. 26. 257
22. Ael. 26. 242

CHAPTER 6

1. Penn. 1. 104
2. L.J. 7. 255; Vicars 3. 39;
   E. 10. 6; E. 271. 3
3. Vicars 3. 91
4. E. 271. 22; E. 269. 4;
   E. 256. 21
5. Irish Sword 2. 6. 83
6. Tanner 60. 1
7. MacNeill 185;
   Vicars 3. 117. 120

8. Vicars 3. 110
9. Cal. S.P.D. 1645. 279
10. Lewis 48
11. L.J. 329. 327
12. L.J. 7. 373
13. Penn 1. 107; Raw-C. 416;
     Cal Clar. S.P. 1. 1971. 2070
14. Coate 184-5
15. E. 285. 16; E. 286. 17
16. K.W. 418; Add. MSS. 5461

CHAPTER 7

1. Penn. 1. 112. 115. 119
2. Penn. 1. 132;
    Irish Sword 2. 5. 83
3. Bagwell 2. 93
4. Port. I. 255
5. Port. I. 255; E. 278. 6
6. E. 293. 24
7. E. 26. 11; E. 294. 11
8. E. 293. 1
9. Raw. C. 416
10. Penn. 1. 142
11. Sprigge 63. 108
12. L.J. 7. 593; Tupper 272
13. Rinuccini 80; Carte 5. 226
14. H.M.C. Ormonde 1. 101-4

CHAPTER 8

1. M.M. Vol. 40. 1; Penn. 159-210;
    Carte 6. 568; MacNeill 215
2. Port. I. 339; Vicars 3. 370
3. Sprigge 168. 178; Vicars 3. 386;
    Cal. S.P. Ven. 1646. 245
4. Chester 25. 82; Vicars 3. 362;
    E. 325. 30
5. Vicars 3. 386; Sprigge 203
6. Main. 1. 301; Oliver 39
7. Tanner 59. 37
8. Cal. Clar. S.P. 1. 2162
9. Chev. 1. 303
10. Tupper 292
11. Chev. 1. 237
12. Chev. 1. 310
13. Chev. 1. 311

14. Chev. 1. 334; E. 340. 4
15. Sprigge 304
16. Main. 1. 310; E. 353. 4
17. Port. I. 392; E. 353. 4
18. E. 1346. 2
19. E. 340. 31
20. E. 325. 7
21. E. 340. 31
22. Ael. 26. 132
23. K.W. 607
24. Ael. 26. 132-3; Gardiner 3. 144
25. Ael. 26. 140; E. 382. 7
26. Ael. 26. 136
27. Ael. 26. 140; E. 382. 7
28. Ael. 26. 188; E. 382. 7
29. Penn 1. 269
30. Ael. 26. 118
31. Carte. 3. 279. 282
32. Penn 1. 235
33. Chev. 1. 400

CHAPTER 9

1. Penn 1. 231
2. Penn 1. 234
3. Penn 1. 235
4. Chev. 1. 403
5. Chev. 1. 415; Hoskins 2. 18
6. C.J. 5. 154
7. Penn. 1. 239
8. Port. I. 437; E. 386. 12
9. Port. I. 437; E. 386. 12
10. Cal. S.P. Ven. 1647. 318
11. Cal. Clar. S.P. 1. 2511
12. Chev. 1. 460
13. Chev. 1. 463
14. L.J. 9. 409
15. Penn 1. 245-6
16. Penn 1. 247
17. E. 393. 33
18. E. 404. 38; E. 409. 3;
    E. 518. 21. 23
19. L. J. 9. 433; E. 405. 6
20. Penn 1. 250; Penn 1. 267
21. Penn 1. 267
22. Hamilton 188
23. Penn 1. 267
24. Clarke Papers 1. 245
25. Penn. 1. 252

26. L.J. 9. 526
27. L.J. 9. 615
28. L.J. 9. 615
29. Abbott 1. 575
30. E. 401. 3; E. 433. 34
31. L.J. 9. 469; E. 433. 34
32. Chev. 1. 491
33. Chev. 1. 502

CHAPTER 10

1. Cal. S.P.D. 1648. 586
2. Tanner 58. 707;
   H.M.C. Ormonde 1. 121
3. Hoskins 2. 193
4. Leach 103. 126. 193
5. Tanner 58. 721
6. Cal. S.P.D. 1648. 44
7. E. 433. 5. 12
8. E. 434. 11
9. Cal. S.P.D. 1648. 40
10. Cal. S.P.D. 40
11. Penn 1; Tanner 57. 46;
    MacNeill 290;
    Add. MSS. 3048. 5058
12. L.J. 10. 233
13. Tanner 57. 45
14. E. 786. 22; Tanner 57. 50
15. E. 786. 22
16. E. 626. 14
17. Tanner 57. 55
18. L.J. 10. 235
19. E. 435. 9
20. Phillips 1. 401; E. 438. 2
21. E. 441.26; E. 443. 18. 21
22. E. 446. 23
23. Abbott 1. 618
24. Abbott 1. 613
25. Hamilton 188
26. C.A.M. 2. 945. 1052
27. Penn 1. 271
28. Add. MSS. 9305. 40; E. 426. 19
29. Hamilton 221
30. Tanner 57. 91; L.J. 10. 274
31. L.J. 10. 289; Tanner 57. 91
32. Tanner 57. 100
33. Carter 40-60; Tanner 57. 115;
    Arch. vol. 40. 35

34. E. 445. 32
35. E. 445. 32
36. Penn 1. 258
37. Tanner 57. 115
38. L.J. 10. 297
39. L.J. 10. 297

CHAPTER 11

1. Port. I. 459
2. Port. I. 462
3. Cal. S.P.D. 1648. 99. 111. 209
4. Port. I. 457;
   Cal. S.P.D. 1648. 124
5. Cal. S.P.D. 1648. 118
6. L.J. 10. 313
7. M.M. Vol. 9. 2. 36
8. Cal. S.P.D. 361
9. Cal. S.P.D. 1648. 267
10. L.J. 10. 313
11. Cal. S.P.D. 1648. 366
12. Hamilton 221
13. Penn 12. 2. 268; E. 460. 13
14. L.J. 10. 344; S.P. 516. 118
15. Pepysian MSS. 294
16. Cal. S.P.D. 1648. 174. 197
17. S.P.D. 515. 118
18. L.J. 10. 399
19. Cal. S.P.D. 1648. 181
20. Cal. S.P.D. 1648. 200
21. E. 499. 20
22. Port. I. 489
23. Cal. S.P.D. 1648. 368
24. Cal. S.P.D. 1648. 367
25. Pepsyian MSS. 271
26. E. 457. 142
27. L.J. 10. 432
28. L.J. 10. 401
29. Cal. S.PD. 1648. 232
30. Hamilton 237
31. Port. I. 494
32. E. 495. 3
33. Cal. S.P.D. 1648. 256
34. Clar. S.P. 2881. 2879
35. Add. MSS. 17; 667. 182, 186
36. Clar. S.P. 2881
37. E. 464. 23
38. Clar. S.P. 2881

39. L.J. 10. 489
40. L.J. 10. 489
41. L.J. 10. 489
42. L.J. 10. 489
43. Clar. S.P. 2881
44. Clar. S.P. 2879
45. Clar. S.P. 2878

CHAPTER 12

 1. L.J. 10. 489. 495
 2. Cal. S.P.D. 1648. 267
 3. Cal. S.P.D. 1648. 269
 4. Cal. S.P.D. 1648. 280. 300
 5. Chev. 1. 589
 6. Cal. S.P.D. 1648. 283
 7. Cal. S.P.D. 1648. 284. 268
 8. L.J. 10. 495
 9. Tanner 57. 278;
     Tanner 57. 308; E. 526. 42
10. L.J. 10. 522
11. L.J. 10. 495; Tanner 57. 276;
     Cal. S.P.D. 1648. 288
12. Tanner 57. 334; Cary. 2. 13;
     Carte's Letters I. 174
13. L.J. 10. 523

14. Cal. S.P.D. 1648. 293
15. E. 526. 46
16. Tanner 57. 334
17. War. 1. 531;
     Pepysian MSS. 235
18. Chev. 2. 589. 593. 609
19. A.S.G. 5937
20. L.J. 10. 595
21. War. 3. 235
22. Main. 1. 330
23. L.J. 10. 595
24. War. 3. 254
25. War. 3. 265
26. L.J. 10. 625
27. Port. I. 441
28. L.J. 10. 625
29. Tanner 57. 431; Cary. 2. 60
30. Cal. S.P.D. 1648. 332
31. Cal. S.P.D. 1648. 337
32. L.J. 10. 626
33. Tanner 57. 449
35. Carte's Letters I. 200
36. War. 3. 274
37. Spalding 27; M.M.: 14. 321-3
38. Carte's Letters I. 208
39. War. 3. 281

Index of Persons, Places, and Political Parties

(B = Battle, S = Siege)

Abingdon, 63, 134
Admiralty, Commissioners of, 29, 42, 91, 123, 129, 137, 143, 147, 163, 166
Adwalton Moor, 41 (B)
Agitators, 137
Allen, Captain Thomas, 182, 187
Amsterdam, 41
Amy, Captain Thomas (Privateer), 121, 136, 144
Angle Bay, 59, 73
Argyle, Marquis of, 148
Arundell, John, 120
Ashley, Lord Jacob, 125, 126
Assheton, Ralph, 40
Auldearn, 92 (B)
Ayscue, Captain Sir George, 122, 178

Badiley, Captain Richard, 188
Badnedge, Colonel, 101
Ball, Captain Andrew, 156, 173
Banbury, 63
Barbados, 62
Bargraves, The, 157, 158
Barnstaple, 33, 43, 92, 110, 120
Barry, Colonel, 147
Bartlett, Captain John, 26
Bartlett, Captain Thomas, 26, 110
Basing House, 80 (S)
Basse Isle, 39
Bassett, Sir Francis, 27, 92
Batten, Admiral William, 7, 14, 21, 27, 30, 37, 42, 73, 75, 90, 105, 107-10, 119, 120, 122, 125-29, 138-40, 143, 152-54, 161, 166-70, 174, 181-86
Beale, Captain, 86, 87
Beaumorris, 58, 72
Bedall, Captain Thomas, 136
Belle Isle, 52
Bence, Alexander, 178, 180, 184
Berwick, 4, 16, 150
Bideford, 46, 54, 92
Black Rock, 71

Blake, Colonel Robert, 65-7, 105, 118, 180
Blandford, 68, 94
Bohemia, Queen of, 187
Bodmin, 31, 74
Bonner, Captain, 163
Bonratty, 111-7 (S)
Bolingbroke Castle, 49
Bougogne, 135, 136
Bowden, Captain George, 28, 51, 121
Braddon Down, 33 (B)
Braithwaite, Captain, 187
Brandley, Captain William, 167
Brentford, 30 (B)
Brereton, Sir William, 40, 50, 51, 57, 95, 125
Bridgeman, Orlando, 50
Bridgewater, 39, 63, 105, 106 (S)
Bridlington, 19, 37
Bright, Captain, 77
Bristol, 13, 40, 43 (S), 44, 46 (S), 49, 54, 92, 94, 106, 107 (S), 111, 129, 150, 152, 167, 168, 178
Broghill, Lord Roger, 116, 129
Brook, Captain, 44-6
Broughton, Colonel, 58
Brown, General Richard, 74
Buller, Sir Richard, 27, 181
Burley, Captain, 20, 44
Burley, Barnabe, 25, 187
Burrell, Andrews, 124
Bushell, Browne, 24, 37, 38, 136, 150
Bushell, Henry, 37
Bushell, James (Gunner), 76
Bushell, Thomas, 143
Byron, Lord John, 57, 63, 95

Calais, 165
Canaston Bridge, 105 (B)
Cannon, Captain (Privateer), 133
Cant, Andrew, 128
Canterbury, 153, 155, 163

Carbery, Earl of, 45, 58
Cardiff, 26, 106, 119
Cardigan, 78(S), 85(S), 93
Carew, Sir Alexander, 46
Carisbrooke Castle, 25(S)
Carlisle, Countess of, 154, 166, 169
Carmarthen, 151(S)
Carnarvon, Earl of, 46
Carnarvon, 78
Carne, Colonel, 118
Carrickfergus, 6, 54, 58, 83, 97
Carteret, Captain George, 14, 136, 143, 181
Carteret, Sir Phillip, 28
Cary, Peter, 108
Castle Cornet, Guernsey, 28, 121, 144
Castlehaven, Earl of, 50, 97-104
Cattwater, 35, 52, 83, 85
Cavendish, Lieut. General, 40, 46
Cawsand, 51
Ceeley, Thomas, 65
Chamberlain, Captain (Privateer), 133, 136, 143
Chard, 39
Charles I, 4-8, 10-13, 16, 19-21, 29, 30, 45, 49, 50, 63, 68, 74-78, 80, 94, 95, 106, 108, 125-28, 134, 141-43, 188
Charles, Prince of Wales, 94, 108, 119, 120, 136, 143, 165, 166, 168, 170-75, 178
Charmouth, 67, 69
Chatham, 9, 161
Chelmsford, 163, 164
Cheriton, 63(B)
Chester, 29, 50, 51, 95, 108, 119(S)
Cholmley, Sir Hugh, 31, 57, 90
Chudleigh, Major General James, 28, 35
Clarke, Captain Robert, 110
Coachman, Captain Gervaise, 78
Colby Moor, 105(B)
Colchester, 164(S), 167(S), 171(S)
Colster, Captain, 23
Committee of Both Kingdoms, 65, 68, 93, 94, 139, 148
Commons, House of, 71, 138, 143
Conway, 50, 119, 128
Cook, Thomas (Boatswain), 75

Coote, Colonel, 119
Coppin, Captain William, 28, 115, 164
Copredy Bridge, 74(B)
Corfe Castle, 41
Cornish Tin Trade, 27-28, 92-93
Cork, 6, 49, 76, 87, 103, 104, 114
Corkbush Field, 141
Crisp, Sir Nicholas, 92
Croisie, 52
Cromwell, Oliver, 41, 46-9, 73, 80, 81, 94, 95, 118, 127, 133, 140-42, 157, 175, 179
Crowther, Admiral John, 104, 113, 149, 150-7
Culpepper, Sir John, 94, 121

Danes, 12, 16, 25, 38, 42
Dansk, Captain Ralph, 39
Dare, Captain Robert, 167
Dartmouth, 28, 51(S), 53, 69, 92, 119(S)
Daventry, 95
Deal, 135, 155, 157, 163(S), 165, 167, 169(S)
Deane, Admiral Richard, 188
Deptford, 9
Derby House Committee, 148, 154, 169, 173, 179, 180, 183-85
Diamond, Captain, 122
Dieppe, 52, 136
Digby, Lord, 59, 94, 95
Dirkin (Principal Gunner), 163
Doddington, Sir Francis, 181
Dogger Sands, 36
Dorchester, 70, 90
Dorislaus, Doctor Isaac, 176
Dover, 4, 121, 147, 163(S)
Downs, 9, 20, 92, 133, 164, 165, 167-70, 184, 187, 188
Driver, Captain William, 18
Dublin, 6, 26, 49, 50, 58, 78, 90, 110, 128
Duncannon, 77, 86-89(S)
Dunkirk, 5-7, 25, 26, 52, 72, 92, 129
Dunster, 39, 63
Dutch, The, 4, 5, 23, 31, 36, 178, 179, 183, 188
Dyve, Sir Lewis, 16, 90

Eastern Association, 40, 47, 56, 63, 80
Edgehill, 29(B)
Egerton, General Randolph, 105
Elizabeth Castle, Jersey, 28, 62,
    121, 181
Esmond, Lord, 77, 87-89
Essex, Earl of, 29, 30, 43, 48, 49, 68,
    69, 72, 74, 75, 80, 90
Evans, Cornelius, 154, 155
Exeter, 30, 39, 46(S), 74, 120(S)

Fairfax, Lord, 30-32, 40, 41, 48, 49, 73
Fairfax, Sir Thomas, 30, 31, 40, 41,
    49, 56, 73, 90, 94, 95, 105, 107, 108,
    119, 120, 140-43, 150, 160, 164, 167,
    169
Falmouth, 27, 28, 38, 108, 120-21(S)
Fleming, 148, 151
Flint, 51
Fogge, Captain, 20
Fortescue, Colonel Sir Faithful, 122
Forth, Earl of, 63
Fowey, 75
Fox, Captain, 23
Franklyn, James (Seaman), 88

Gainsborough, 47(B), 49, 119
Galway, 40, 44(S), 118, 119, 137
Gerard, Sir Charles, 71, 77, 78, 85,
    93, 95
Gernet, Captain (Privateer), 136, 144
Gillingham, 161
Gilson, Captain John, 106, 120, 124
Glamorgen, Earl of, 108, 126, 128
Gloucester, 32, 46(S), 49
Godolphin, William, 28
Goffe, Doctor Stephen, 28
Goree, 176-78
Goring, Colonel George, 13, 24, 25, 31,
    40, 83, 94, 95, 160, 164
Gosfright, Andrew, 138
Green, 133, 138
Grenville, Sir Bevill, 35
Grenville, Lieut. General, 74, 83
Guernsey, 28, 51, 61, 62, 69, 179
Gunfleet, 174
Gun-runners, 18, 23, 28, 31, 47
Gwynne, Colonel David, 61

Haddock, Captain Richard, 47, 54, 57,
    178, 182, 185
Haesdonck, Captain John Van
    (Privateer), 92, 108
Halstock, John (Surgeon), 122
Hamilton, Marquis of, 4, 139, 148
Hampden, John, 5, 30
Hammond, Captain, 158
Hammond, Colonel, 120, 141
Hampton Court, 141
Harris, Captain, 158
Harrison, Captain, 185
Harrison, Colonel Thomas, 141
Harwich, 157, 164, 167, 168
Haverfordwest, 59, 61, 93, 105
Harve, 52
Heane, Colonel, 184
Helvoetsluys, 165, 167, 176, 181
Henderson, Sir John, 31
Henrietta Maria, Queen, 12, 16, 18,
    36-8, 40, 41, 73, 119
Hereford, 22
Hertford, Marquis of, 26, 40
Hessle, 22
Hinckman, Mr., 166
Holland, Henry Rich, Earl of,
    160, 176
Holmby, 128, 134
Holms Islands, 106
Holyhead, 49, 72
Hooper, Major, 115, 117, 119
Hopton, Sir Ralph, 26, 27, 30, 31, 38,
    63, 108, 120
Horton, Colonel, 140, 151
Hotham, Sir John, 12, 16, 17, 32, 41
Hotham, John, Jr., 41, 50
Howett, Captain Samuel, 97, 102
Hull, 12, 13, 16-8(S), 41(S), 47,
    48(S), 49, 168, 177
Hyde, Sir Edward, 181

Inchiquin, Earl of, 49, 77, 87, 89,
    129, 149
Independents, 127, 129, 130, 139, 140,
    142, 145, 148, 157, 188
Irish Affairs, Committee for, 6, 131

Jelf, Captain (Privateer), 121, 129
Jermyn, Lord Henry, 28

Jersey, 28, 59, 61, 62, 123, 135, 136, 143, 181
Jervoise, Captain, 161, 162
Jones, Colonel Michael, 130
Jones, Captain Thomas, 65
Jones, Captain (Privateer), 121, 136
Jorey (Clerk), 169
Jordan, Captain Elias, 25, 166, 170-72, 181, 186
Jordan, Captain Joseph, 44, 61, 106, 124, 170, 179
Joyce, Cornet, 134

Kearse, Captain John, 107
Kentish Gentlemen, 153-58, 166
Kettleby, Captain Thomas, 27, 133
Kem, Samuel (Chaplain), 126, 128, 147, 152-54, 158
Kilkenny, Catholic Confederacy, 49, 113
Kinsale, 26, 114, 150

La Rochelle, 109
Lalue (French engineer), 86
Lamming, Captain Roger, 138, 139
Land's End, 28, 93, 118, 129, 147, 150, 179
Landguard Fort, 157
Langdale, Sir Marmaduke, 150, 175
Langport, 63, 105
Larcan, Lieutenant, 77-88
Laud, Archbishop, 6
Lauderdale, Earl of, 137, 169
Laugharne, Colonel Rowland, 45, 58, 59, 61, 71, 78, 85, 86, 93, 105, 108, 119, 151, 161
Laugharne, 78
Launceston, 27, 74
Lawson, Captain John, 150
Legge, Captain, 12
Leicester, 95
Leigh, 167
Lendal (Boatswain), 152, 154, 156, 158, 164, 169
Levellers, 134, 140, 141, 145
Leven, Earl of, 44, 73, 94
Lichfield, 40
Limehouse, 166
Limerick, 113, 115, 137, 143

Lincoln, 47, 49
Lindsey, Earl of, 22
Lipson Fort, 52
Lisle, Lieutenant Thomas, 151, 157
Liverpool, 50, 51, 129
Lloyd, Sir Francis, 59
Loftus, Colonel, 101
London, 3, 5, 13, 29, 40, 42, 45, 47, 50, 53, 63, 142, 148, 152, 156, 157, 167, 168
L'Orient, 52
Lords, House of, 142
Lords Justices, 26
Lort, Captain Roger, 45, 58
Lostwithiel, 74
Louis XIV, 7
Lundy Island, 143
Lurting, William, 50
Lyme, 16, 63-71(S)

MacAdam, Colonel, 111-19
Macdonnel Clan, 43
Maidstone, 160, 163(B), 164
Manchester, Earl of, 47, 73, 80, 81
Mann, Captain John, 66, 106, 124
Margate, 168
Marlborough, Earl of, 53, 61
Marston Moor, 73(B)
Massey, Colonel Edward, 46, 94, 138
Maudlyn Fort, 52, 83
Maurice, Prince, 23, 46, 51, 63, 69, 187
May (King's page), 19, 20
Mazarin, Cardinal, 109, 136
Medway River, 161, 164
Meldrum, Sir John, 22, 47, 48, 90
Mennes, Admiral Sir John, 12, 20, 51, 187
Mersea Island, 167
Mervyn, Admiral Sir Henry, 10
Middleton, Sir Thomas, 95
Mildford Haven, 28, 40, 43, 44, 52, 59, 61, 72, 74, 90, 136, 148, 150
Minehead, 26, 49, 63, 129
Mitchell, Andrew (Boatswain), 151, 166
Moizer, Edward, 68
Montrose, Earl of, 94, 108
Moorish Pirates, 67
Mootham, Abraham (Seaman), 88

Morlaix, 39, 52
Morland, Mr., 163
Mostyn, 50, 72
Moulton, Admiral Robert, 28, 40-42,
    45, 71, 77, 104, 107, 112, 118, 159,
    168, 185, 188
Mount Batten, 85
Mount Edgecombe, 31
Mount Orguiel, Jersey, 28
Mount Stamford, 35, 52, 62, 83
Moyer, Captain, 18, 41
Mucknell, Captain John, 106, 107
Munro, Colonel, 54
Muskerry, Earl of, 111-18

Nantes, 52
Nantwich, 40, 57(B)
Naseby, 95(B)
Navy Board, 9
Navy Commissioners, 21, 123, 124, 139
Navy, Parliamentary Committee
    for, 9
Newark, 31, 40, 46, 49, 63(B)
Newbury, 49(B), 80(B)
Newcastle, Earl of, 18, 31, 40, 46, 47,
    49, 73
Newcastle, 16, 23, 28, 31, 37, 57(S),
    73(S), 78(S), 126, 150, 157, 179
Newcastle Emlyn, 86
New Model Army, 4, 5
Nixon, Captain Robert, 155
Northumberland, Earl of, 10, 11, 14,
    19, 20, 29
Nottingham, 29, 41

Oaze Shoal, 172
Orange, Prince of, 6, 16
Organey, River, 111
Orkney Islands, 38
Ormonde, Earl of, 49, 50, 57, 72, 78,
    125, 147, 149
Orquendo (Spanish Admiral), 5
Osborne, Sir Peter, 28, 121
Owen, Admiral Richard, 135
Oxford, 29, 30, 40, 43, 45, 63, 68, 69,
    73, 80, 94, 95(S), 108, 125

Pacey, Captain Thomas, 159
Palmer, Sir Henry, 19

Parliament, 1, 3, 6, 14, 16-18, 20, 24,
    32, 37, 38, 40, 43, 44, 46, 53, 62,
    76, 82, 83, 90, 96, 110, 122, 124,
    126, 130, 133, 137, 140, 153, 157,
    158, 161, 163, 166
Parraulx, 122
Pattison (Master), 174
Paul, 18, 22
Paulet, Sir John, 49
Pearse, Captain John, 166
Pembroke, 28, 45, 58, 90,
    148(S), 151(S)
Penarth, 118, 150
Pendennis, 27, 52, 120-22(S)
Penn, George, 131
Penn, Admiral William, 83, 97-104,
    107, 111-18, 129, 131, 136, 137, 149
Pennington, Sir John, 5, 14, 19, 20,
    43-45, 58, 92, 93
Penrose, Captain Francis, 156-60, 185
Pepys, Samuel, 10
Percy, Captain Abraham, 77
Peters, Hugh, 122, 151
Pett, Captain Phineas, 21, 124, 125,
    161-63
Philliphaugh, 106(B)
Phipps, Mr., 166
Pill, 45, 58, 59(S)
Plunket, Captain Thomas, 89, 109-10
Plymouth, 4, 13, 26, 27, 36, 38, 39, 46,
    51(S), 53, 48, 74, 83(S), 106, 108,
    119(S), 147, 181, 184
Plympton, 35
Plymstock, 57
Polhill, Captain, 39
Popham, Admiral Edward, 188
Portishead, 101
Portland, 36, 75, 90, 120, 184
Portsea Island, 24
Portsmouth, 4, 9, 24(S), 83, 108, 135,
    165-67, 170, 172, 173
Powell, Colonel Rice, 85, 86, 151, 161
Poyer, John, 58, 90, 104, 148, 161
Pratt (Gunner), 163
Presbyterians, 80, 126, 130, 134,
    137-39, 142, 148
Preston, General Thomas, 77, 86-89,
    104
Preston, 175(B)

Privateers, 6, 7, 25, 28, 38-40, 51, 52, 62, 72, 77, 78, 90, 129, 133, 134, 136, 137, 143, 144, 147, 150, 184
Providence Company, 12
Public Safety, Committee for, 27, 29
Putney, 140
Pym, John, 3, 5, 11-13, 20, 43, 57

Quay Island, 113-18
Queensborough, 154

Raglan, 106, 108
Rainsborough, Colonel Thomas, 48, 107, 132, 133, 139-44, 147, 150-55, 167
Reading, 40, 63, 80
Reeve, Captain William, 179
Rew, Captain William, 45, 107
Rich, Captain Stephen, 119
Rich, Colonel, 163, 169
Richelieu, Cardinal, 7
Rinunccini, (Papal Nuncio), 109-13. 131
Robartes, Lord John, 74-76, 85
Rochester, 154, 161
Rosewell, George (Seaman), 182
Rotterdam, 31, 167
Roundway Down, 43(B)
Rowton Heath, 108(B)
Royston, 137
Rupert, Prince, 23, 29, 30, 40, 63, 72-74, 94, 107, 165, 174, 181, 183-88
Russell, Governor of Guernsey, 108, 121
Ruthin, Colonel, 30

Sandwich, 138, 154
St. Albans, 137
St. Fagans, 151(B)
St. Malo, 61, 92, 122, 179
St. Mawes, 27, 120
St. Michaels Mount, 120
St. Nicholas Island, 35, 46
Saltash, 31, 33(B), 35
Saltmarshe, John, 41
Sandown Castle, 157, 169
Sark Island, 122
Saybrook Colony, 12
Scarborough, 23, 28, 31, 37(S), 57, 73, 90(S), 168

Scillies, 119, 120, 121(S), 136, 176, 179
Scots, 44, 56, 57, 62, 80, 123-28, 139, 142, 148, 153
Shannon River, 111, 113, 119
Ship-Money Fleet, 4, 7
Shoeburyness, 172
Shrewsbury, 58, 63
Skinner, Captain (Privateer), 121, 176, 181
Skippon, General Sir Phillip, 30, 75
Slanning, Sir Nicholas, 27, 28
Slingsby, Captain, 20, 21
Sluice, The, 182
Smith, Thomas (Admiralty Secretary), 29, 139
Smith, Sir Percy, 97-104
Smith, Admiral William, 44, 59, 71, 78, 87-89, 97
Somaster, Captain, 65
Sourton Down, 38(B)
Southsea Castle, 24
Spain, 4-6, 38, 52, 94, 129, 136
Sprigham, John (Chaplain), 138
Stackpool House, 58
Stamford, Earl of, 33, 38
Stapledon, Sir Phillip, 137
Stevens, Captain Tristram, 53
Steyton, 59
Strachen, Captain, 18
Stradling, General Sir Edward, 105
Stradling, Captain Henry, 27
Strafford, Earl of, 6
Stratton, 38(B)
Strickland, 16, 179, 186
Swanley, Captain George, 16
Swanley, Admiral Richard, 24, 25, 44, 45, 54, 58-61, 71, 78, 80, 86-89, 93, 94, 97, 103, 104, 125, 131, 136, 137
Swansea, 151
Sweden, 38, 135
Swin, 173
Sydenham, Colonel William, 90

Tate, Zachery, 81
Taunton, 39, 63, 94, 105(S)
Tavistock, 35

Tenby, 28, 45, 59, 61(S), 90, 93, 149-51
Thomas, Captain William, 39, 85, 105, 129, 131
Thomond, Earl of, 111
Tillier, Colonel Henry, 58
Trafford, Colonel, 72
Trefloyne House, 58
Trevanion, Sir Charles, 92
Trenchfield, Admiral, 22, 26
Tromp, Admiral, 4, 5, 23, 24, 179, 181, 185
Turnham Green, 30(B)
Turpin, Captain, 42
Tynemouth, 27, 47, 127

Upnor Castle, 161, 163
Urbino, Juan de, 131
Urry, Sir John, 94
Ushant, 52

Vane, Sir Henry, 21, 29
Vane, Henry, Jr., 43, 44
Vasacour, Colonel Sir John, 49
Victuallers, 10, 54, 62, 72, 76, 90, 153, 168, 180, 184, 185
Villiers (King's Page), 19, 20

Wake, Captain Baldwin, 20, 21, 50, 57, 120, 121
Waller, Sir Hardress, 176
Waller, General Sir William, 24, 43, 68, 69, 74, 80, 81, 137

Walmer, 157
Wardlaw, Colonel James, 46, 52
Warwick, Robert Rich, Earl of, 5, 6, 14, 16, 20, 21, 23, 29, 30, 38, 39, 41-43, 52, 53, 55, 67-69, 71, 72, 75, 76, 81, 90, 91, 156-60, 165-88, passim.
Waterford, 90, 109, 129, 131, 136, 137
Were, Colonel John, 65, 67
West Riding, 30, 31
Wexford, 26, 38, 50, 77, 78, 90, 129, 136, 137
Weymouth, 28, 46, 53, 69, 90, 107, 179, 184
Whalley, Major Edward, 141
Wheeler, Captain Abraham, 75, 179
Whitty, Captain, 61
Widdrington, Sir William, 49
Wight, Isle of, 25, 141, 142, 153, 170
Wilkinson (Gunner), 75
Williams, Captain Reeve, 143
Willoughby, Colonel, 44, 71
Willoughby, Lord, 46, 48, 167, 172, 181
Winceby, 49(B)
Windsor, 94, 150
Winnal, Captain Thomas, 123
Woodward, Captain Andrew, 135
Worcester, 29, 68, 94
Wrexham, 51

Yarmouth, 26, 164, 167, 168
York, James, Duke of, 16
York, John, Archbishop of, 50
Youghal, 16, 76, 90, 95-104(S), 118

CPSIA information can be obtained
at www.ICGtesting.com
Printed in the USA
BVHW07s1423030718
520749BV00016B/152/P